IMAGES
of America

REMEMBERING ARKANSAS CONFEDERATES *and the* 1911 LITTLE ROCK VETERANS REUNION

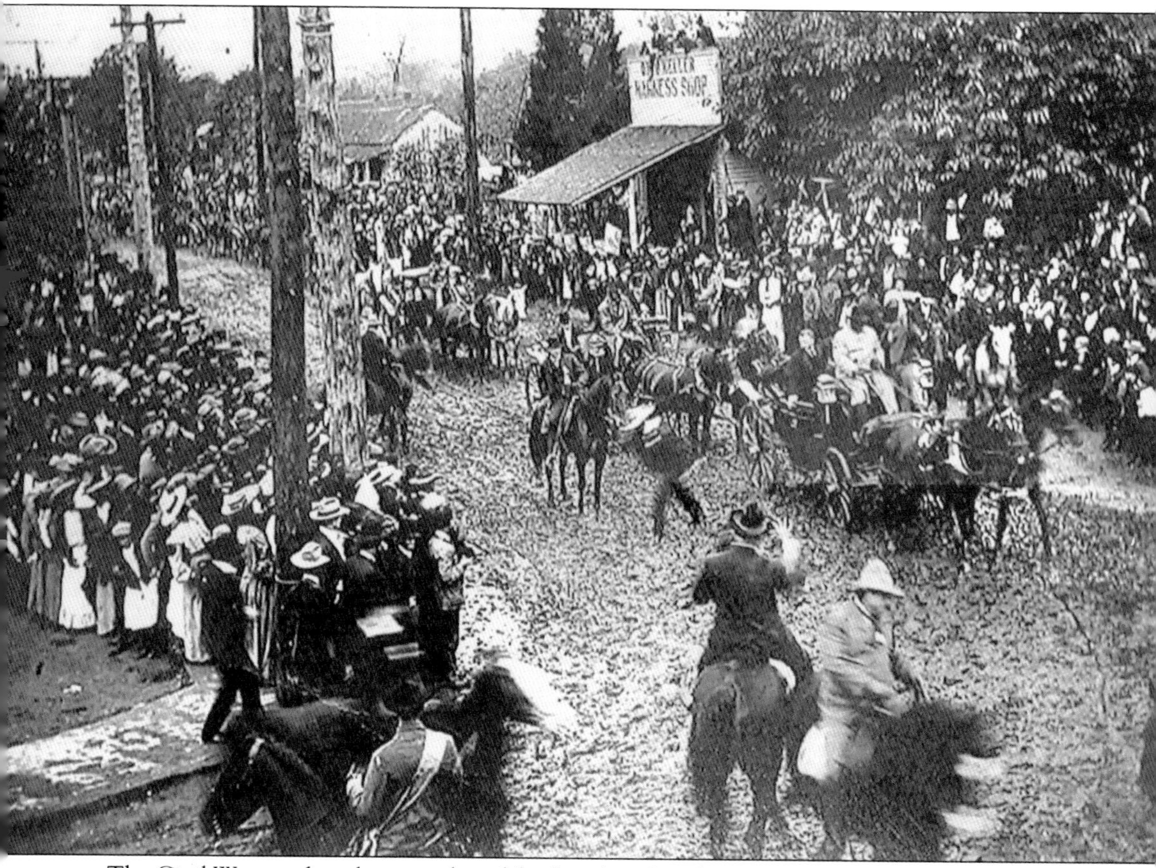

The Civil War was keenly remembered for decades after the war ended. In 1905, Pres. Theodore Roosevelt visited Arkansas, fresh from having settled the war between Russia and Japan. Seen here parading through Argenta (today's North Little Rock), Roosevelt's procession included mounted Arkansas veterans of both the Confederacy and the Union army. "It does my heart good to see the blue and gray riding side-by-side," the president commented. (Courtesy of North Little Rock History Commission.)

ON THE COVER: The largest crowd in the history of Arkansas (not exceeded until the election of Bill Clinton as president in 1992) was that of 100,000 who gathered for the United Confederate Veterans (UCV) convention in 1911. Among the 12,000 old soldiers who attended were those seen in the cover photograph, taken in Camp Shaver, the veterans' encampment located in Little Rock's City Park.

IMAGES
of America

REMEMBERING ARKANSAS CONFEDERATES *and the* 1911 LITTLE ROCK VETERANS REUNION

Ray Hanley and Steven G. Hanley

ARCADIA
PUBLISHING

ISBN 978-0-7385-4298-0

Published by Arcadia Publishing
Charleston, South Carolina

Printed in the United States of America

Library of Congress Catalog Card Number: 2006925668

For all general information contact Arcadia Publishing at:
Telephone 843-853-2070
Fax 843-853-0044
E-mail sales@arcadiapublishing.com
For customer service and orders:
Toll-Free 1-888-313-2665

Visit us on the Internet at www.arcadiapublishing.com

We dedicate this book to all those brave men, whether they wore the gray or the blue, who shed their blood on Arkansas soil for a cause in which they believed. May they be united in peace.

Contents

ACKNOWLEDGMENTS

The authors take great pride in having produced this history of Arkansas and the Civil War, but we owe a debt of thanks to many who contributed, including Jon LeMay Photography of Little Rock, Stephen McAteer of the MacArthur Museum of Arkansas Military History, Mark Christ of the Arkansas Historic Preservation Department, Roger Williams of the Quapaw Quarter Association, and Lynn Ewbank and Bob Devan of the Arkansas History Commission. Thanks also to the North Little Rock History Commission, the Butler Center, University of Arkansas at Little Rock (UALR) Archives, Chuck Durnette, Don Hamilton, Bill Terry, the members of the Arkansas Division of the Sons of Confederate Veterans led by Comdr. Danny Honnoll, and Diane Hanley for her editing skills. Unless otherwise noted, historical images are from the authors' personal collections.

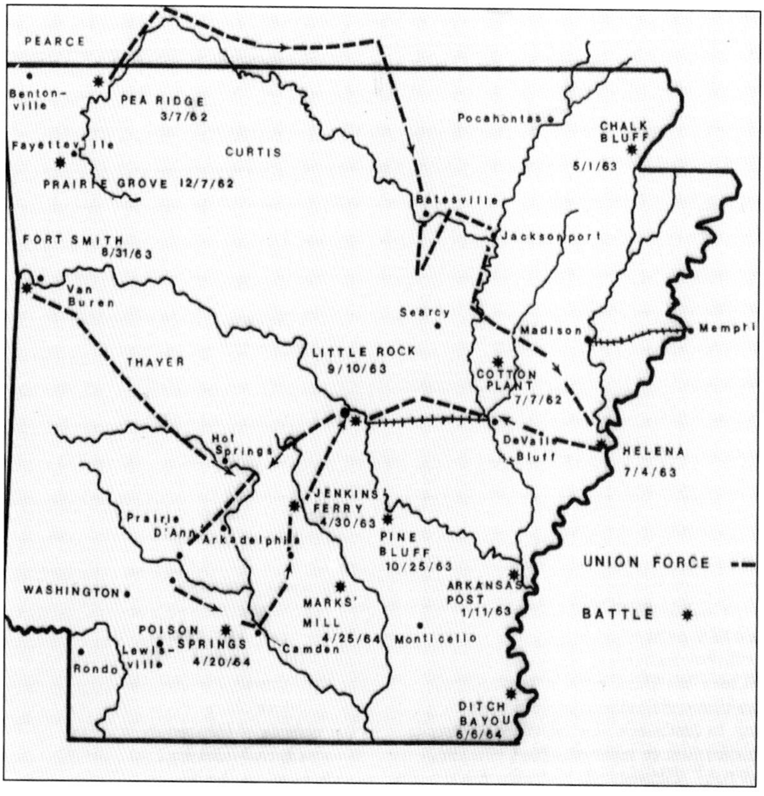

This map by UALR professor Gerald Hanson illustrates the pattern of the Civil War in Arkansas, from battles at Pea Ridge and Prairie Grove in the northwest to the Union march down through Batesville to Helena, opening the way for the invasion of Little Rock. In the war's final year, Union troops marched into Southwest Arkansas and faced defeat at Poison Springs and Jenkins Ferry. (Courtesy of North Little Rock History Commission.)

INTRODUCTION

On May 6, 1861, the secession convention meeting at the State House in Little Rock voted 65 to 5 for Arkansas to leave the Union and join the Confederacy. "Enough votes have been cast to take us out of the Union," proclaimed Chairman David Walker. "Now since we must go, let us all go together, let the wires carry the news to all the world that Arkansas stands as a unit against coercion." Four of the five dissenters eventually reversed their "no" votes; only Isaac Murphy, a 62-year-old teacher and lawyer from Madison County, refused to make the decision unanimous. "I have cast my vote after mature reflection and have duly considered the consequences, and I cannot conscientiously change it," Murphy told the convention. "I therefore vote no!"

With the decision made, most Arkansans rallied to the cause of Southern independence. While slavery was the key flashpoint of the war, only one Arkansas family in five owned slaves; to most the war was not about slavery. Like most Southerners, they answered the call to arms for such reasons as "states' rights" and to protect their homes and families against a "Yankee invasion." Few who enlisted had ever been to war, and most felt the fighting would be over quickly. Many young men saw the war as a once-in-a-lifetime opportunity to prove their manhood and to defend the honor of the South. By the end of the conflict, more than 60,000 Arkansas men would serve in the Confederate army.

At the war's inception, the *Van Buren Press* described the Arkansas citizens turned soldiers: "Our citizens have been accustomed to the use of arms from infancy—they possess a love of country—they are emphatically a fighting people." However, the reality was that, as brave and anxious to defend their homeland as these men were, few had military training or an understanding of battle tactics. Many regiments' officers were elected upon mobilization, more as an honor than because of military experience; hence a daunting challenge lay ahead.

For Arkansas, the war opened in 1862 with a failed attempt to control Missouri, its neighbor to the north. This led to the clash at Pea Ridge in Northwest Arkansas, the largest battle that would be fought west of the Mississippi River. The fierce two-day battle was a victory for the Union, giving an early lesson in the advantages of Northern artillery.

With Missouri firmly in Union hands, most Confederate troops and supplies were sent east of the Mississippi River to the major battlefronts. Arkansas was left defenseless; the Union army threatened Little Rock and took its river port of Helena in 1862. An angry Gov. Henry Rector wrote Pres. Jefferson Davis that, if measures were not taken to secure the state, Arkansas might secede from the Confederacy and "build a new ark and launch it on new waters, seeking a haven somewhere, of equality, safety, and rest."

President Davis sent the memorable Maj. Gen. Thomas Hindman, a Mexican War veteran from Helena, to raise a new army and take charge of operations in Arkansas. Hindman stirred controversy by making difficult decisions like declaring martial law, enforcing the Conscription Act, executing deserters, and even commandeering Texas soldiers crossing the state toward Mississippi. With the new troops, he set up workshops to manufacture weapons and ammunition and sanctioned the creation of irregular bands of civilian volunteers to harass the enemy.

Hindman engaged the Union army first at Prairie Grove in December 1862, with a hard day's battle leaving a stalemate. Low on ammunition and food, the Confederates faced disaster the next day. However, the "Billy Yanks" sleeping on the battlefield awoke to find that the "Johnny Rebs" had slipped away under a decoy flag of truce, in a plan by which Hindman saved most of his army to fight another day.

Savage guerrilla warfare would rage in much of the mountain region throughout the war. While most of the able-bodied men were away at war, organized bands of renegades terrorized the countryside, committing arson, murder, rape, and robbery. Many hill people, including most of the population of Hot Springs, abandoned the state during the war.

Across Arkansas, life on the home front grew increasingly grim. Without manpower, fields went unplowed and crop production plummeted. Older men and women, mothers, and children often went to bed hungry. Those who did have food and other scarce goods had to hide these from the soldiers of both armies and from roving bands of thieves. Women worked long hours to support the troops, caring for the sick and wounded, rolling bandages, and making uniforms. It was a hard four years for most Arkansans.

By January 1863, the war had opened up in Eastern Arkansas: a fleet of Union gunboats attacked Arkansas Post, where the massive earthen Confederate Fort Hindman had been erected to guard the approach to Little Rock. Greatly outnumbered, the garrison put up a brave fight, surrendering only when one regiment raised a white flag without authorization from the fort's commander. The town of Arkansas Post was abandoned and would never be rebuilt.

A Confederate force, seeking to relieve pressure on Vicksburg, launched an assault on the Union-occupied town of Helena on July 4, 1863. A series of poor decisions by the Confederate commander canceled out the heroic valor under fire by such soldiers as those in Gen. James Fagan's command, and the battle was lost on the same day Vicksburg fell and Robert E. Lee lost at Gettysburg.

After Helena, the war became one of attrition. In September 1863, the Union army overcame a last Confederate stand at Bayou Fourche and marched into Little Rock from the east, while Gov. Harris Flanigan and the Confederate army headed southwest to reestablish a new Confederate capital in Washington, Arkansas.

In December 1863, President Lincoln issued guidelines for the creation of loyalist governments in Union-held areas of the South. If 10 percent of those who had voted in the 1860 election would swear a loyalty oath, they could establish a new civil government. By March 1864, Isaac Murphy, the lone dissenter on secession in 1861, became one of two governors—he in Little Rock and Confederate governor Flanigan in Washington, Arkansas.

The dream of an independent Dixie was dying, although in Arkansas, impressive Confederate victories would still be won at Poison Springs and Jenkins Ferry. In 1864, shortly before his death at the battle of Franklin, Tennessee, Maj. Gen. Patrick Cleburne of Helena lamented in a letter to Jefferson Davis, "Surrender means that the history of this historic struggle will be written by the enemy; that our youth will be trained by Northern school teachers; will learn from Northern school books their version of the war; will be impressed by all the influences of history and education to regard our gallant dead as traitors, and our maimed veterans as fit subjects for derision."

However, General Cleburne would be pleased to know today that time has proven him wrong. The examples of courage and sacrifice shown by those who fought for the Lost Cause live on in the diaries, letters, and memoirs they penned, in the annual reunions of the United Confederate Veterans, in the war stories swapped at veterans' reunions and passed down to children and grandchildren, and in the chronicles of historians such as Bell Wiley and Shelby Foote. As long as courage and sacrifice are valued, these heroes' gallant words and deeds will continue to inspire.

One

Arkansas Goes to War

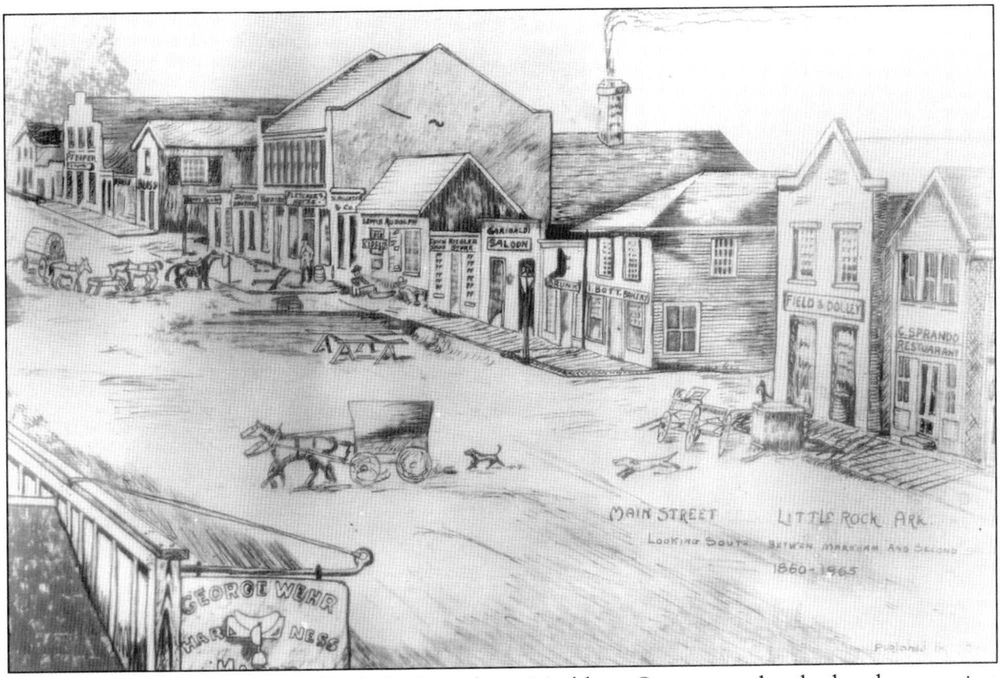

Arkansas's capital city of Little Rock, looking down Markham Street, was sketched as the secession debate raged. The state's population then was estimated at 324,000 white citizens and 111,000 black persons, mostly slaves. Outside the Delta, Arkansas was in some ways as much a Western state as Southern. In early 1861, it was not certain that Arkansas would follow the states of the Deep South out of the Union until President Lincoln's call for troops to fight sister Southern states triggered secession in May of that year. One Arkansas soldier, Fred Peak, upon marching off to war in 1861, stated, "So inpatient did I become for starting that I felt like a thousand pins were pricking me in every part of my body and started off a week in advance of my brothers."

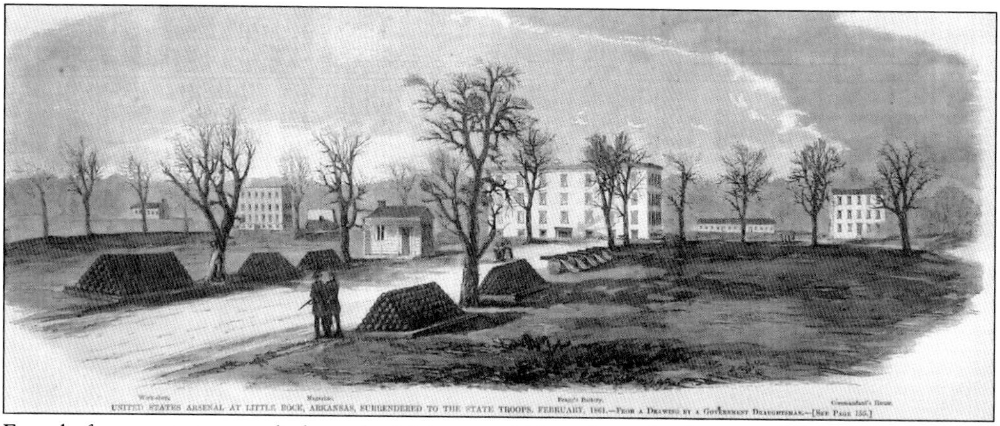

Even before a vote to secede from the Union would be taken, the desire to fight was so strong in Arkansas that, under orders of Gov. Henry Rector, the state militia seized the federal arsenal and all its munitions on February 8, 1861. The arsenal's commander, Capt. James Totten, surrendered rather than risk bloodshed. The central building of the arsenal still stands today, now the MacArthur Museum of Arkansas Military History. (Courtesy of MacArthur Museum of Arkansas Military History.)

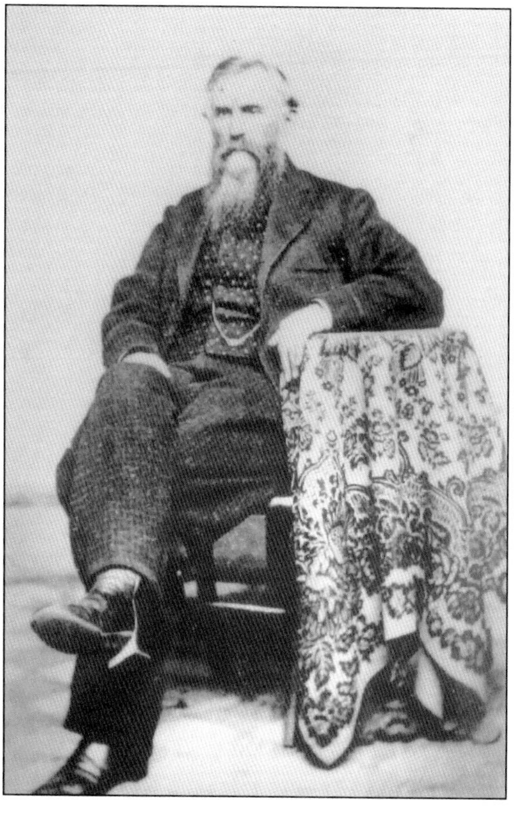

Henry Rector, elected governor in 1860, unsuccessfully pressed for secession in early 1861. After Fort Sumter, when President Lincoln called for 75,000 volunteers to put down the rebellion, Rector sent this reply: "no [troops] will be furnished. The demand adds insult to injury. The people of this commonwealth are freemen, not slaves, and will defend to the last extremity their honor, lives and property, against northern mendacity and usurpation." (Courtesy of MacArthur Museum of Arkansas Military History.)

Arkansas had refused the first bid to secede, as most Arkansans had little stake in slavery. However, after the April 1861 firing on Fort Sumter, the next vote to secede passed 69 to 1. Arkansas left the Union to defend against a feared Northern invasion. The *Philadelphia Enquirer* headlines made prominent mention of the state's action: "Secession of Arkansas" was listed just under the report "Washington to be Attacked."

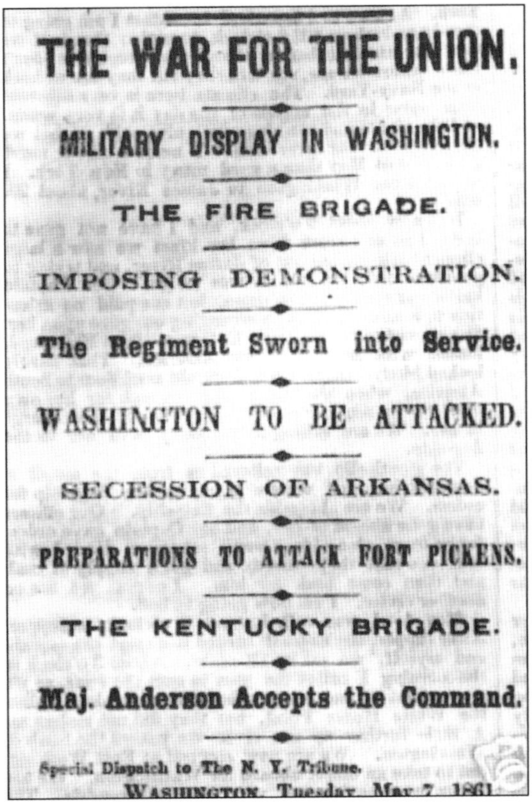

THE WAR FOR THE UNION.

MILITARY DISPLAY IN WASHINGTON.

THE FIRE BRIGADE.

IMPOSING DEMONSTRATION.

The Regiment Sworn into Service.

WASHINGTON TO BE ATTACKED.

SECESSION OF ARKANSAS.

PREPARATIONS TO ATTACK FORT PICKENS.

THE KENTUCKY BRIGADE.

Maj. Anderson Accepts the Command.

Special Dispatch to The N. Y. Tribune.

WASHINGTON, Tuesday, May 7, 1861.

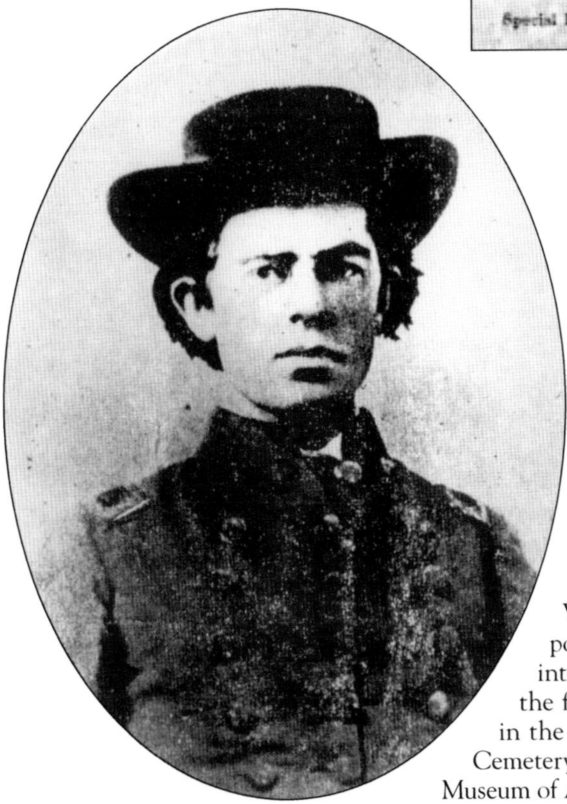

The toll of war was first levied on Arkansas at the Battle of Wilsons Creek, a Confederate victory in Southwest Missouri, on August 10, 1861. Lt. Omer Weaver of Little Rock was at his cannon post when a Union artillery round slammed into his chest. Lieutenant Weaver was likely the first Arkansas Confederate soldier to die in the Civil War; he is buried at Mount Holly Cemetery in Little Rock. (Courtesy of MacArthur Museum of Arkansas Military History.)

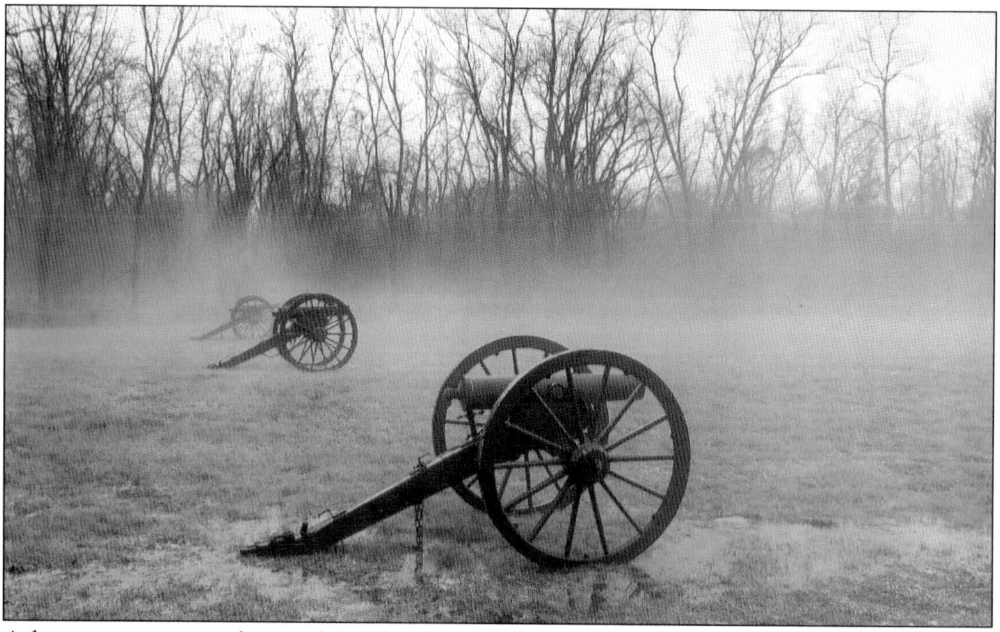

Arkansas guns were silent early in the Civil War; the Confederates controlled Arkansas and Southwest Missouri, while most Arkansas soldiers fought in the East. In early 1862, Confederate general Sterling Price hoped to take St. Louis but was driven from Springfield, Missouri, by Union general Samuel Curtis. A remote Ozark hilltop named Pea Ridge for its wild peas became the site of the bloodiest battle ever fought in Arkansas. (Photograph by Ray Hanley.)

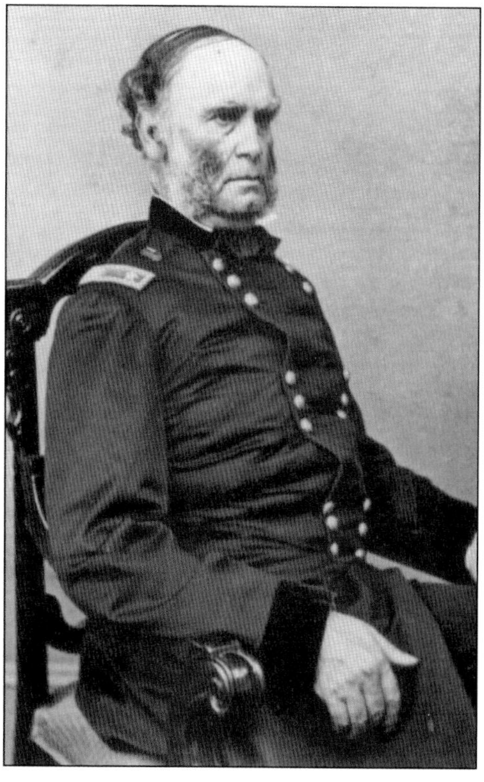

Union general Samuel Curtis reached Bentonville on February 12, 1862, breaking the state's aura of safety. A Mexican War veteran, former St. Louis mayor, and three-term congressman, Curtis resigned his seat at age 56 to take a command when the Civil War began. As his troops stepped over the state line, a band played "The Arkansas Traveler," while the general proclaimed, "The flag of our Union again floats over Arkansas."

General Curtis had driven Gen. Sterling Price's Confederates out of Missouri, invading Arkansas in order to engage him again and win a Union foothold in the state. Price, described as tall and handsome, was a prominent tobacco planter in Missouri and a brigadier general in the U.S. Army during the Mexican War. He cast his allegiance with the South and had won an earlier battle at Wilsons Creek in Missouri.

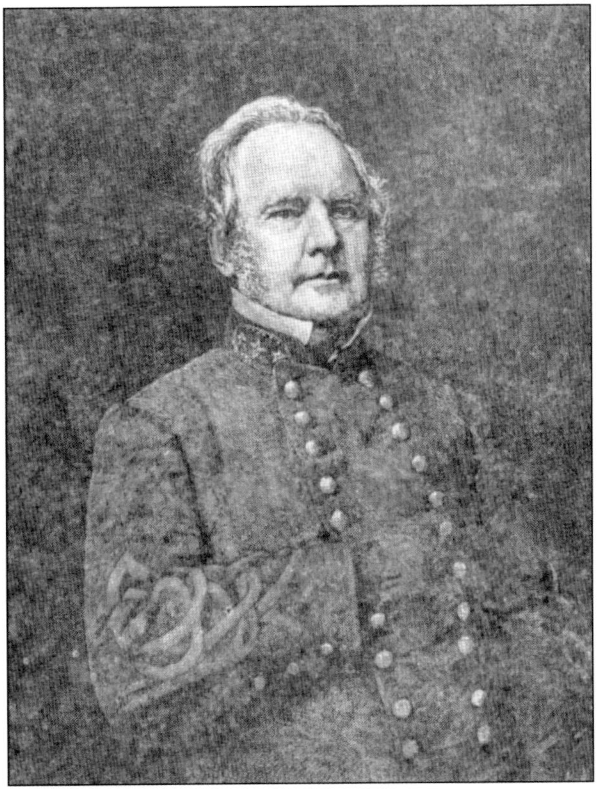

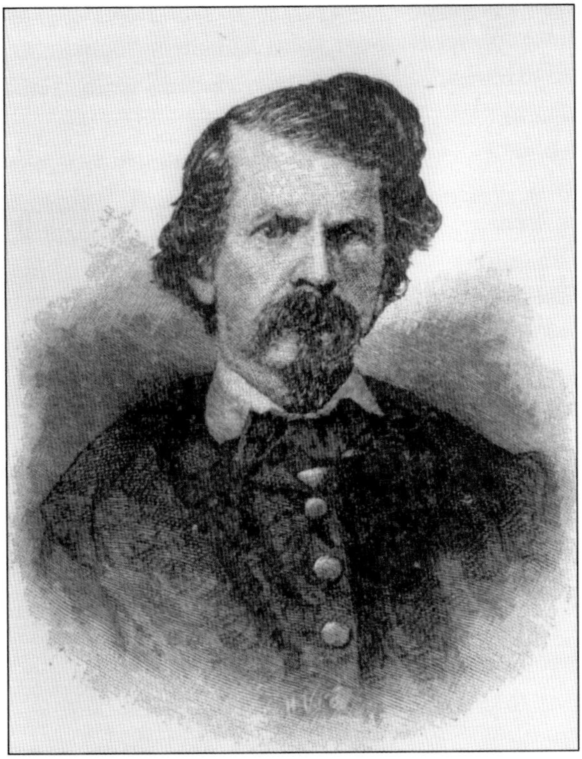

Primary command of the Confederates awaiting battle shifted to Gen. Earl Van Dorn, commander of the Confederate Trans-Mississippi Department, which encompassed Missouri, Arkansas, Western Louisiana, Texas, and the Indian Territory of Oklahoma. Van Dorn, a West Point graduate, former U.S. Army officer, and noted Indian fighter, was described as "handsome, trim, elegant in appearance, and a ladies' man"; he was reportedly killed by an irate husband in May 1863.

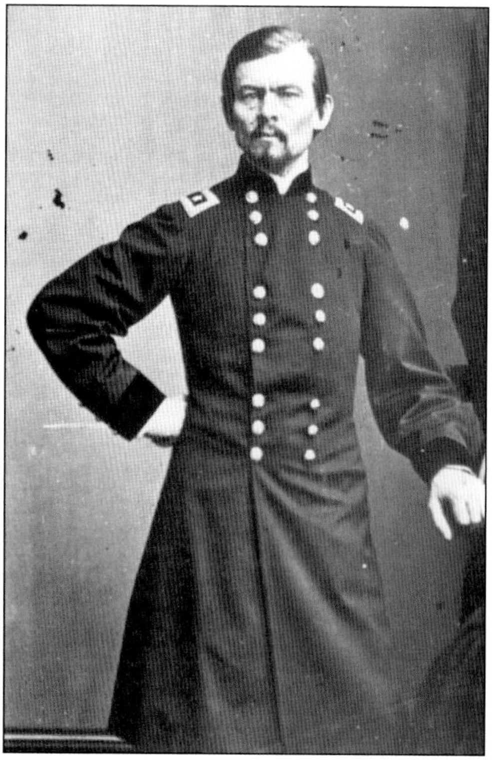

Confederate general Van Dorn was challenged at Pea Ridge by Gen. Franz Sigel. Sigel had fled Europe in 1847 after an unsuccessful German revolution against Prussia. He was a St. Louis schoolteacher when the war began but quickly rose to the rank of major general after helping rally German-Americans to the Union cause. The highlight of his military career would be at Pea Ridge, commanding two divisions under General Curtis, perhaps redeeming his hasty flight from the Battle of Wilsons Creek a few months earlier.

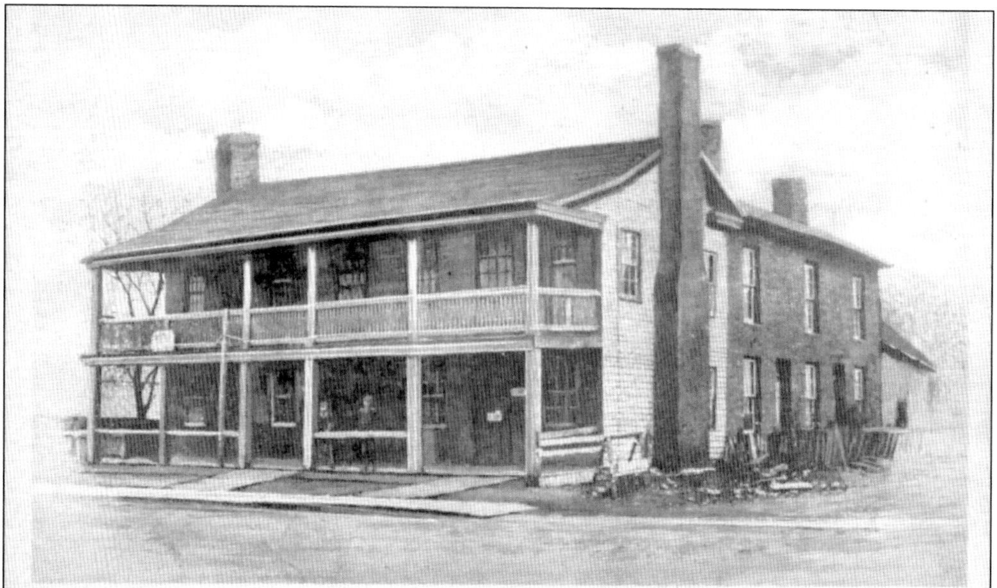

OLD EAGLE HOTEL. BUILT IN 1841. BENTONVILLE, ARK.
Siegel's Headquarters, March 1862.

Two Union divisions lingered in Bentonville as the Confederates moved to engage them. Gen. Sigel was having breakfast at the Eagle Hotel until his men waiting outside saw the approaching rebels; Sigel and his troops were chased out of town and barely evaded capture. Sigel returned in 1887, stayed in the same hotel room, and finally finished his breakfast before visiting the battlefield with some former Confederates, now friends.

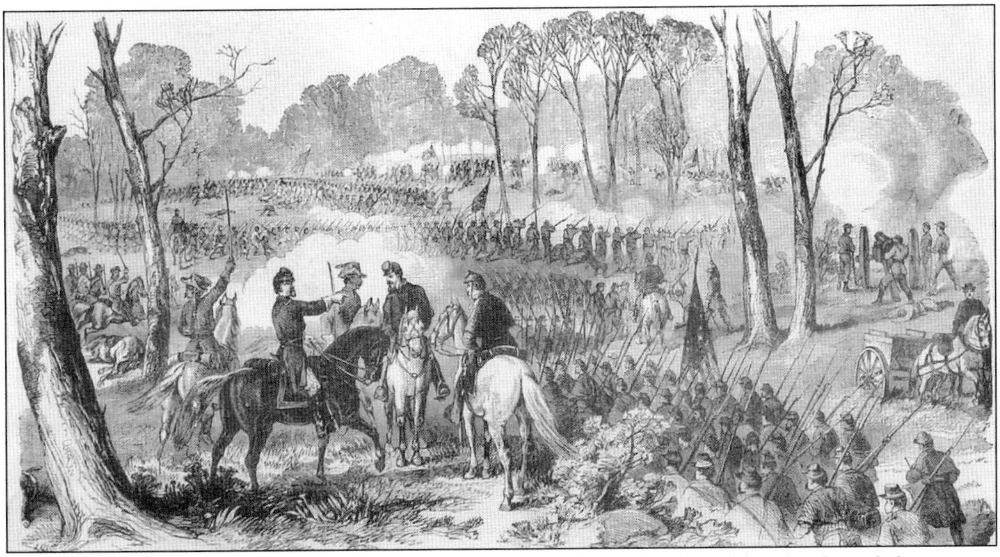

Van Dorn planned to strike the Union forces at Pea Ridge "quick and hard," though his troops were fatigued from marching north. Union general Curtis was prepared for Van Dorn's two-pronged attack around each end of Elkhorn Mountain. The flank led by Sterling Price initially fared well, pushing the federals back and capturing Elkhorn Tavern. However, the other flank was pounded by Union forces, as illustrated here by *Harpers Weekly*.

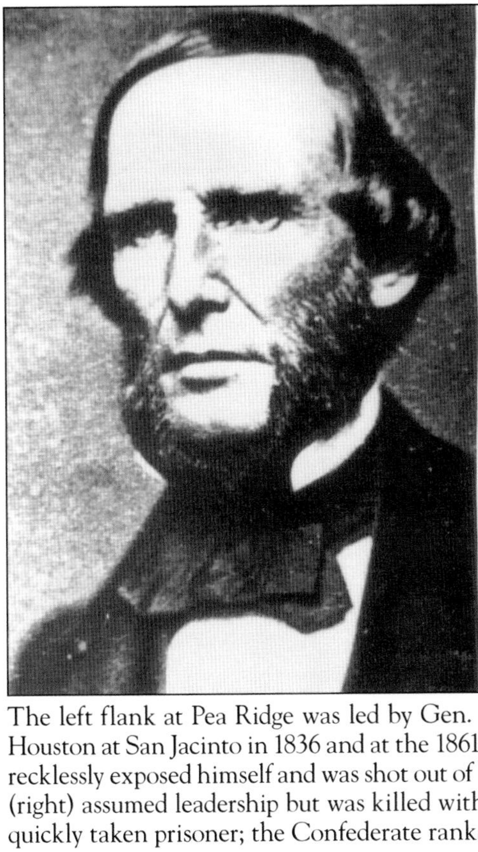

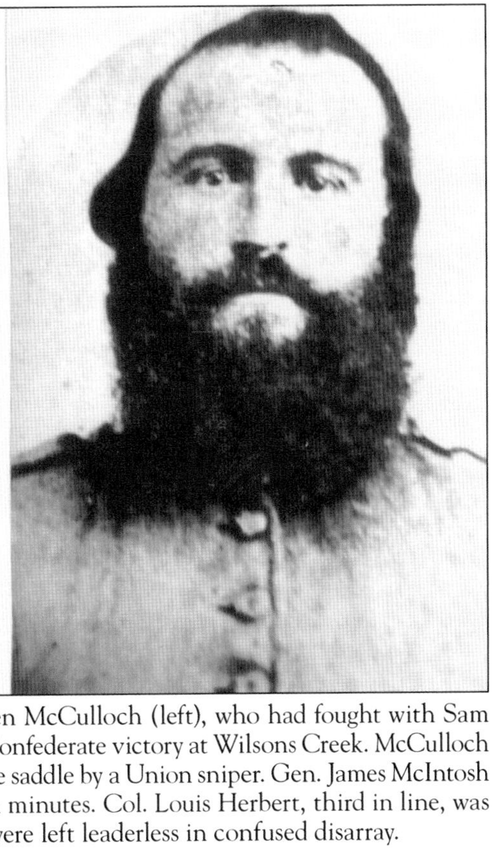

The left flank at Pea Ridge was led by Gen. Ben McCulloch (left), who had fought with Sam Houston at San Jacinto in 1836 and at the 1861 Confederate victory at Wilsons Creek. McCulloch recklessly exposed himself and was shot out of the saddle by a Union sniper. Gen. James McIntosh (right) assumed leadership but was killed within minutes. Col. Louis Herbert, third in line, was quickly taken prisoner; the Confederate ranks were left leaderless in confused disarray.

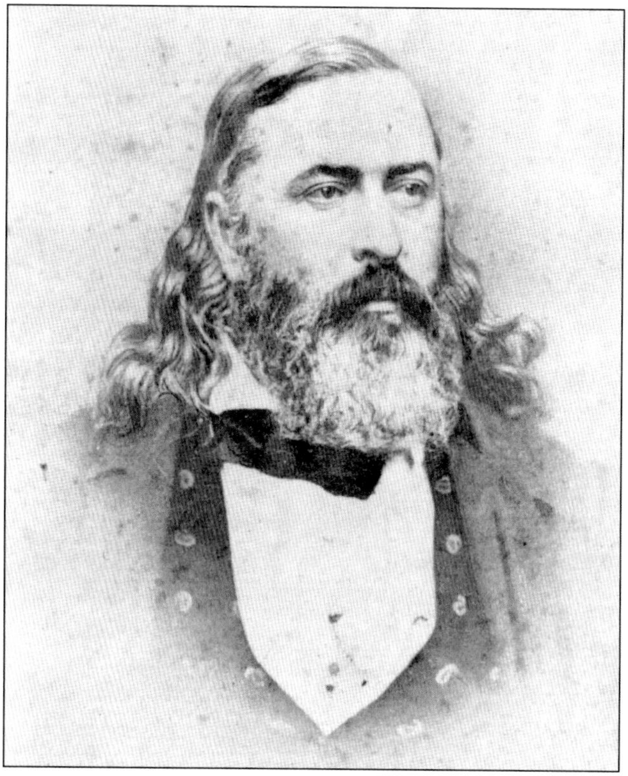

One of the commanders under General McCulloch at Pea Ridge was the 300-pound brigadier general Albert Pike, who was a renowned poet, lawyer, planter, and newspaper publisher, but not a particularly effective military leader. (Courtesy of Butler Center for Arkansas Studies.)

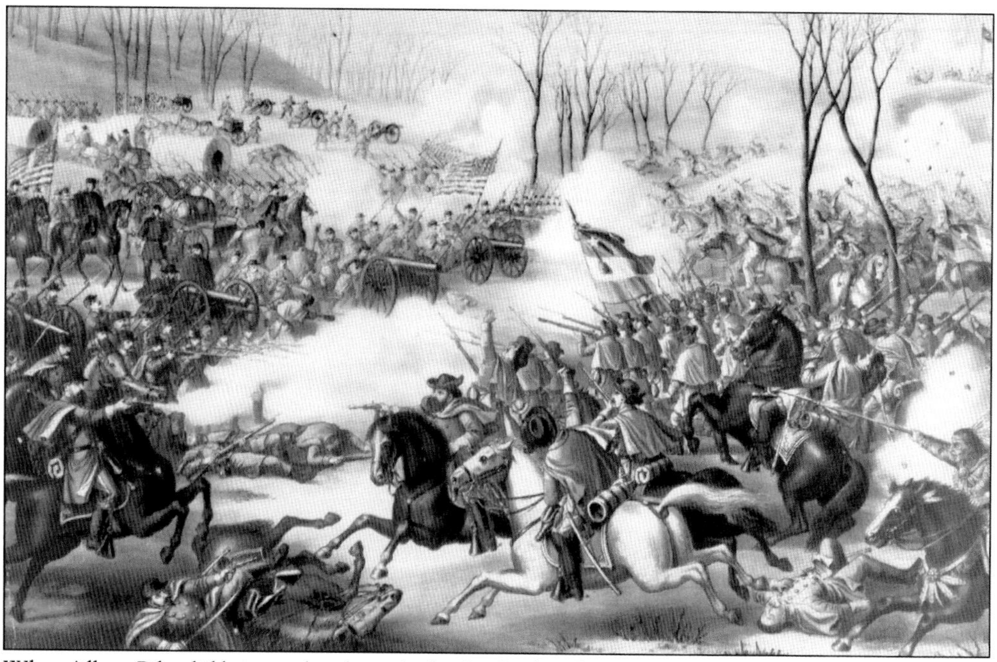

What Albert Pike did bring to battle under his leadership, however, were more than 1,000 Cherokee Indians, as well as members of a few other tribes. This somewhat overly dramatized illustration from *Harpers Weekly* shows the charging Confederates with the Native Americans among their ranks. (Courtesy of University of Arkansas at Little Rock Archives.)

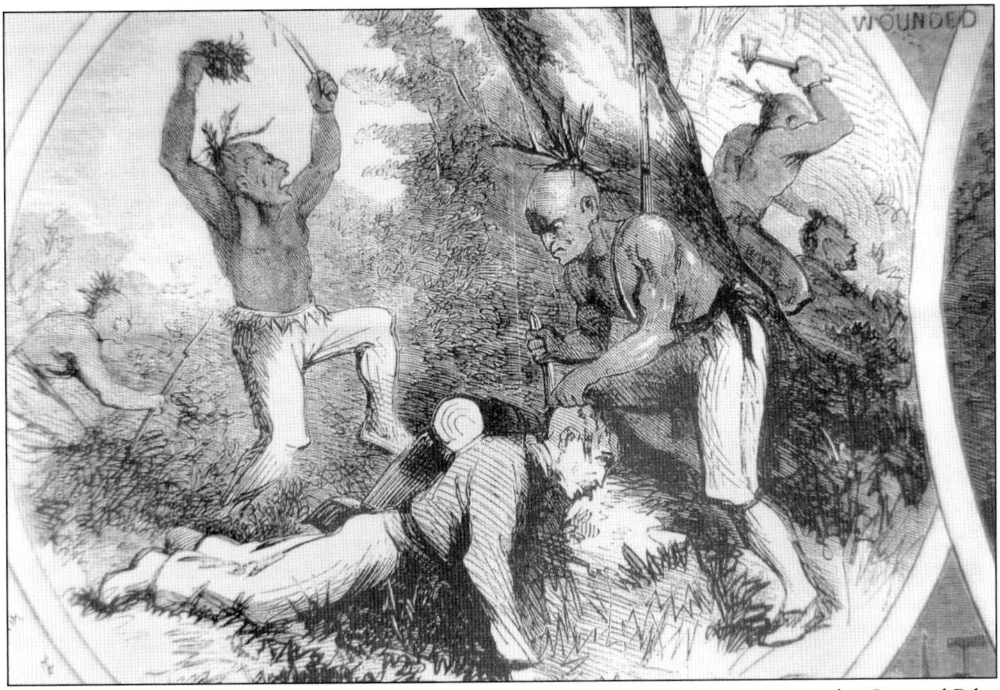

Field dispatches from Union general Curtis alleged that the Native Americans under General Pike had scalped and mutilated some of his dead and wounded soldiers. The poorly equipped Native Americans were armed mainly with tomahawks, and a few incidents of scalping apparently occurred. *Harpers Weekly*, a few weeks after the battle, inflamed Northern readers with this illustration dramatizing the stories; the episode followed Albert Pike for the remainder of his life.

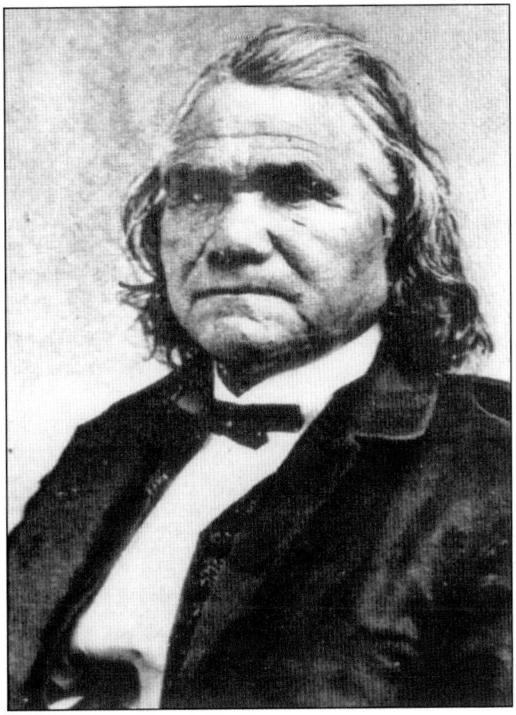

Pike's Cherokees were also led by Col. Stand Watie, the only Native American to become a Confederate general. Born in Georgia, Watie had signed onto the agreement sending the Cherokees on the Trail of Tears to Oklahoma. Watie influenced many of his people to align with the Confederacy and formed the Cherokee Mounted Rifles. Watie proved to be a daring cavalry raider, and he was the last Confederate general to surrender.

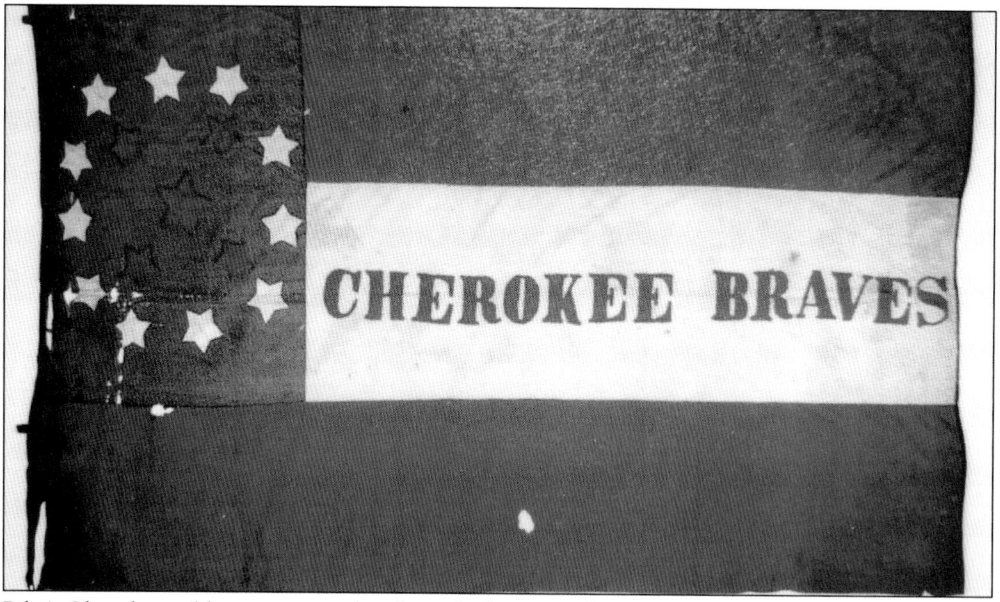

Pike's Cherokee soldiers went into battle with their own flag at Pea Ridge, under which they had early success. In the first charge, the Cherokees captured a Union battery, whooping and setting fire to the wooden portion of the cannon. They soon came under blistering Union artillery fire and found themselves fighting in a fashion for which they lacked training; they scattered, retreated, and were held in reserve for the balance of the battle.

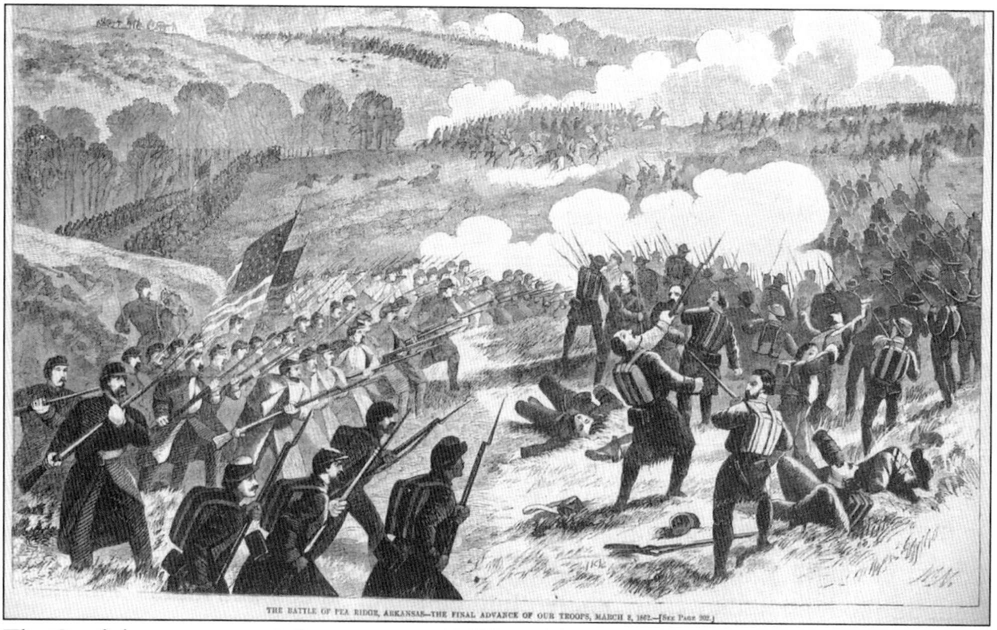

The Confederates captured the area around Elkhorn Tavern, a remote country inn, on March 7. The next morning, Union general Curtis counterattacked with superior massed artillery, as illustrated by *Harpers Weekly*. The Confederates held their ground until ammunition ran low; Van Dorn retreated south to Van Buren, but the victorious Union troops were too battered to pursue. Missouri was secure from rebellion, and a Union foothold was established in Arkansas. (Courtesy of Butler Center for Arkansas Studies.)

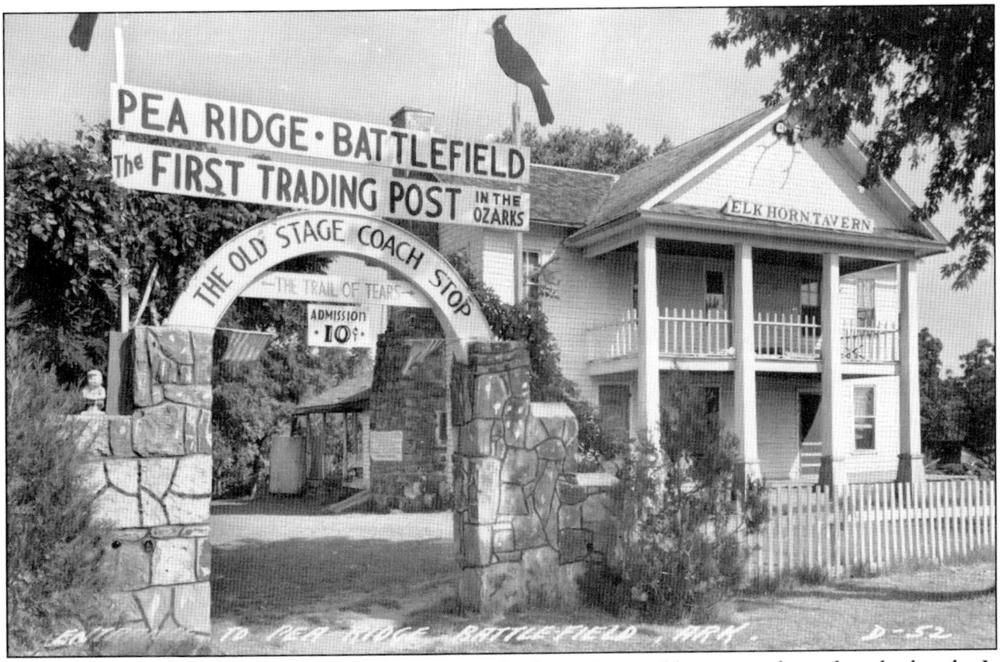

The landmark Elkhorn Tavern, where so many died, was burned by marauders after the battle. It was twice rebuilt around the original 1833, bullet-flecked chimney. By the 1940s, Elkhorn Tavern was a 10¢ tourist attraction promoting both the Civil War battlefield and the nearby route of the Cherokee Trail of Tears. Today restored to its 1862, pre-battle condition, the building is a centerpiece of the Pea Ridge National Military Park.

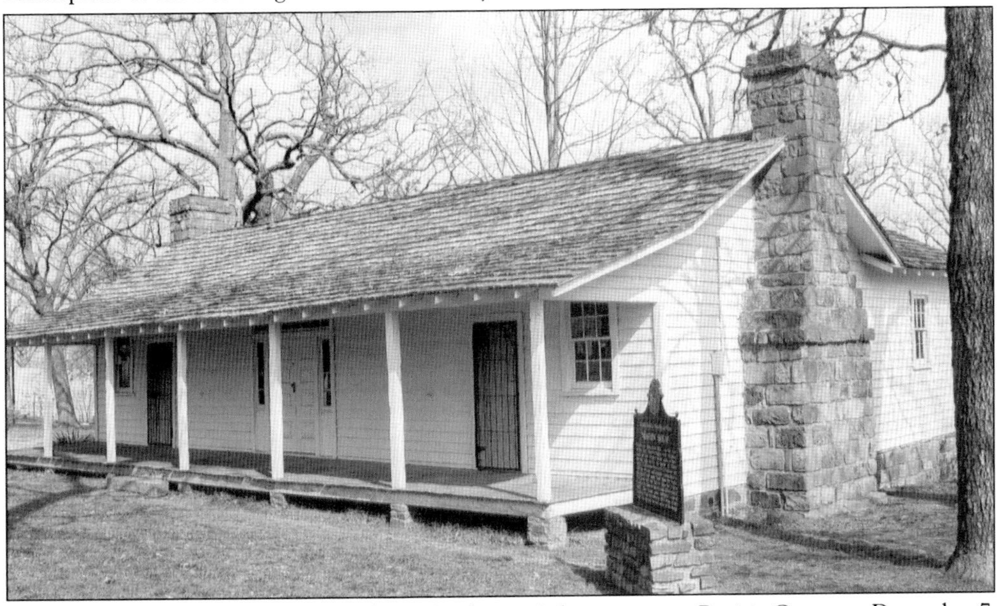

After Pea Ridge, the next major battle in Northwest Arkansas was at Prairie Grove on December 7, 1862. Confederate general Thomas Hindman of Helena, leading the Trans-Mississippi Division, organized a new army and gambled on one last chance to retake Northwest Arkansas. The night before the battle, he convened his officers in the home of John Morrow, marching out at 4:00 a.m. The house stands today at Prairie Grove State Park. (Photograph by Ray Hanley.)

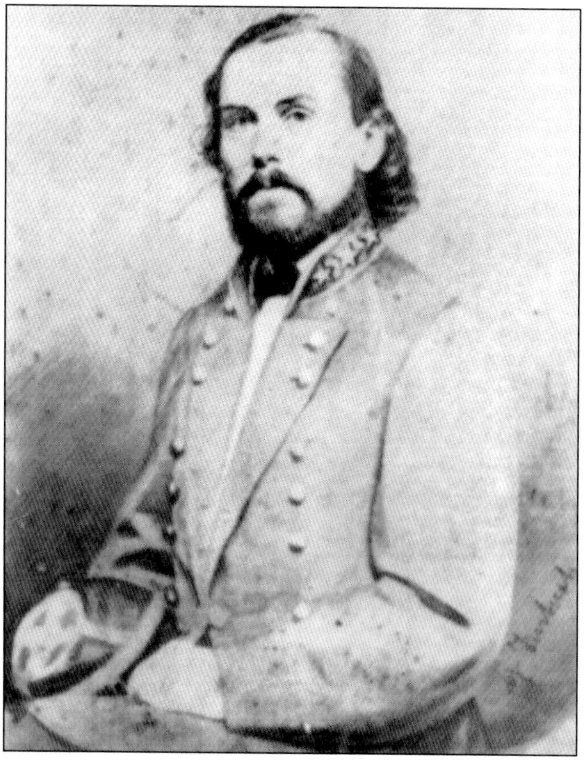

Hindman, the highest-ranking Confederate general from Arkansas, was a U.S. congressman who pushed for secession as the war began. He was wounded at Shiloh in April 1862 and twice more during the war. Hindman's vigorous and controversial enforcement of conscription and martial law alienated many. At the war's end, he fled to Mexico to farm coffee, but in 1867, he returned to Helena—where he was assassinated in his home.

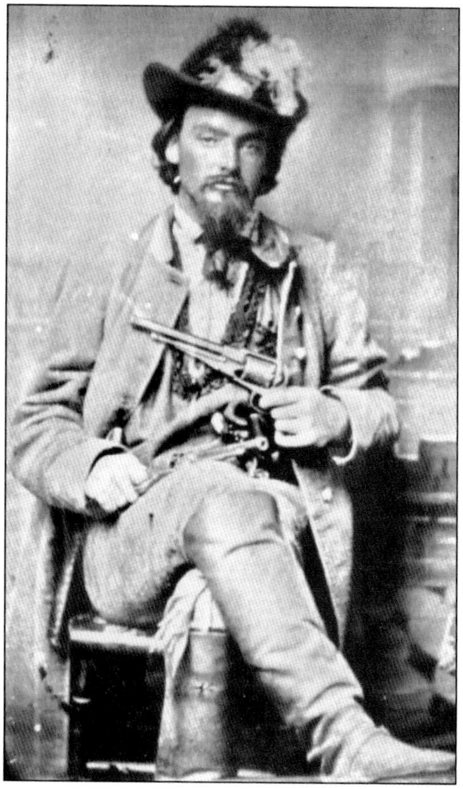

As Hindman and the Confederates moved out in the predawn darkness at Prairie Grove, they were led by an advance guard of William Quantrill's raiders. Quantrill's chief scout, the flashy George Maddox (posed here), was teamed with the Confederate cavalry led by Gen. John Marmaduke and initially drove back the advancing Union forces. (Courtesy of Arkansas Sons of Confederate Veterans.)

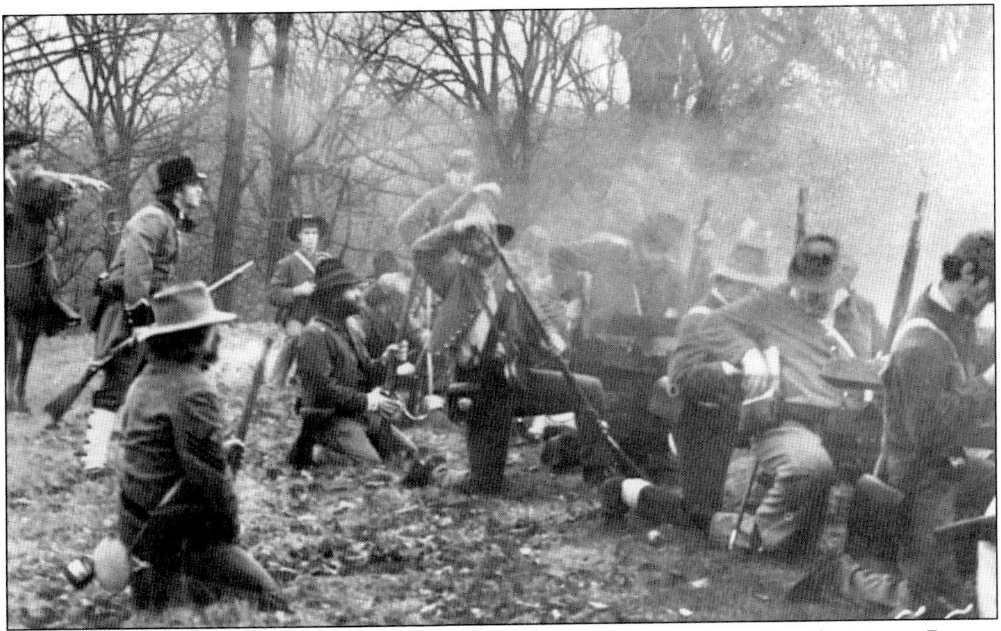

The fighting went on all day, as re-created here by reenactors in an annual event at Prairie Grove. Hindman likely had victory within his grasp had he followed up on his early advantage. Instead he took a defensive position, which allowed time for Union reinforcements under Gen. James Blunt to arrive and shift the tide of battle back to the federals. (Courtesy of Prairie Grove State Park.)

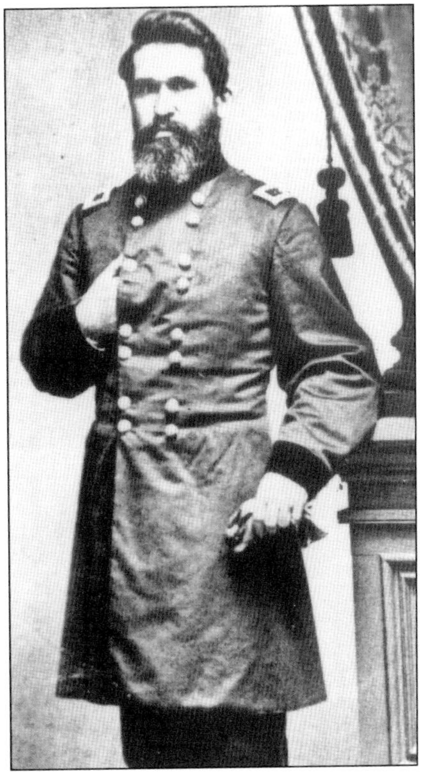

Hindman's Union counterpart, Gen. James Blunt, was a Kansas physician and ardent abolitionist before the war. Prairie Grove would be the apex of his military career; the low point was losing 90 troops, mostly black soldiers, to rebel raiders in 1863. A favorite of Abraham Lincoln, Blunt later worked to recruit black soldiers along the frontier. He ended his days in a Washington, D.C., hospital for the insane, dying in 1881.

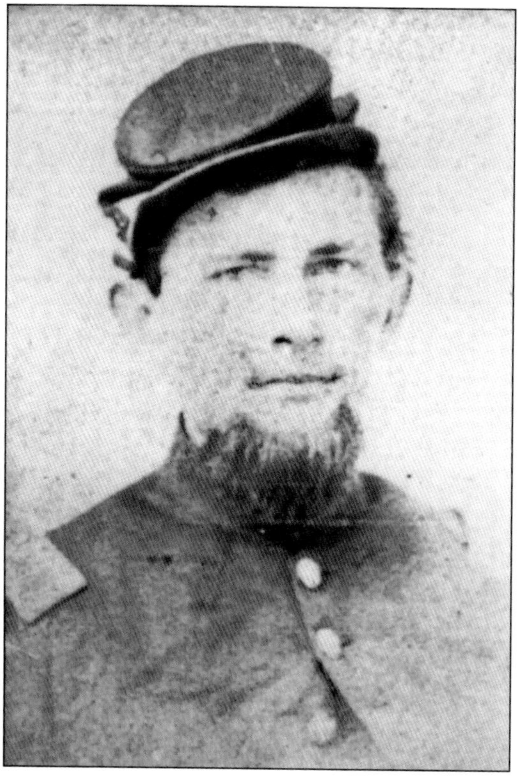

Union lieutenant Charles Dewolf of the 7th Missouri Cavalry kept a journal of his service. He recorded that the cold on the morning of the battle was like "Greenland"; weak from dysentery, he had his breakfast of canned oysters and sardines interrupted by the attacking rebels: "I moved onto the field with them, and all the splendors and horrors of a battlefield lay before me." Dewolf survived the battle and lived until 1915.

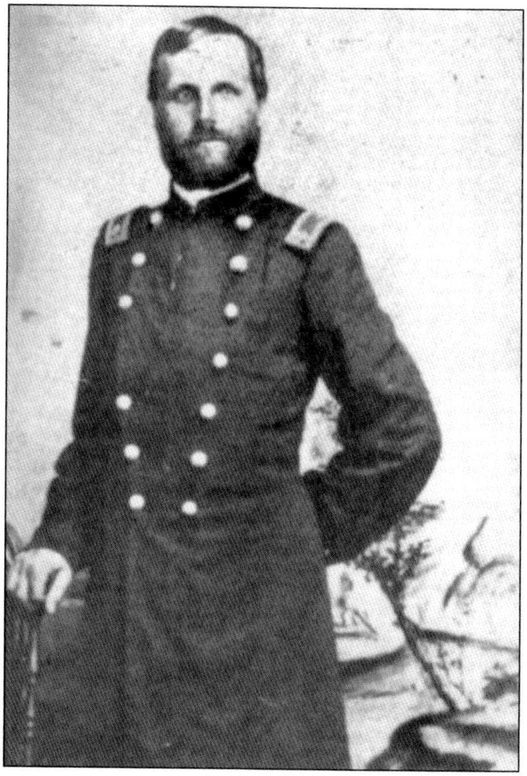

Lieutenant Dewolf also wrote of the death of his superior, Maj. Eliphalet Bredett: "a heavy volley was fired at him and he fell from his horse," dying on the cold ground. Dewolf continued, "[The rebels] lay in heaps on top of the slope. Many were killed by cannon shot, I noticed one was struck in the middle cutting him in two. His eyes were open as though he died before he could close them. Many had their hands full of dirt and leaves, grasped in their death agony. It was a horrid sight." Under a decoy flag of truce, Hindman saved his army to fight another day, retreating south to Van Buren.

Two

WAR COMES TO EASTERN ARKANSAS

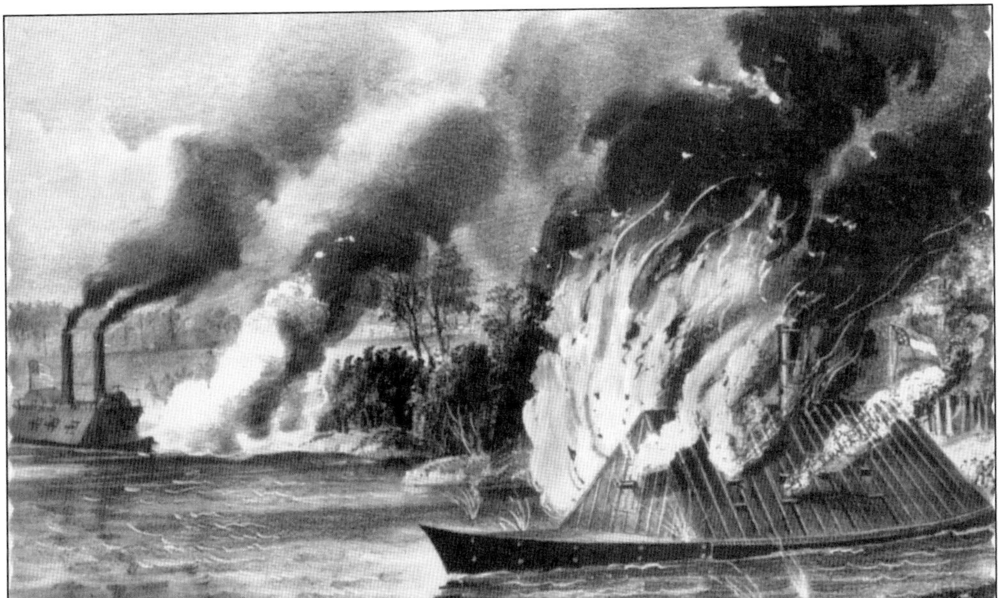

"Destruction of Rebel Ram - 'Arkansas'" - October 4, 1862

Through 1862 and into 1863, the tide of war was again rising toward Arkansas. Gen. Ulysses S. Grant was intent on taking control of the Mississippi River on the eastern border of Arkansas. The Confederate forces defending Arkansas expected the Union army would then move overland and by rivers to stage an attempt to take Little Rock. One obstacle to the Union's control of the Mississippi River had been the armored CSS *Arkansas* ram, named for its iron prow. Carrying 200 men and 10 guns, the ironclad's luck ran out on October 4, 1862, when its engines failed near Baton Rouge while pursued by the Union's ironclad *Essex*. The *Arkansas*'s crew set her afire, abandoned ship, and let her sink rather than be captured. The Currier and Ives painting was widely displayed in Northern homes.

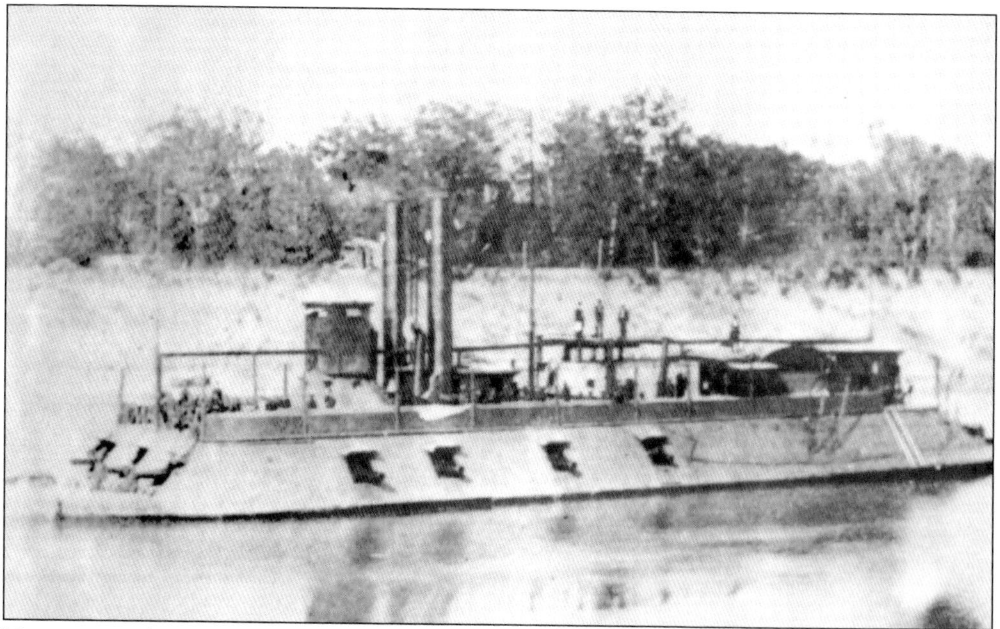

Union general Samuel Curtis had prevailed at Pea Ridge early in 1862 and was determined to invade Little Rock, heading overland out of Missouri. Bogged down and low on supplies, Curtis was counting on the Union army and navy taking the White River and reaching him in Jacksonport in Northeast Arkansas. The Union forces brought in six new ironclad steamers, like the *Mound City*, specially designed to navigate Southern rivers.

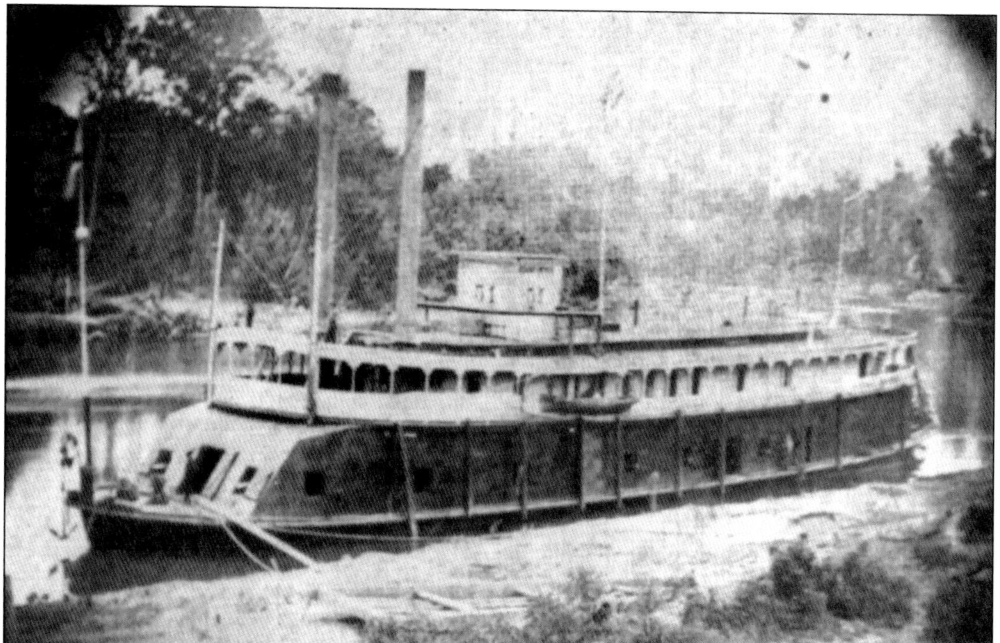

The Confederacy lacked the naval resources of the North and went to great lengths to try to defend the river routes that led to its important cities. Confederate Gunboat No. 51, seen here on the White River, was actually a converted passenger steamer that had been armored with available sheets of steel and fitted with cannons.

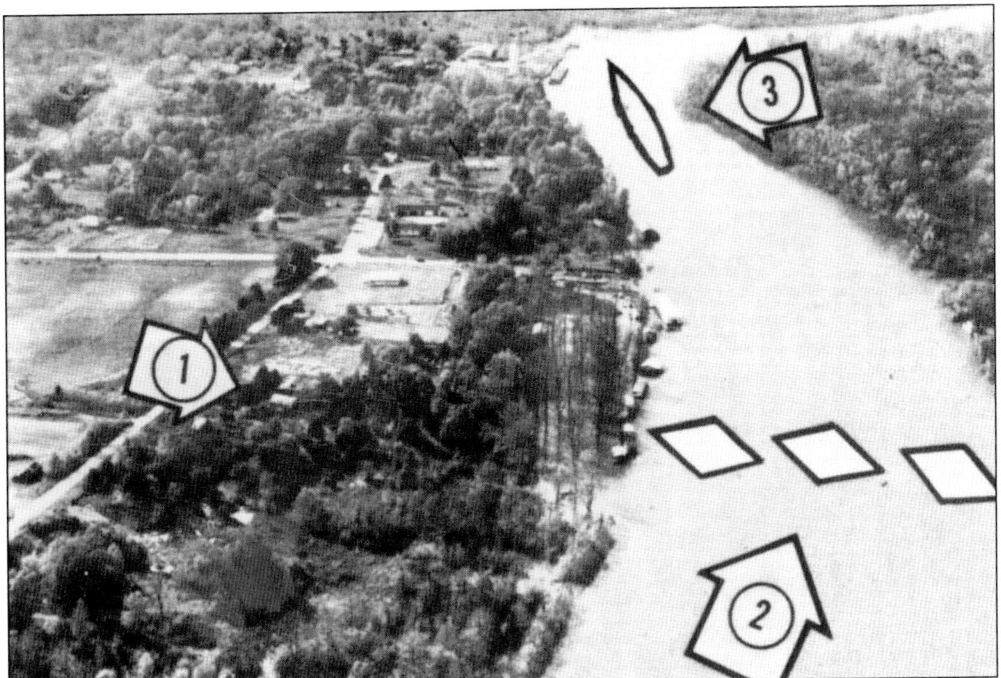

The Confederates attempted in June 1862 to halt the enemy's armada at tiny St. Charles, set above a bend in the White River, by blocking the river channel with three sunken steamboats, as shown in this 1962 illustrative aerial photograph. The Union gunboats, led by the *Mound City*, started steaming toward the Confederate river blockade at 6:00 a.m. on June 17, 1862. Capt. Augustus Kilty steamed in the *Mound City* to within 600 yards of the Confederate artillery as the air filled with screaming shells going in both directions. The highest-fatality single shot of the Civil War, a 32-pound shell, struck the steam drum of the ship, killing or wounding all but 26 of the *Mound City*'s crew of 175. *Harpers Weekly* illustrated the encounter and also reported that some who dove overboard were allegedly killed by Confederate sharpshooters. (Above image by Garner Allen, courtesy of *Stuttgart Daily Leader*. Below image courtesy of Butler Center for Arkansas Studies.)

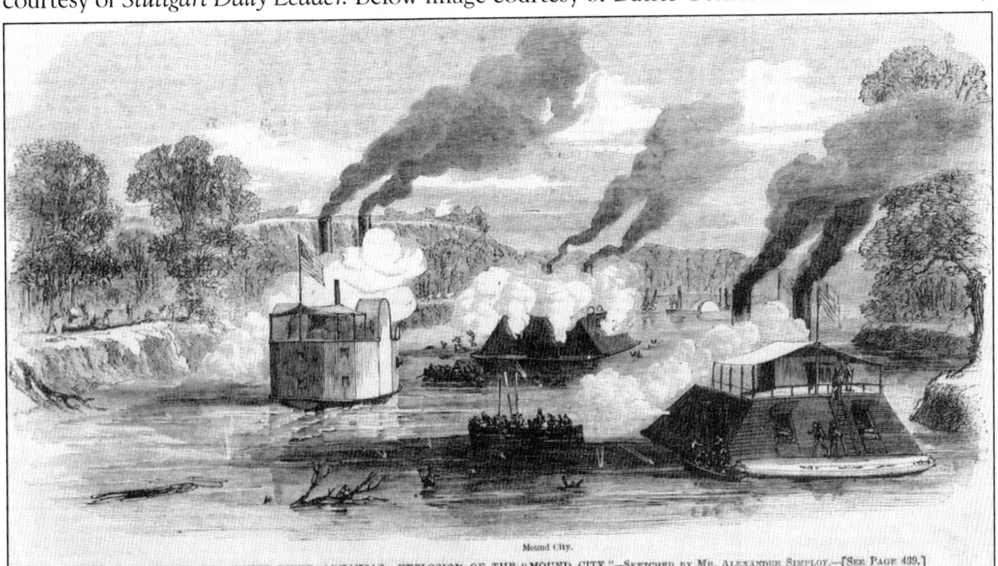

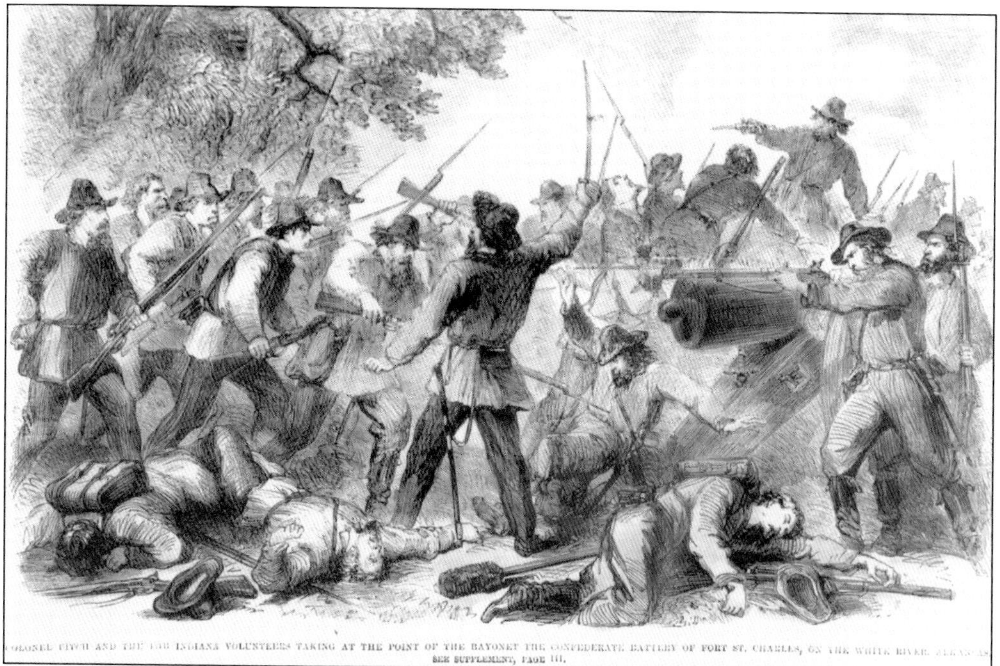

Despite the loss of the *Mound City*, the remaining Union gunboats soon silenced the Confederates' artillery; a regiment of Indiana Volunteers overcame the remaining defenses. The Union had won the battle but lost almost 150 men to the Confederates' half-dozen casualties. Many of the initial survivors of the *Mound City* later died slow, painful deaths from their scald burns; the ship was repaired and put back into service. (Courtesy of Butler Center for Arkansas Studies.)

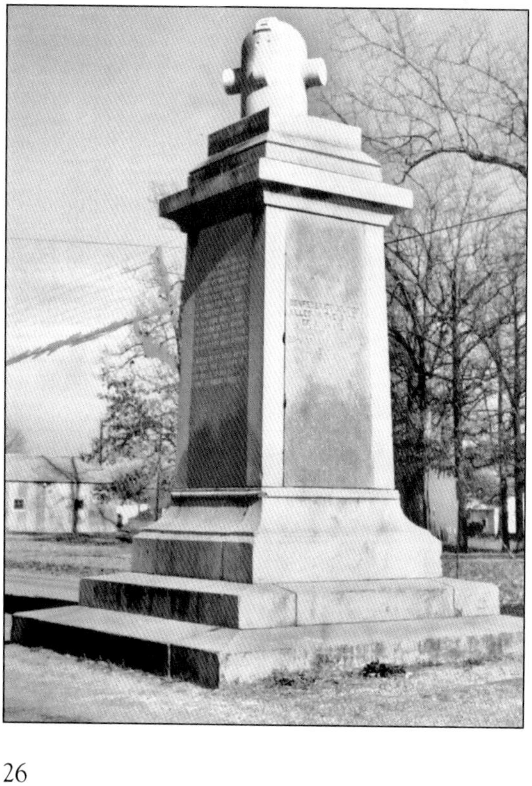

Standing today in St. Charles is this monument paid for and erected in 1919 by a Northerner in memory of a relative killed in the blast, William Hickman Harte. The monument lists both the Union dead and the six Confederates killed. This inclusion may have been at the town's insistence or because the benefactor was reportedly moved by meeting the townsman who had cared for his wounded relative. (Courtesy of Butler Center for Arkansas Studies.)

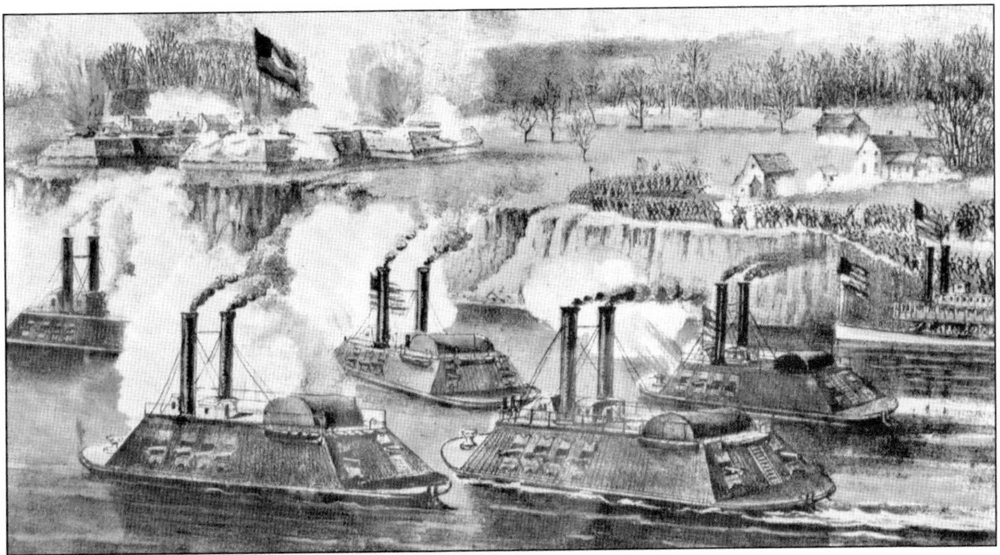

The strongest of all Confederate forts in Arkansas was built at Arkansas Post, 50 miles up the Arkansas River from its juncture with the Mississippi. Fort Hindman was a huge earthen fortification intended as a base for harassing Union efforts on the Mississippi and also served to help guard Little Rock, 117 miles upstream. In January 1863, 32,000 Union troops set sail on transports up the river, intent on taking the fort. Currier and Ives depicted the flotilla of Union gunboats shelling the entrenched Confederates on January 10. The Union bombardment put the Confederate artillery largely out of action, allowing Gen. S. G. Burbridge to lead an infantry charge into the fort's earthworks. The planting of the Union flag and the waving of the Confederate white flag of surrender were dramatized by an artist who had apparently accompanied the Union army. (Courtesy of Butler Center for Arkansas Studies.)

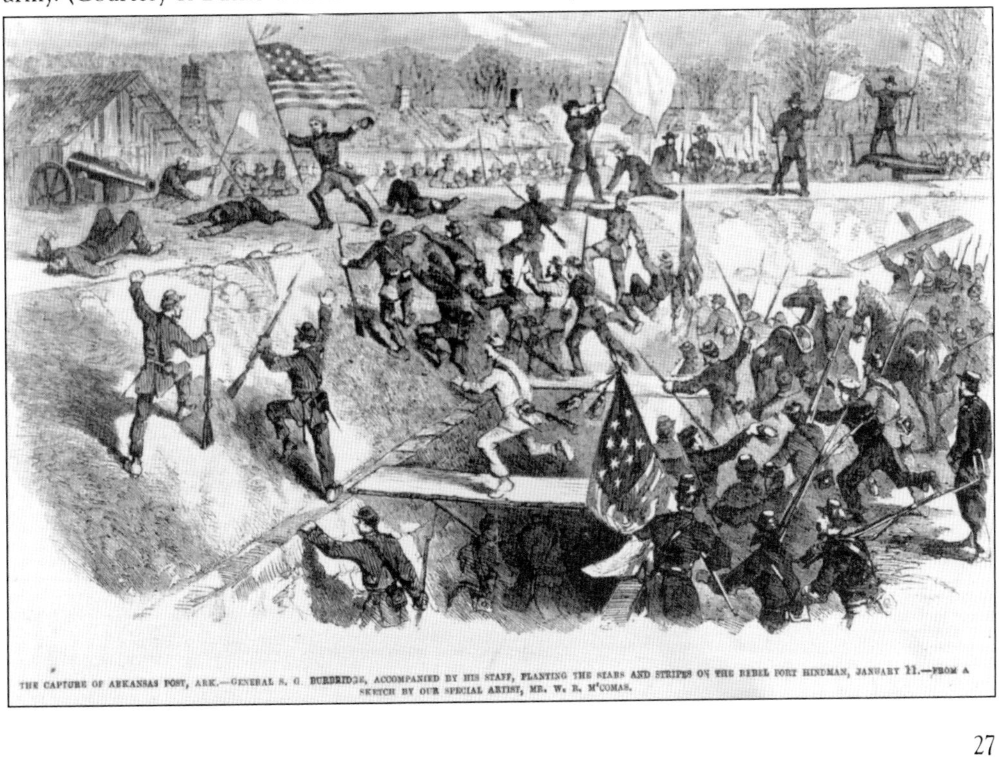

THE CAPTURE OF ARKANSAS POST, ARK.—GENERAL S. G. BURBRIDGE, ACCOMPANIED BY HIS STAFF, PLANTING THE STARS AND STRIPES ON THE REBEL FORT HINDMAN, JANUARY 11.—FROM A SKETCH BY OUR SPECIAL ARTIST, MR. W. R. M'COMAS.

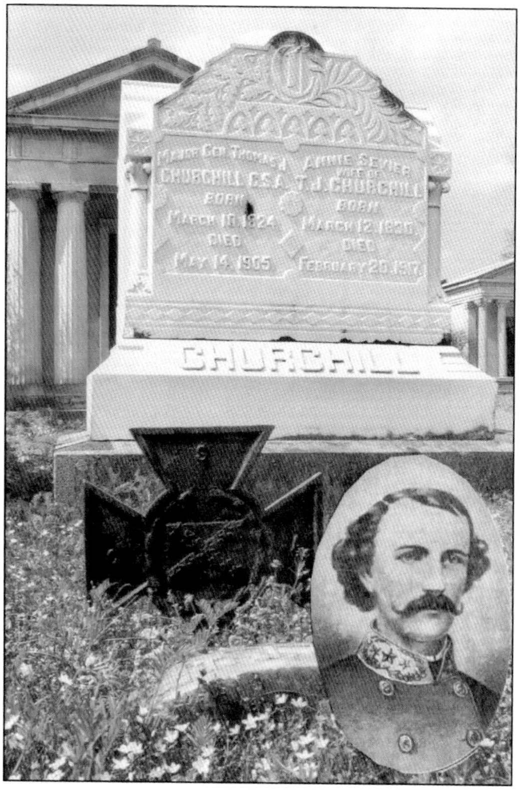

Fort Hindman's 4,900 Confederates were commanded by Gen. Thomas J. Churchill of Little Rock. Churchill had fought well at Pea Ridge and at Richmond, Kentucky, the year before. He was taken prisoner along with his men but was later exchanged for Union prisoners and returned to the war. Churchill served as Arkansas's governor in 1881–1883 and died in Little Rock in 1905 at age 81; he is buried in Mount Holly Cemetery.

The devastating impact of the Union gunboats' pounding of Fort Hindman was illustrated by *Harpers Weekly*; the sketch shows the fort's casement and nine-inch gun wrecked and the crew decimated. Confederate casualties approached 150, while the Union lost over 1,000 infantrymen due to the blistering small-arms fire mounted by the fortified Confederates. The site of the fort has today been reclaimed by the river, which undermined its bluff location. (Courtesy of Butler Center for Arkansas Studies.)

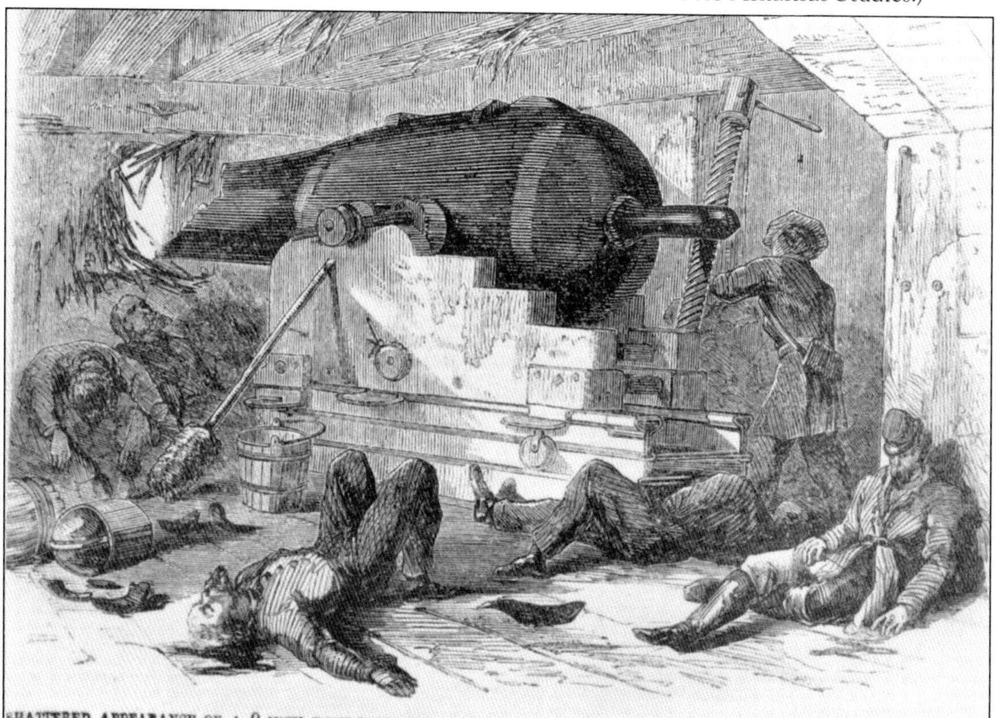

SHATTERED APPEARANCE OF A 9-INCH DAHLGREN GUN, IN THE PRINCIPAL CASEMATE OF FORT HINDMAN, ARKANSAS POST. SKETCHED BY OUR SPECIAL ARTIST.

Gen. William Tecumseh Sherman, who helped lead the assault on the fort, walked through the ruins after the battle, commenting: "The fresh made parapet had been knocked down in many places, and dead men lay around very thick. . . . It was as fierce an engagement of six hours as has occurred during the war." Sherman, who famously noted "war is hell," would later be called both hero and tyrant for his scorched-earth march through Georgia.

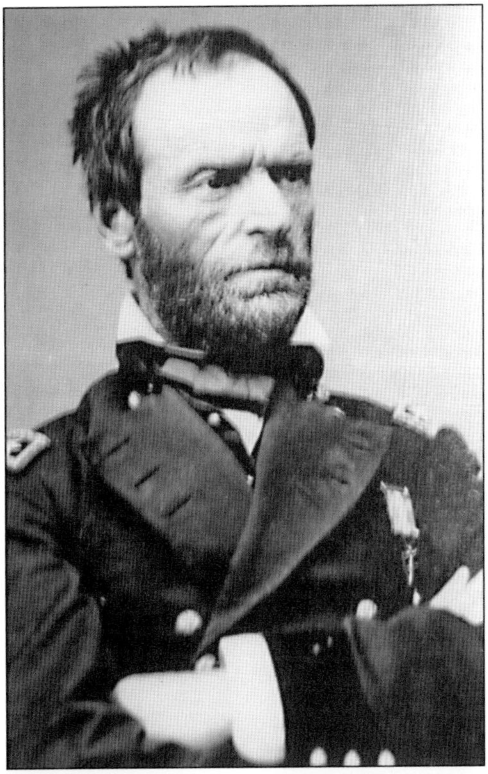

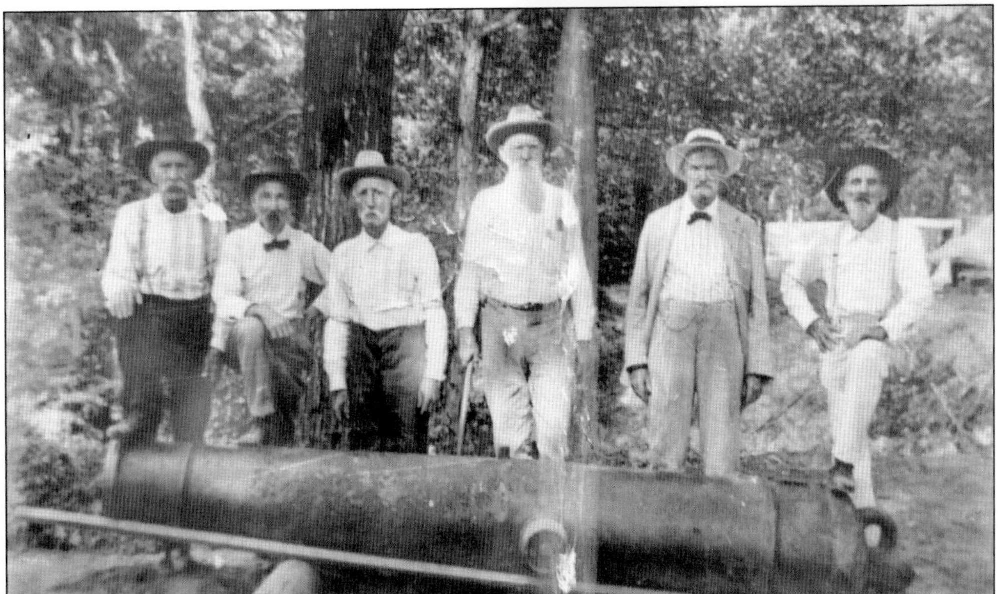

The last six surviving Confederate veterans of the United Confederate Veterans Camp Fagan group are posed at Arkansas Post in 1920 with one of the cannons from the 1863 battle. They were at a reunion encampment at the time, likely speculating on how the battle of Arkansas Post might have ended differently. Felix Allen, far left, from the town of Casscoe, would be the last of the six to die. (Courtesy of Arkansas Post State Park.)

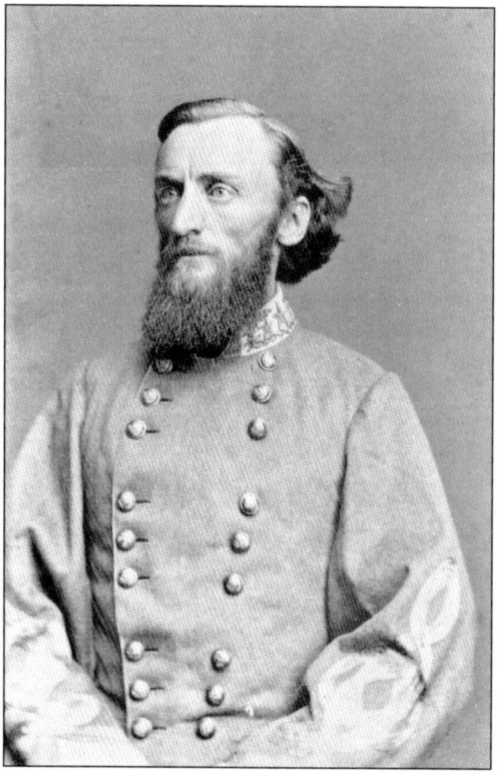

Gen. John Marmaduke, a West Point graduate, served with distinction throughout Arkansas, including the battles at Prairie Grove and Helena and in Southwest Arkansas. In the spring of 1863, he plotted an attack into Southeast Missouri, hoping to rally Southern sympathizers. Captured in 1864, he finished the war as a Union prisoner in faraway Boston. He survived the war and died in office in 1887 while serving as governor of Missouri. (Courtesy of Butler Center for Arkansas Studies, Paul Dolle Civil War Collection.)

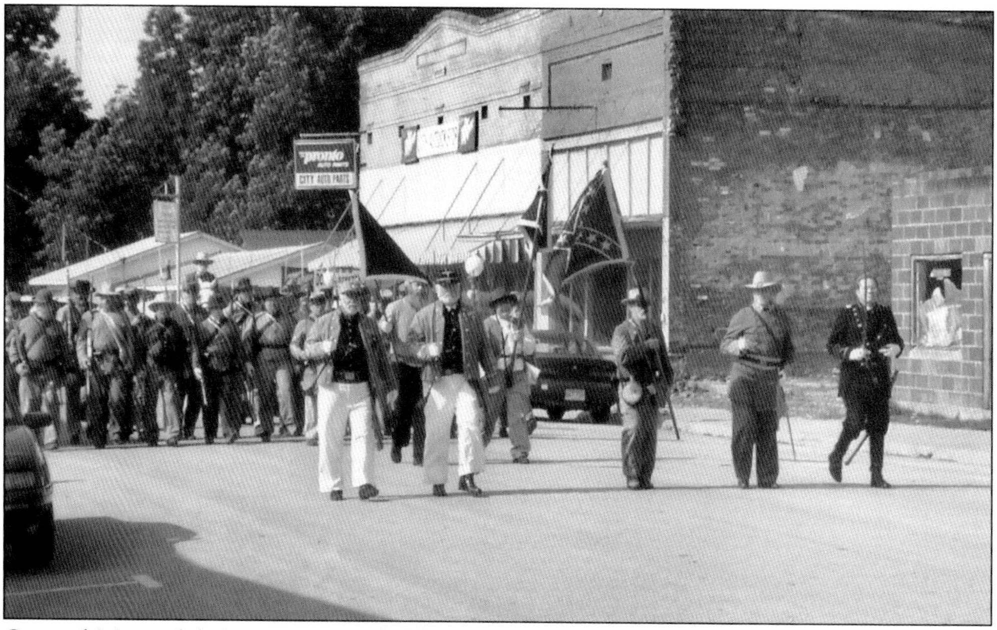

General Marmaduke's memory was held in high esteem in Northeast Arkansas following the Civil War. When it was incorporated, the small town of Marmaduke in Greene County took his name. The Arkansas Sons of Confederate Veterans erected a marker in the general's honor in this small town in 2005 and marched in the Fourth of July parade. (Courtesy of Arkansas Sons of Confederate Veterans.)

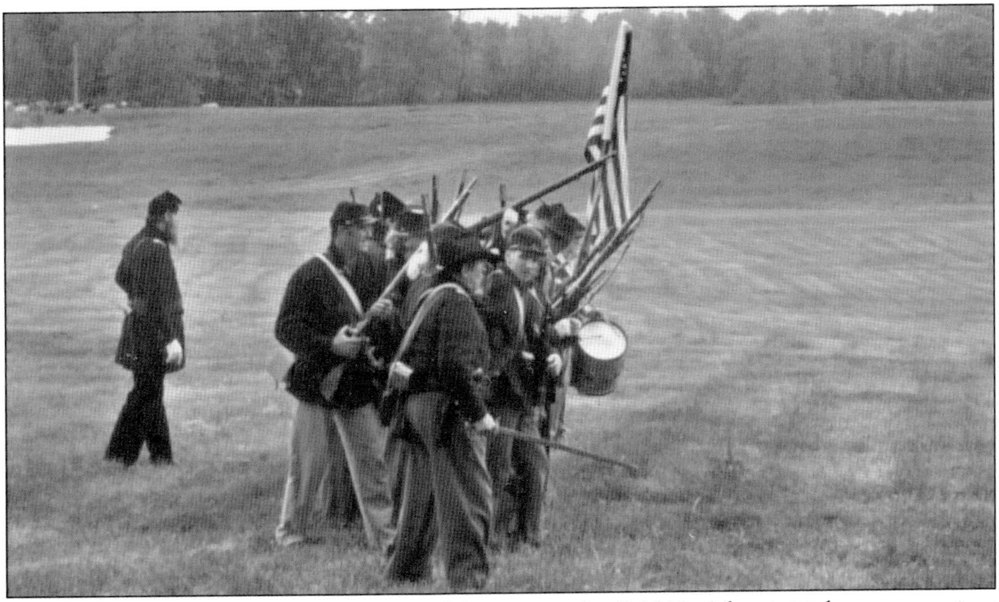

General Marmaduke led 5,000 men into Missouri in April 1863. After initial success against small federal units, Union reinforcements arrived off the Mississippi River. Narrowly evading the pursuing Yankees, Marmaduke retreated into Arkansas by erecting a narrow, bobbing bridge, using grapevines for rope. Most of the troops succeeded in crossing the St. Francis River in this brilliant military and engineering feat. However, the horses were too heavy for the bridge and had to be swum across; many of the fatigued animals drowned and were seen floating downstream for miles. Once over the river, Marmaduke entrenched his troops and artillery, preparing for the approaching federal troops. In the Battle of Chalk Bluff on May 2, 1863, each side reportedly suffered some 200 casualties killed, wounded, or captured. Chalk Bluff State Park, north of Piggott, Arkansas, hosts an annual reenactment, as seen here. (Courtesy of Arkansas Sons of Confederate Veterans.)

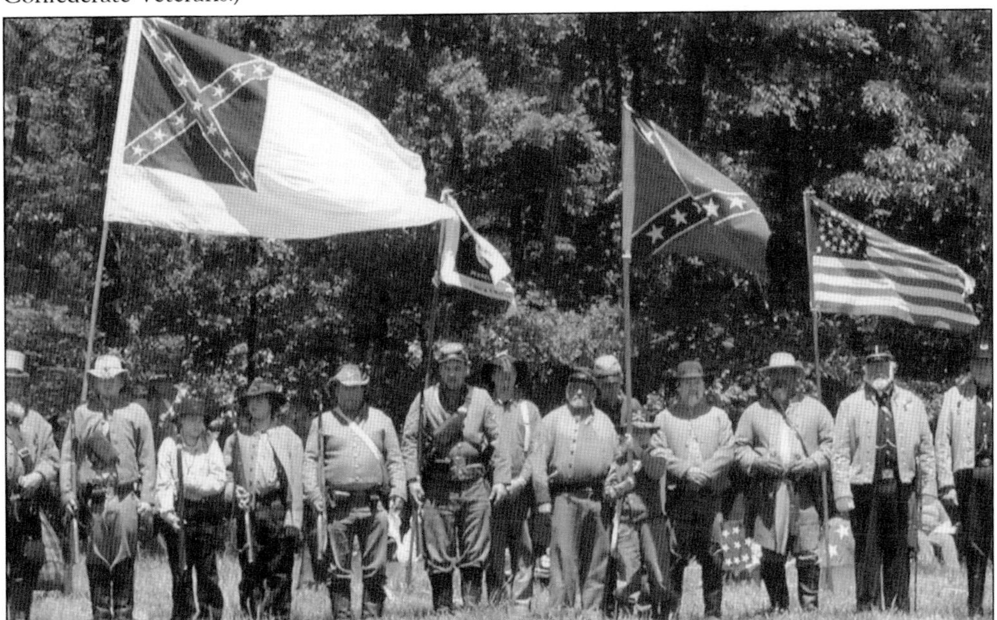

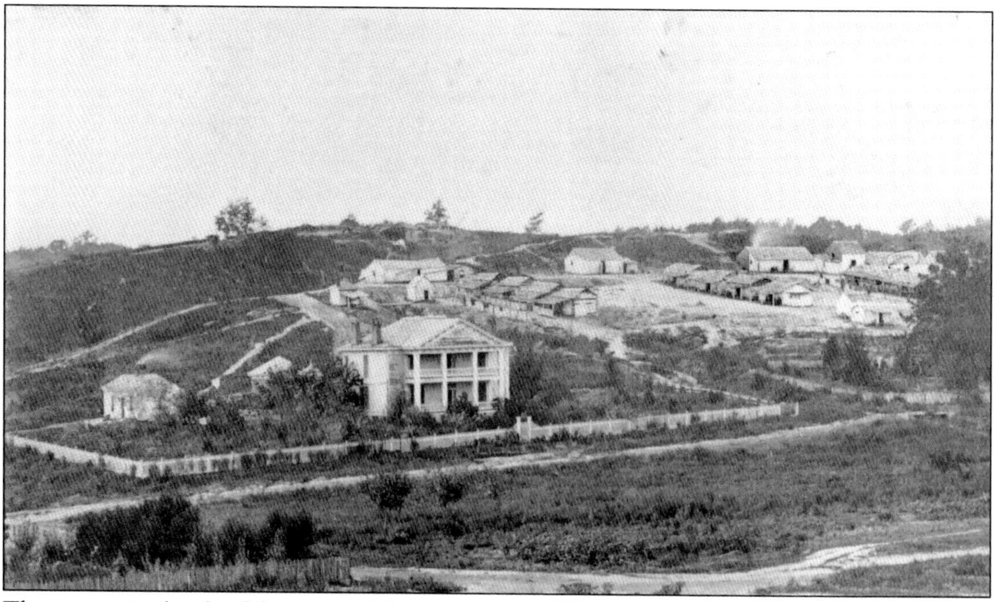

The next major battle of the war in Arkansas came on July 4, 1863, at Helena, the Mississippi river port occupied by Union forces since July 1862. As seen here during the war, the trees had been stripped from the surrounding hillsides to build fortifications. The large home in the center belonged to absent Confederate general James Tappan. The 1850s Tappan mansion was damaged but later restored. (Courtesy of Butler Center for Arkansas Studies, Paul Dolle Civil War Collection.)

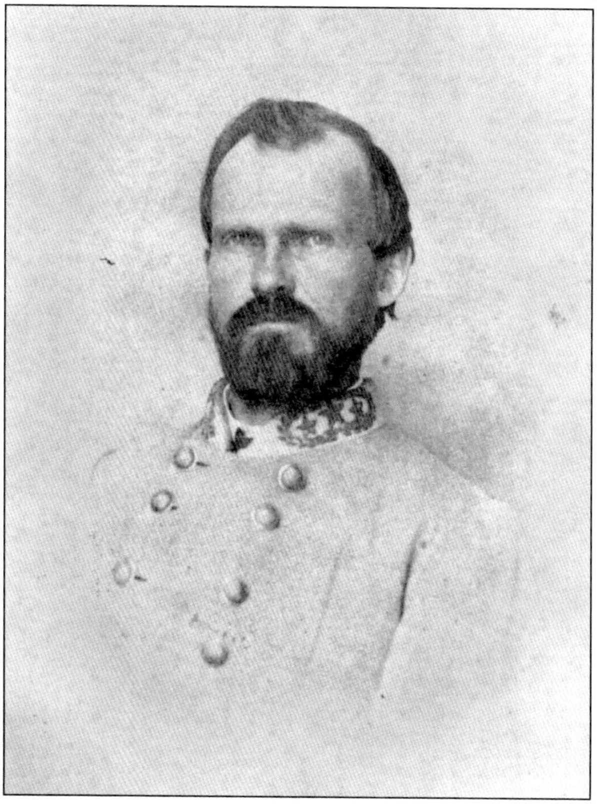

Gen. James Tappan, a Yale graduate, attorney, and one of seven Confederate generals from Helena, was not present at the battle for his hometown, though his house was in the path of shot and shell. Tappan fought in the midst of the "Hornet's Nest" at Shiloh and a number of other battles. After the war, he twice declined the Democratic nomination for governor, instead becoming dean of the Arkansas Bar. (Courtesy of Butler Center for Arkansas Studies.)

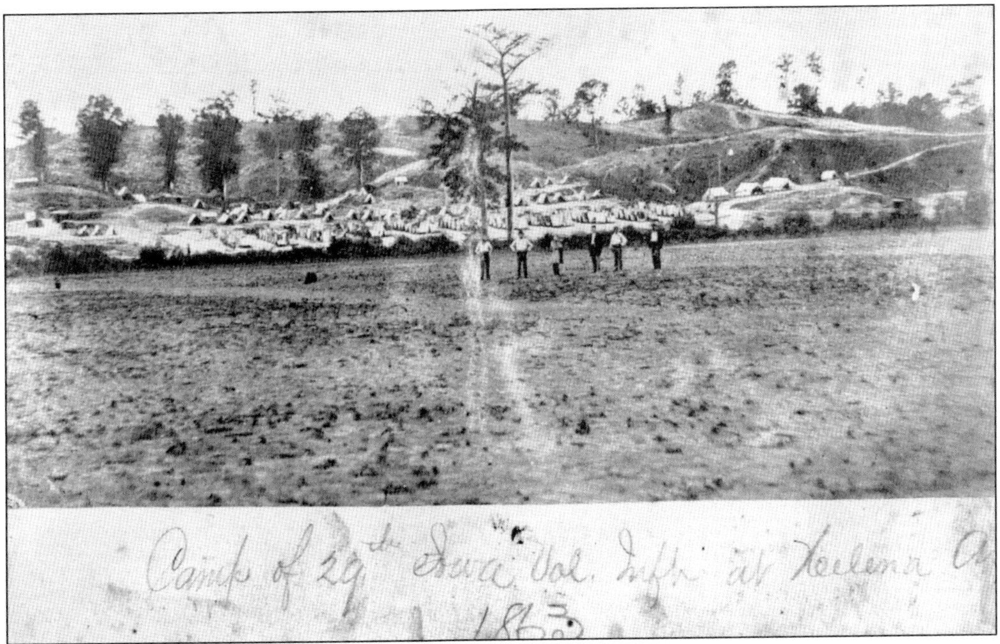

After the 1862 Union occupation of Helena, troops like those of the 29th Iowa Volunteer Infantry used the port city as a supply and staging area to help lay siege to Vicksburg and to move farther into Arkansas. The Confederates, led by Gen. Theophilus Holmes, decided to attack the 4,000 fortified federals, believing that if they could retake Helena, it would offer some relief to besieged Vicksburg down the river.

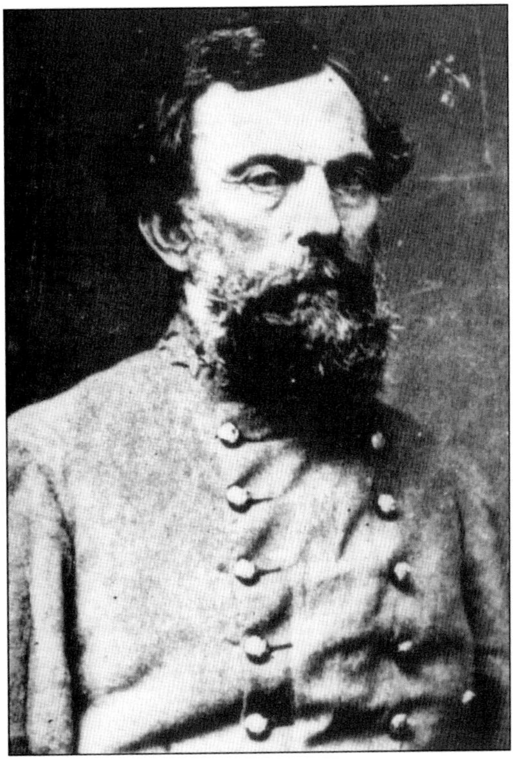

The campaign to retake Helena was entrusted to the leadership of Lt. Gen. Theophilus H. Holmes, a Mexican War veteran from North Carolina. Holmes was held in low esteem by his troops, who nicknamed him "Granny." Historian Shelby Foote described the aging Holmes as a "grim-featured man" whose "rigidity of face, indicative of arteriosclerosis, was matched by a rigidity of mind." (Courtesy of J. M. Heiskell Collection, University of Arkansas at Little Rock.)

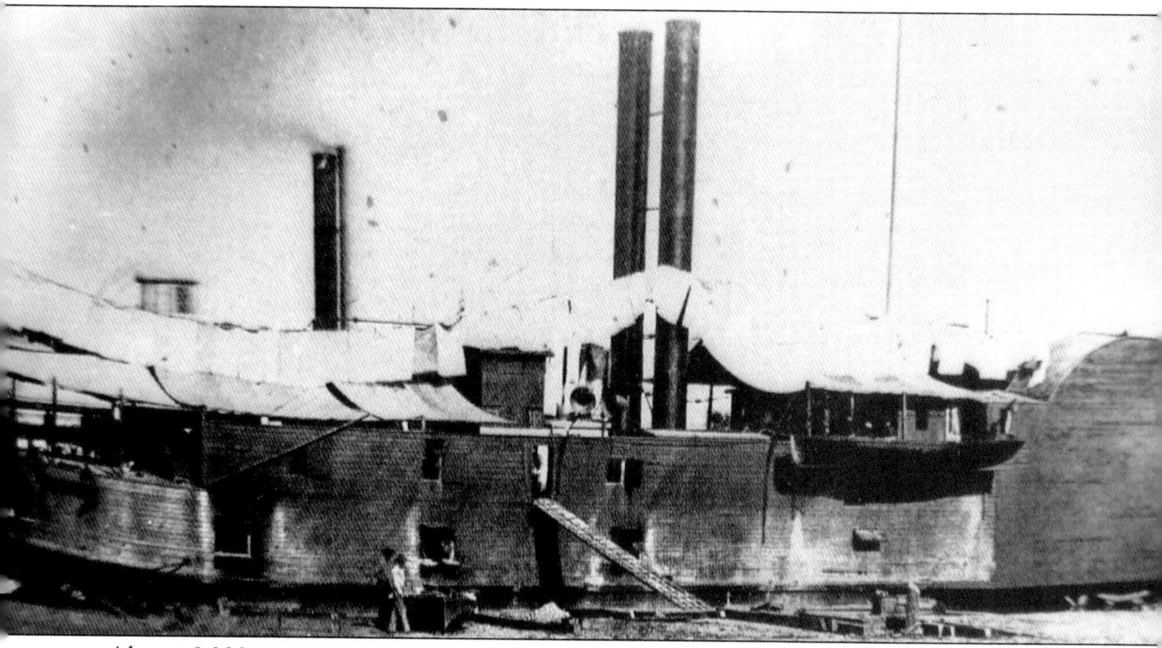

Almost 8,000 weary, rain-soaked Confederates arrived on the outskirts of Helena late on July 3, 1863, confronting half that many well-entrenched Union troops under Maj. Gen. Benjamin Prentiss. The Union commander had reinforced Fort Curtis, an earthen fort, and had also positioned the massive 575-ton sidewheel steamer gunboat *Tyler* for support against the expected attack. Ironically the ship was named for John Tyler, who stayed loyal to his Southern state of Virginia. General Holmes ordered an attack "at daylight" on July 4 led by Price's two brigades, Marmaduke's cavalry, and Fagan's brigade. The coordinated Confederate attack plan broke down on several fronts. Marmaduke's 1,750 dismounted cavalry, pinned down by enemy fire, waited in vain for support from Brig. Gen. Lucius Walker's cavalry brigade. General Fagan believed the orders meant "at first light" and attacked promptly; General Price believed it meant "at sunup" and delayed for almost an hour. Fagan's unsupported troops came under heavy artillery and small-arms fire, but with incredible courage, they advanced to take five outer fire pits. When Price's troops finally moved, the *Tyler*'s guns opened up with devastating effect. Still they charged, taking Graveyard Hill; even Union general Prentiss said they showed "courage and desperation rarely equaled." When Price's third and final assault failed in the July heat, the Confederates had no choice but to retreat through the fallen trees and ravines. The battle of Helena was over, with 239 Union casualties and over 1,600 Confederates killed or wounded—many from the 413 rounds rained down from the *Tyler*. A Wisconsin soldier at Graveyard Hill wrote, "The battlefield is no pleasant place to visit, covered with men wounded in all ways—some with brains exposed, others shot through the body with grape shot, or a large ball still sufficient to nearly cut the body in twain." Another Union soldier wrote, "Just to see the rebels lying in piles where they charged up the hill, it was awful. I never want to spend another such 'Fourth of July.' " Compounding the tragedy, the battle served no real purpose, for on the very same day, Vicksburg fell. Adding further agony to the cause, the Confederacy lost at Gettysburg on that same July 4, 1863.

The bravest sustained effort against blistering enemy fire had come from the 1,339 men under Gen. James Fagan. A Mexican War veteran from Saline County, Fagan was among the first military men in 1861 to recruit a company for the Confederacy. He later distinguished himself in other battles and after the war served as a U.S. marshal. He died in 1893 and is buried in Little Rock's Mount Holly Cemetery. (Courtesy of MacArthur Museum of Arkansas Military History.)

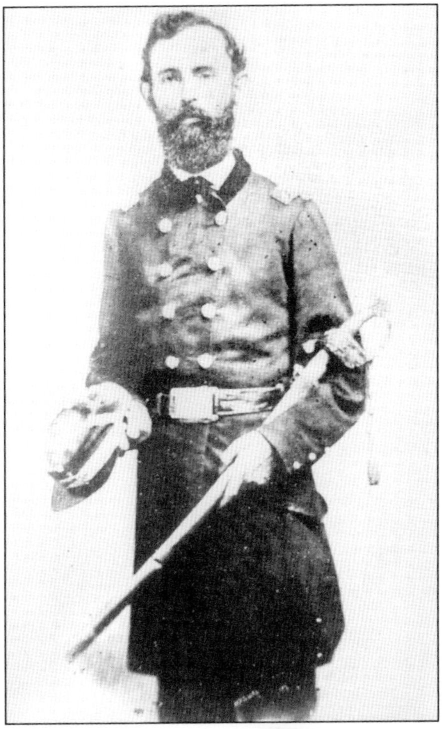

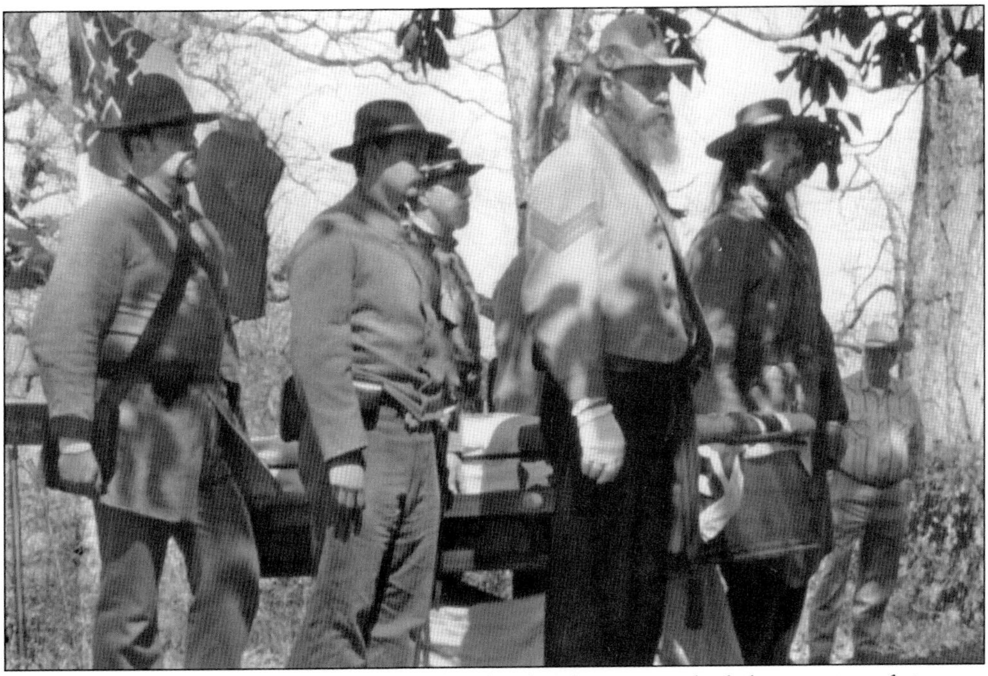

In 2002, a construction crew on the south side of Helena unearthed the remains of six men determined to be some of General Fagan's troops that had fallen in the charge against the Union forces' Battery D. In a 2005 ceremony, the six fallen soldiers were laid to rest in a single casket adorned with Confederate belt buckles as handles in Helena's Confederate Cemetery. (Courtesy of Arkansas Sons of Confederate Veterans.)

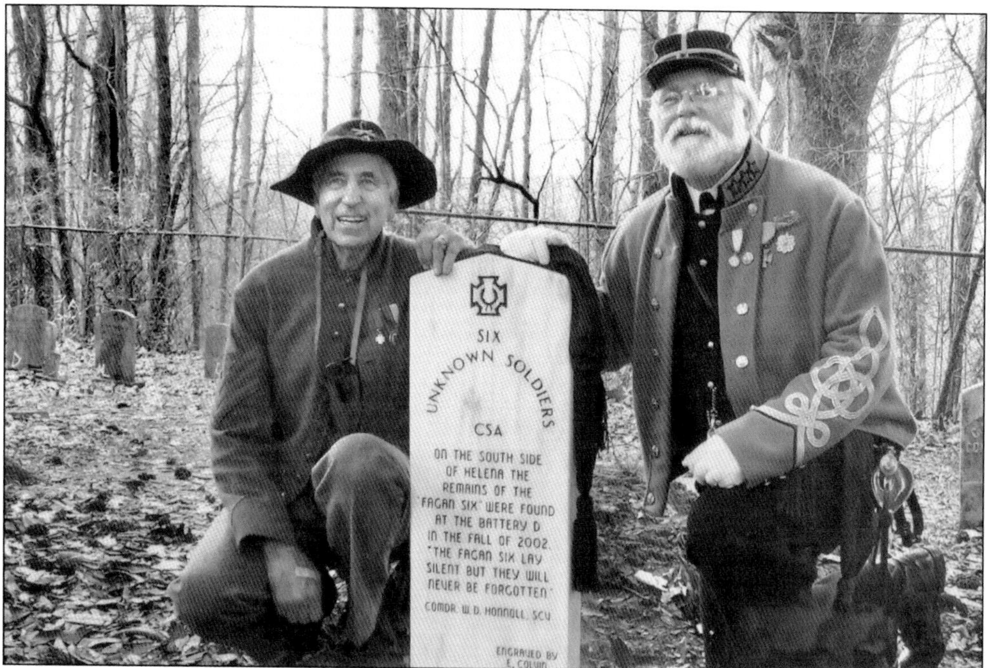

"The Fagan Six lay silent but they will never be forgotten," were the words of W. D. Honnoll, commander of the Arkansas Sons of Confederate Veterans, as the organization led the funeral for the six unidentified soldiers. Commander Honnoll, to the right, posed with engraver Edgar Colvin of Pine Bluff at the installation of the memorial marking the graves of the fallen soldiers. (Courtesy of Arkansas Sons of Confederate Veterans.)

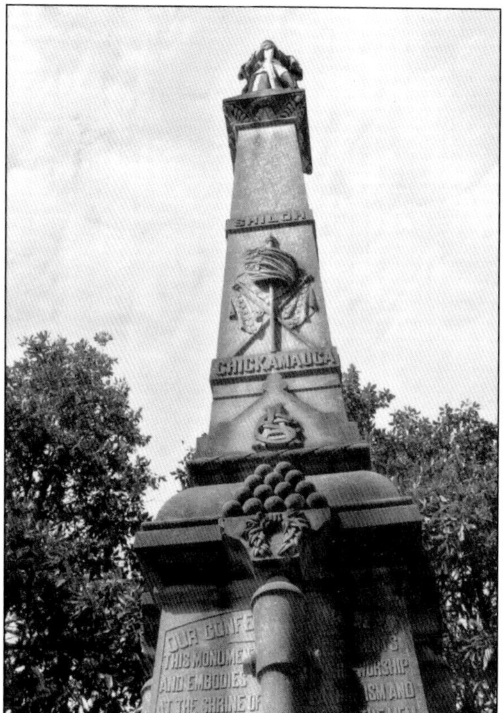

The shrine to the Confederacy in Arkansas is most assuredly atop the highest point in Helena, at the Confederate cemetery where the Fagan Six were belatedly laid to rest. Standing sentinel over the graves of mostly unknown Confederate dead is a stone soldier atop this 37-foot monument of Italian marble, erected in 1892. Honoring the Helena dead, the monument also denotes other battles such as Chickamauga and the Wilderness. (Photograph by Ray Hanley.)

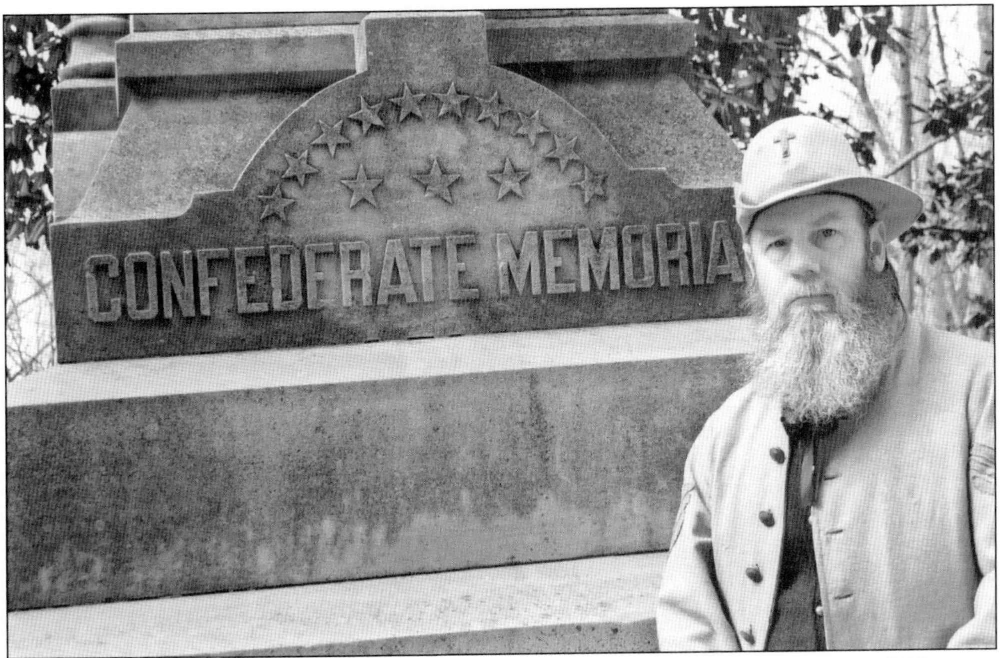

Confederate veteran reenactor Terry Bandy poses by the Confederate monument in Helena on Patrick Cleburne Memorial Day in 2006. The cross on Bandy's hat marks both his profession and the role he sometimes takes in the events hosted by the Sons of Confederate Veterans and in a number of films, where he plays the chaplain's part. Reverend Bandy is an active minister living in Bay, Arkansas. (Photograph by Ray Hanley.)

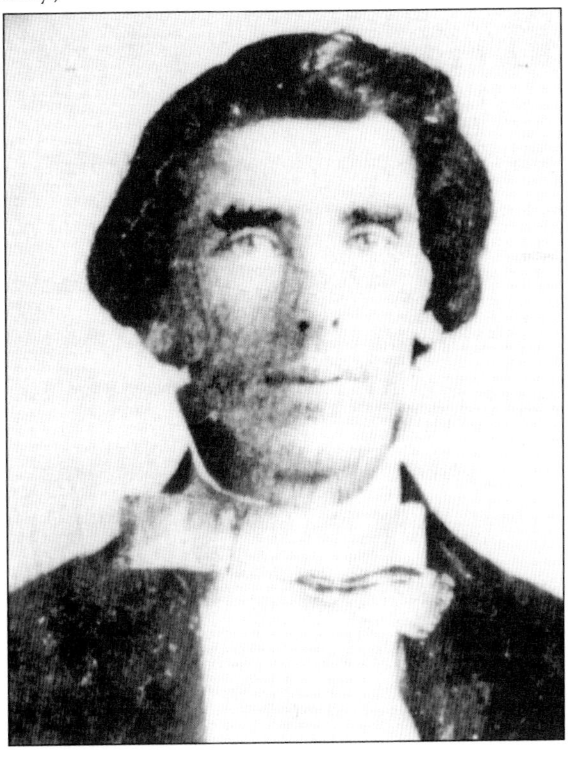

"Stonewall of the West" was the title earned in battle by the most honored Confederate general given by Arkansas. Patrick Ronayne Cleburne was born in Ireland in 1828, beginning his military career with a three-year stint in her majesty's army. Cleburne immigrated to the United States, acquired training as a pharmacist, and entered business in Helena. He is pictured here at the age of 25 shortly after arriving in Helena.

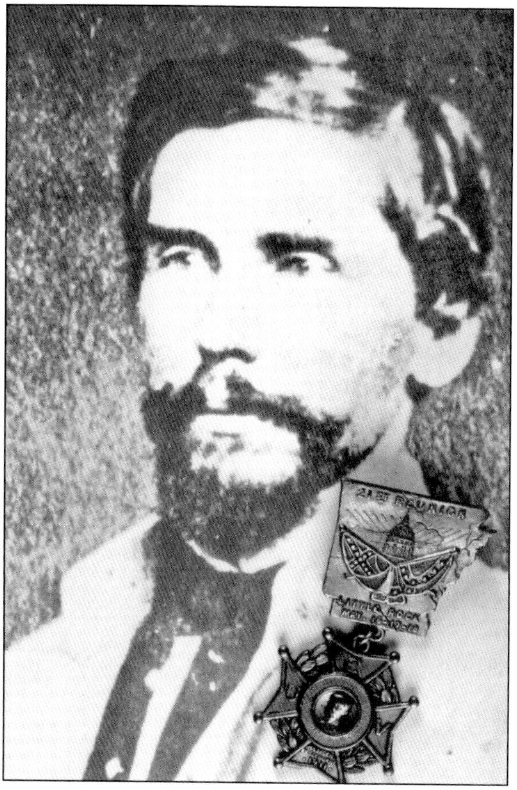

At secession, Cleburne was a successful attorney with considerable property (but no slaves) and was quickly elected colonel of the 15th Arkansas. His bravery and tactics at Shiloh and other battles earned Cleburne a reputation as a superb combat officer and a savage fighter, fearless in battle and widely considered the best division commander in the Confederacy. Along with this March 1864 photograph is a medal bearing his likeness, a souvenir of the 1911 Confederate Reunion.

Cleburne's blue regimental battle flag was known to both sides of the conflict; Union general Sherman later spoke of "tipping [my] hat to that blue flag . . . [for] when it was sighted we knew a fight was coming." The tattered flag, adorned with symbols of battles seen, is today in a Tennessee museum. Following the flag into the 1862 battle of Richmond, Kentucky, Cleburne was shot through the cheek; a minie ball took out two teeth and exited his open mouth. A witness reported "he caught the bullet in his teeth and spit it out."

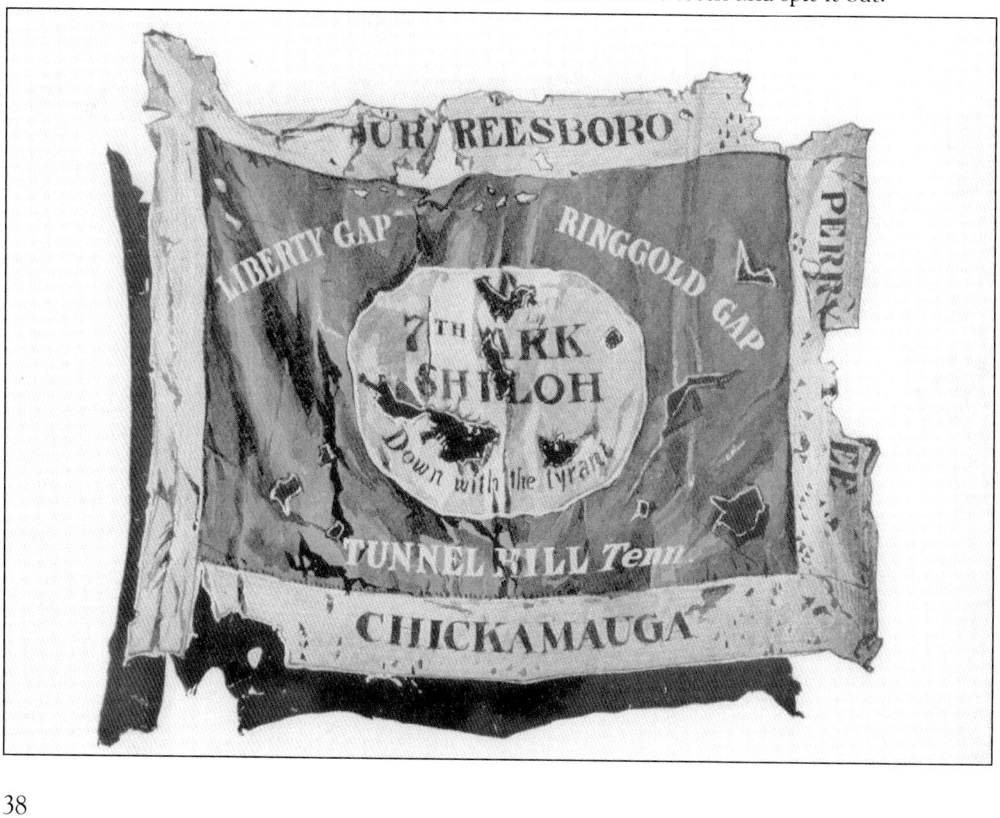

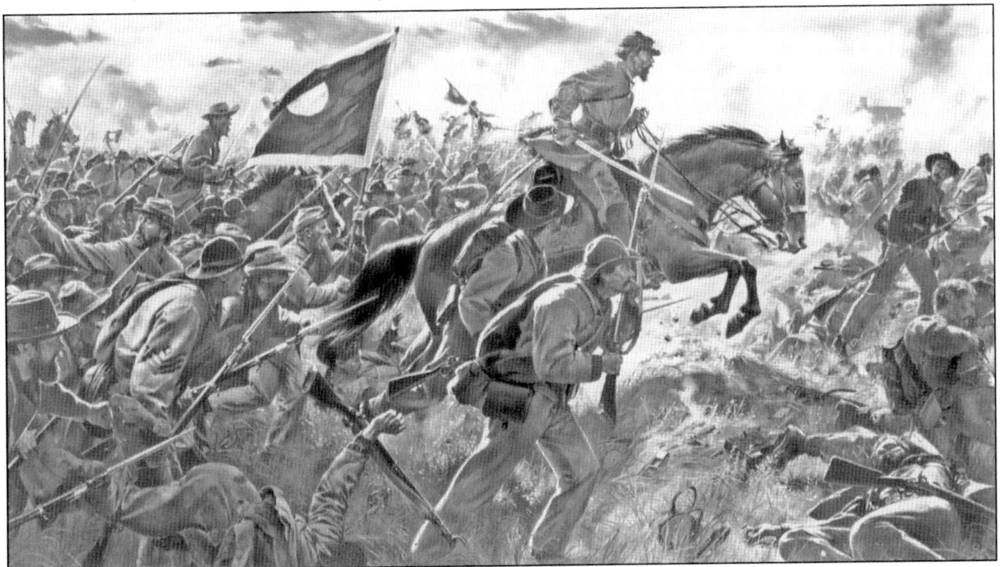

Cleburne's commander and close friend, Gen. William Hardee, would say of him, "When his division defended, no odds could break its lines. When it attacked, no numbers resisted its onslaught." The battle of Franklin, Tennessee, was waged on November 30, 1864, and Cleburne's division was in the thick of it. Gen. Daniel Govan, one of Cleburne's brigade commanders, commented, "General, there will not be many of us that will get back to Arkansas." Cleburne replied, "Well, Govan, if we are to die, let us die like men." In a charge toward the entrenched Union lines, Cleburne's horse went down with a bullet to the head; a second horse was quickly found but was killed by a cannonball as Cleburne put one foot into a stirrup. Waving his sword, Cleburne charged ahead on foot; 50 yards short of the enemy lines, a single bullet pieced his heart, killing him instantly. (Above image courtesy of artist Don Troiani [www.historicalartprints.com]. Below image courtesy of Gallon Historical Art of Gettysburg, Pennsylvania [www.gallon.com].)

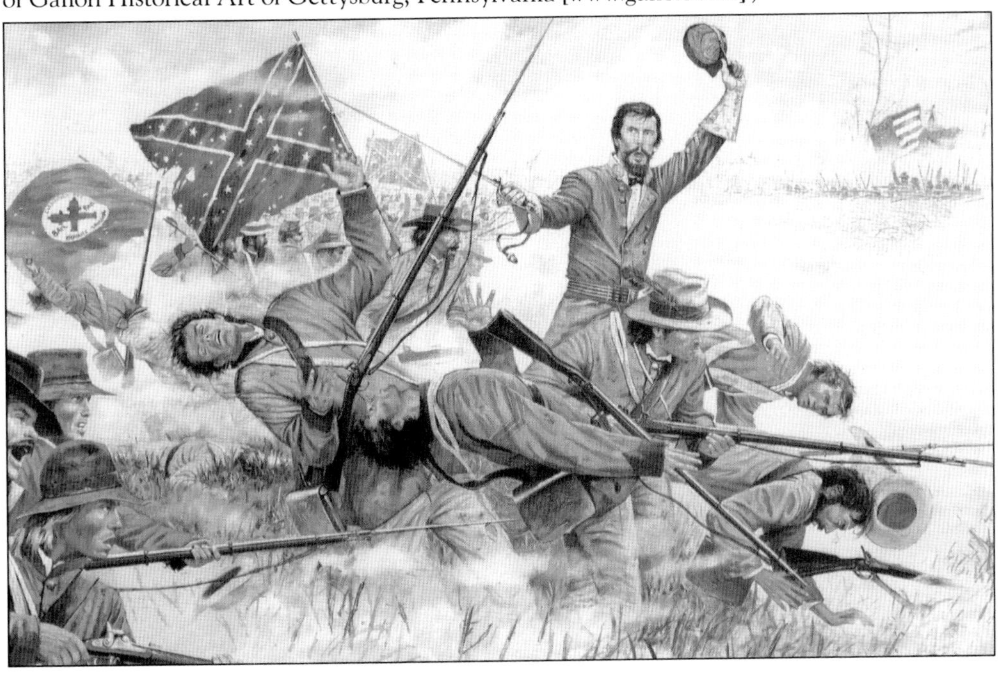

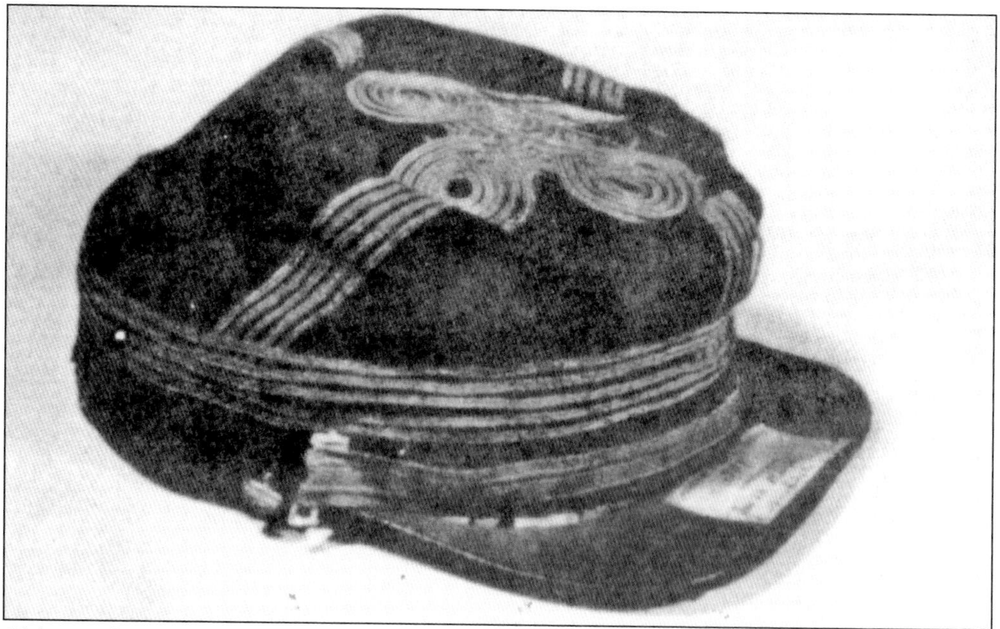

Cleburne's body lay amid the carnage the next morning, his boots and sword gone, one death among thousands and one of five Confederate generals killed that day. The cap he wore in his final charge rests today at the Tennessee Historical Society in Nashville. His sword is in the Confederate Museum in New Orleans. Confederate general George Gordon said, "A truer patriot or knightlier soldier never fought and never died. Valor never lost a braver son or freedom a nobler champion."

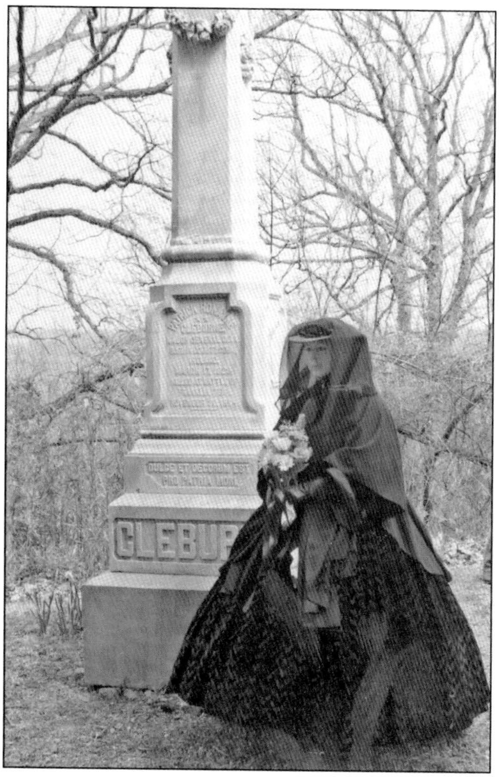

In January 1864, while attending his commander's wedding, Cleburne had been swept off his feet by Susan Tarleton. She agreed to become his fiancée three months later, intending to wed after the war. Devastated by her betrothed's death, she wore mourning garb for a year. Susan's role is portrayed here by reenactor Bobbie Barnett at the 2006 Cleburne Memorial Day ceremony at Cleburne's monument in the Confederate cemetery in Helena. (Photograph by Ray Hanley.)

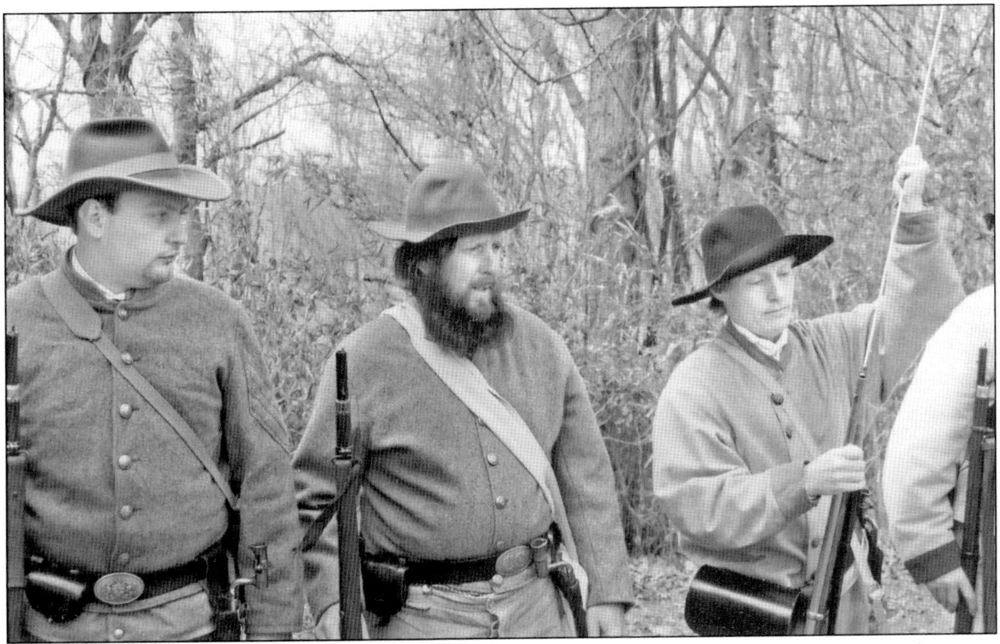

One part of the annual Cleburne memorial service atop the Confederate cemetery in Helena is a salute of cannon and musket fire to the fallen soldiers resting on the hill. Among the reenactors preparing to fire the salute is Marde Clardy, seen here at the far right. She symbolizes in reenactments the Southern women who disguised themselves as men in order to fight the Union invaders of their homeland. (Photograph by Ray Hanley.)

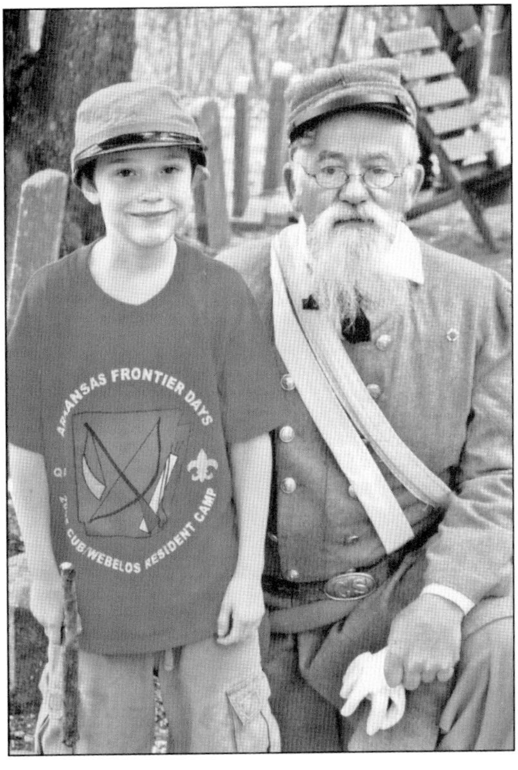

Reenactors like Jim Kincade (right) give of their time and personal resources to re-create the history of their Confederate ancestors in the annual event at Helena and at other sites around Arkansas. Through their efforts, history comes alive for Arkansans of all ages, including children such as seven-year-old Joey Hanley, who attended the 2006 Cleburne Memorial Day events. (Photograph by Ray Hanley.)

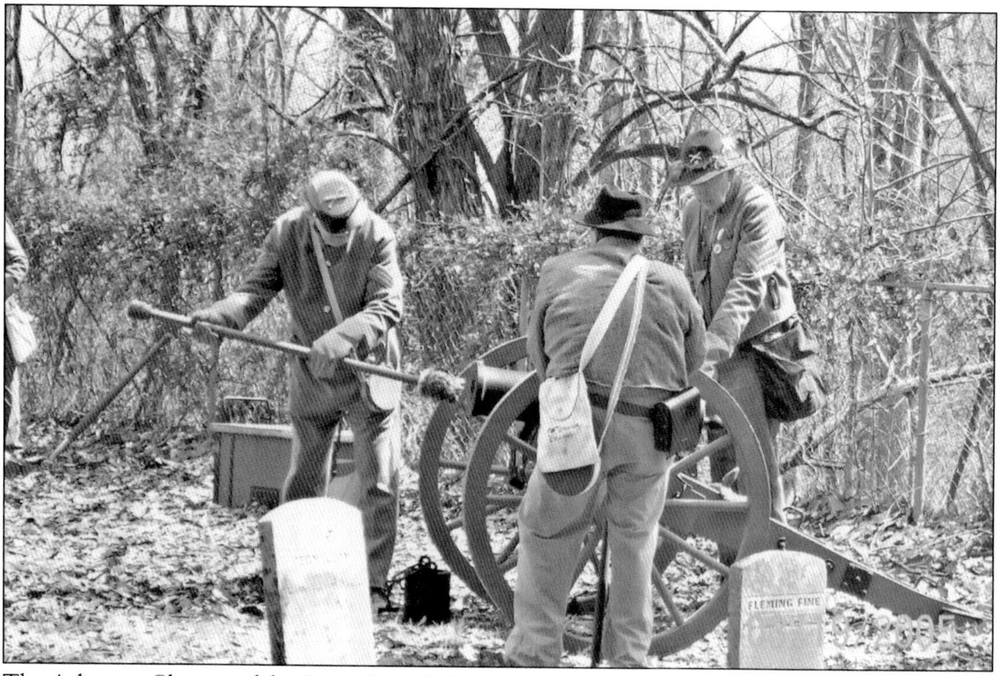

The Arkansas Chapter of the Sons of Confederate Veterans (SCV) has in its arsenal two mountain howitzers that, upon the officer's command, fire booming volleys over the graves of the soldiers atop the hill in Helena. During the Civil War era, the guns were built so that they could be disassembled and transported on horses over the rough countryside in which many battles occurred. The accurate replicas used by the SCV were built at a foundry in Lake Providence, Louisiana. The resounding echo of the guns in the hands of the skilled crew is one of the highlights of the annual Cleburne Day event at Helena. (Photographs by Ray Hanley.)

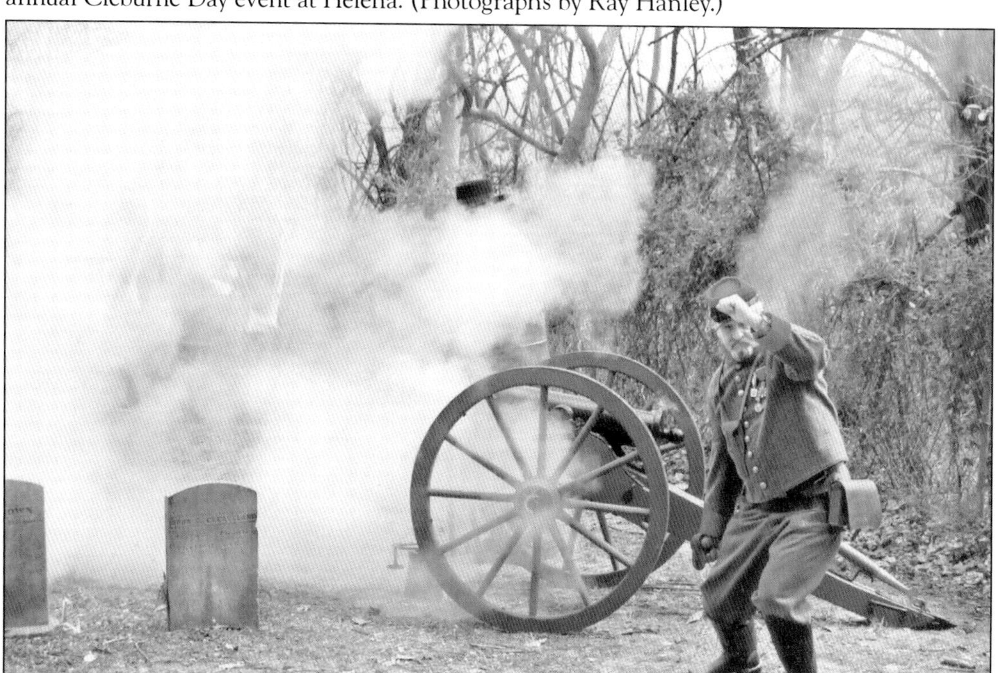

Three

THE UNION DRIVE ON LITTLE ROCK

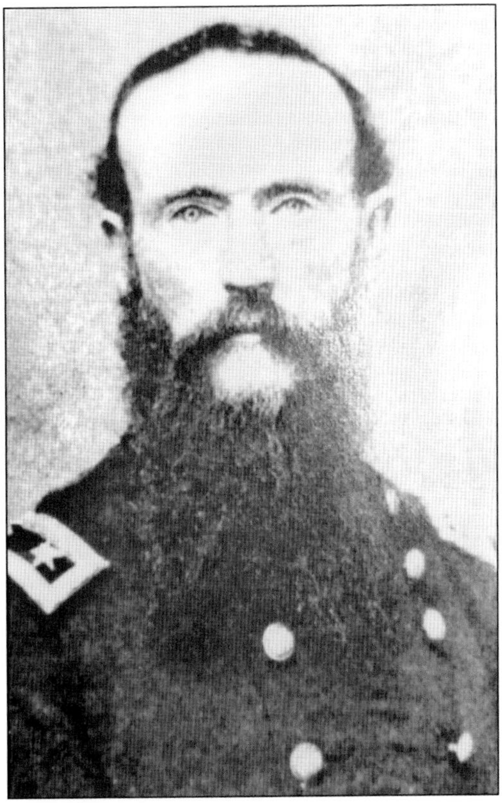

The Confederate government and the citizens of Little Rock began bracing for what they saw as inevitable by the summer of 1863: the Union army's drive to seize Arkansas's capital city. With Vicksburg captured, Union general U. S. Grant turned his attention toward taking Little Rock and the rest of Arkansas. Grant appointed Gen. Frederick Steele, a veteran of the battles of Arkansas Post and Helena, to command all federal forces in Arkansas and to mount the drive on the state's capital. Steele survived the war but died in 1868 in a fall from his carriage after suffering an attack of apoplexy.

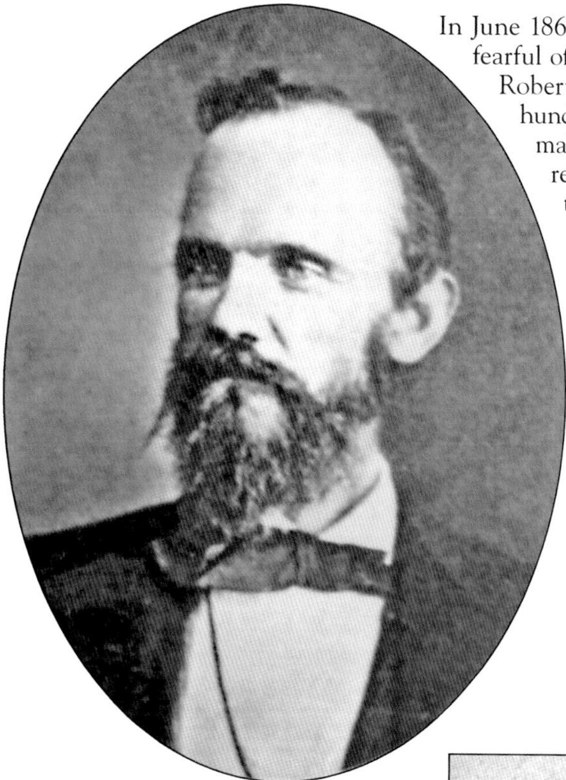

In June 1862, Little Rock was poorly defended and fearful of Union general Curtis's large army. Col. Robert C. Newton concocted a plan whereby hundreds of local women wrote letters to their male relatives fighting in the East, gratefully reporting that thousands of Confederate troops were arriving from Texas to defend Little Rock. The courier carrying the letters passed them into Union hands; General Curtis believed the disinformation and delayed any planned invasion for perhaps a year.

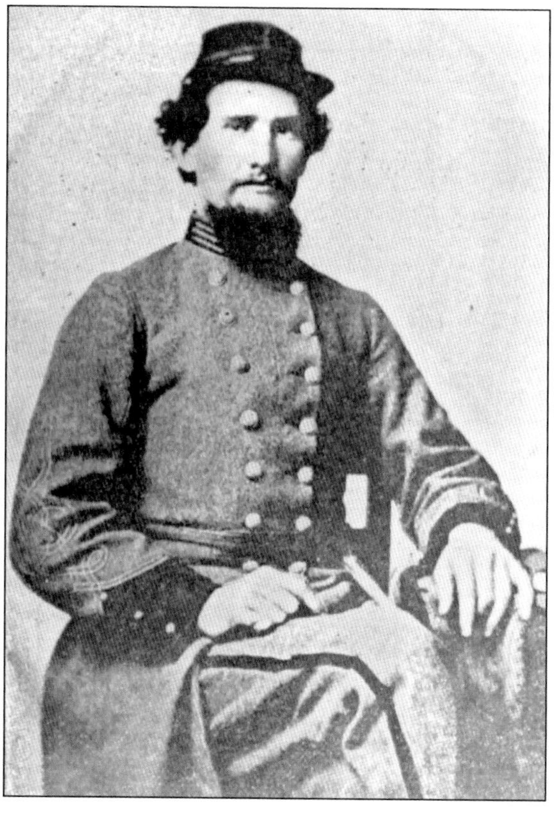

Gen. Sterling Price dug his troops into defensive positions downriver from Little Rock to meet the advancing Union army. Confederate physician Dr. Junius Bragg (pictured) wrote at that time, "Things look rather gloomy about here. . . . All government property is being removed from town. I consider it merely a matter of time when Little Rock falls. . . . Dull apathy sits upon the face of her people. Her chivalry has long since gone from her shores." (Courtesy of Camden Public Library.)

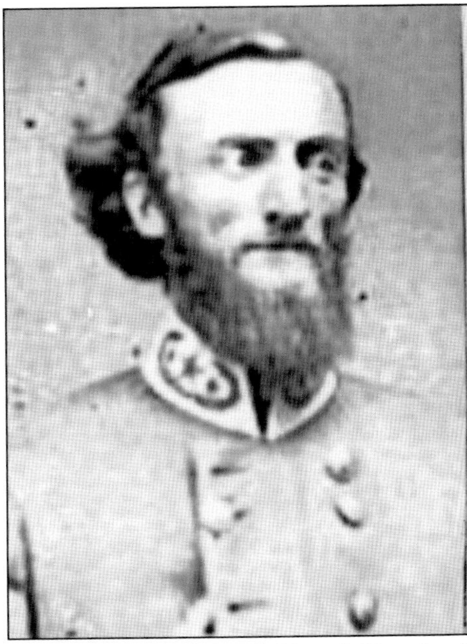

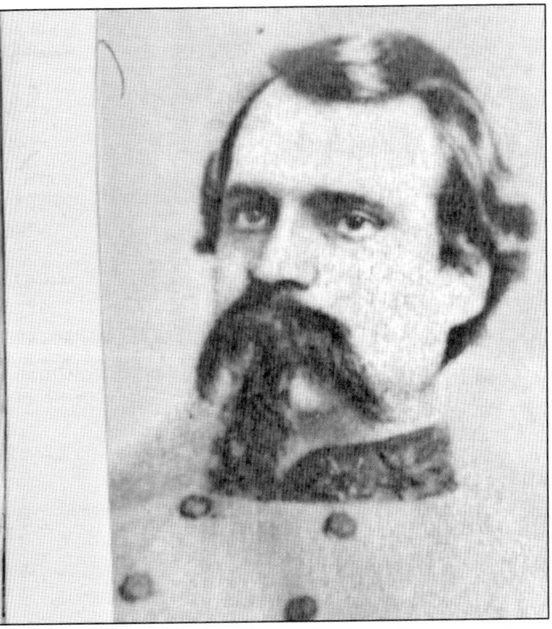

General Marmaduke (left) and Gen. Lucius Walker (right) had been feuding for some time. Marmaduke accused Walker of cowardice; Walker challenged his fellow general to a duel of honor. On September 6, 1863, with 14,000 Union troops approaching, the generals met at dawn on the plantation of Godfrey LeFevre seven miles below Little Rock. The first exchange of shots harmed neither man, but Marmaduke's second bullet apparently severed Walker's spinal cord.

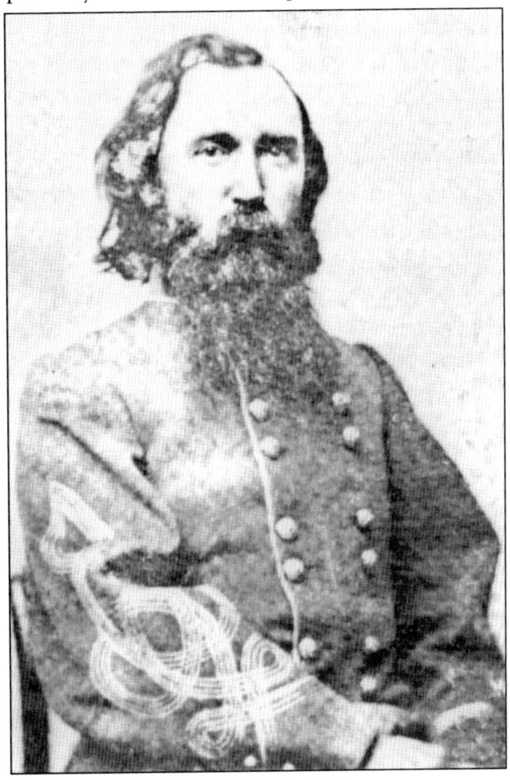

Mortally wounded, Walker asked if he had hit Marmaduke; when told not, he responded, "Thank God, I am glad. He will yet live to do his country's service when I'm dead." Walker died the following day, leaving his command to Gen. Archibald Dobbins, pictured here. Dobbins served with distinction for the remainder of the war, then at war's end immigrated to Brazil, where he disappeared without a trace in 1869.

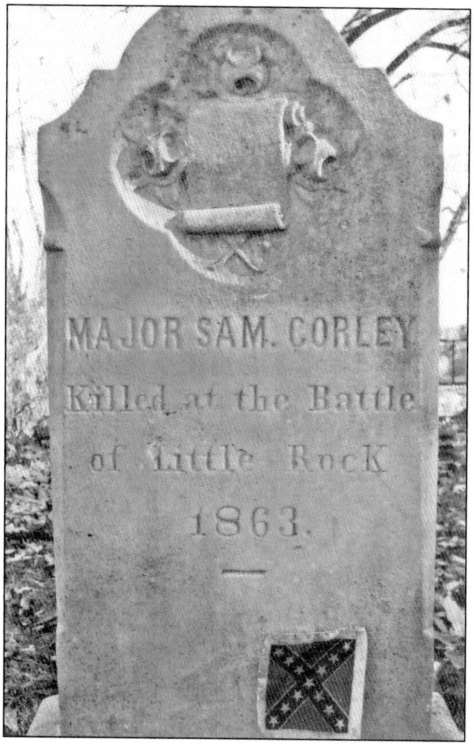

Maj. Samuel Corley was along the last line of Little Rock's defense at Fourche Bayou on September 10. Ordered to hold the line, he prayed, "Blessed be the Lord God, who teacheth my fingers to battle, and my hands to war." Corley was shot in the chest while brandishing his saber; an advancing Union officer stopped to comfort the dying major, promising to get his personal effects to his family.

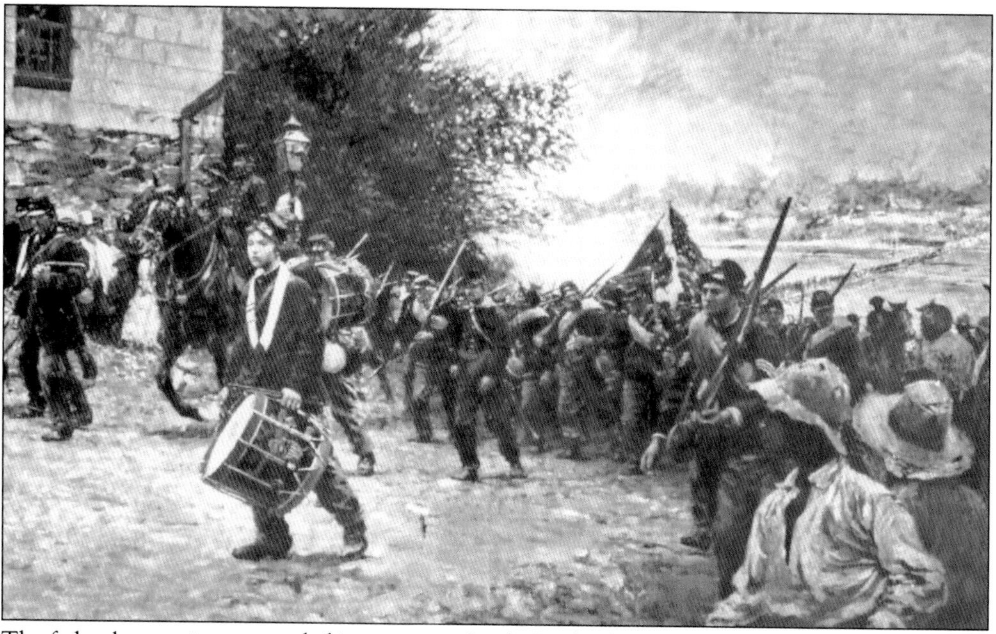

The federal campaign succeeded in capturing Little Rock after 40 days and 137 Union casualties. Among the troops that had spent weeks fighting toward Little Rock, the 3rd Minnesota Volunteer Infantry had seen some of the toughest combat. It was this regiment, selected by General Steele, that helped lead the invading army into Little Rock on September 11, 1863. The painting shown here hangs today in the Minnesota State Capitol. (Courtesy of MacArthur Museum of Arkansas Military History.)

In 1916, the state of Minnesota erected this monument in the Little Rock National Cemetery honoring those from Minnesota who died far from home during the Civil War. It reads: "Erected by The State of Minnesota, in memory of her soldiers here buried who lost their lives in the Service of the United States in the war for the preservation of the Union." (Photograph by Ray Hanley.)

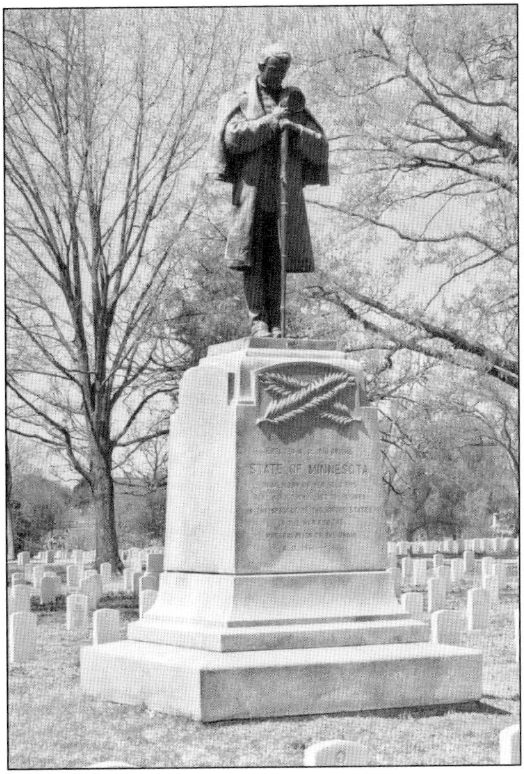

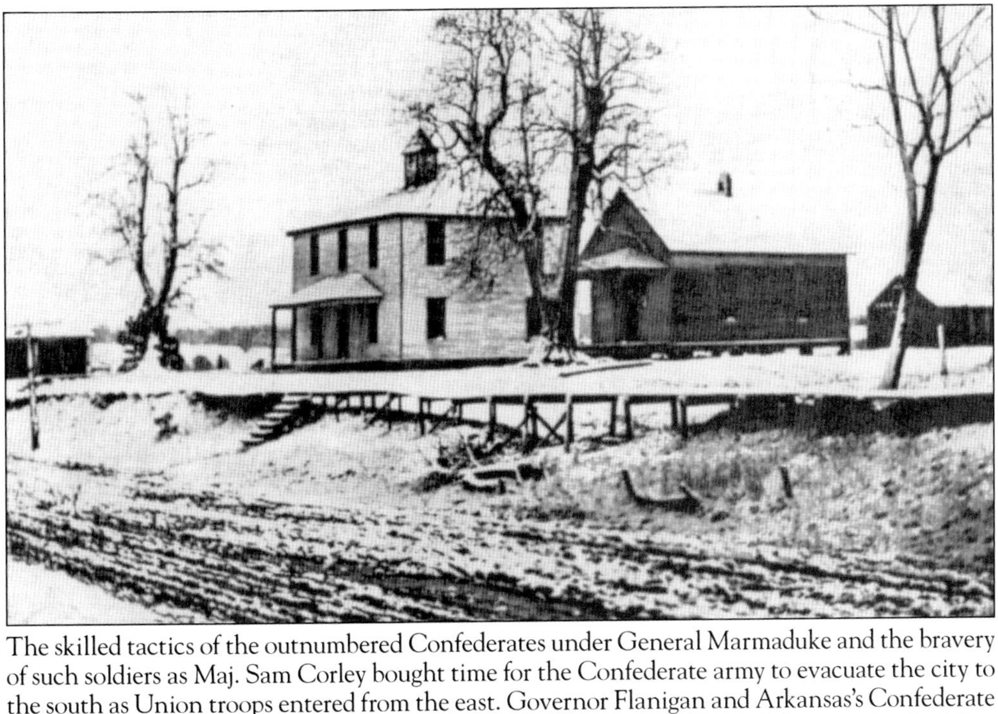

The skilled tactics of the outnumbered Confederates under General Marmaduke and the bravery of such soldiers as Maj. Sam Corley bought time for the Confederate army to evacuate the city to the south as Union troops entered from the east. Governor Flanigan and Arkansas's Confederate government would relocate to the village of Washington in Southwest Arkansas; this building served as the government's capitol building for the remainder of the war.

During the occupation of Little Rock, 17-year-old David O. Dodd was arrested for spying when found with coded papers he refused to explain. Shocking local citizens, General Steele ordered the boy hanged. David wrote to his mother before his execution, "I know it will be hard for you to give up your only son, but you must remember it is God's will. I pray we may meet in Heaven. Goodbye, God bless you all. Your son and brother."

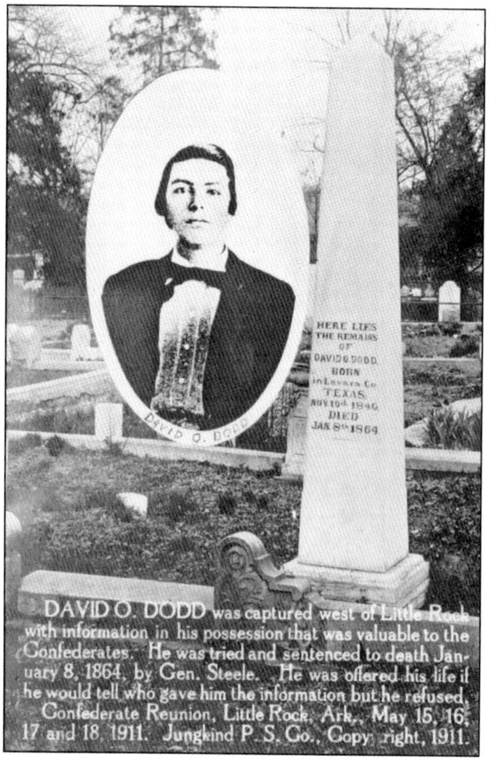

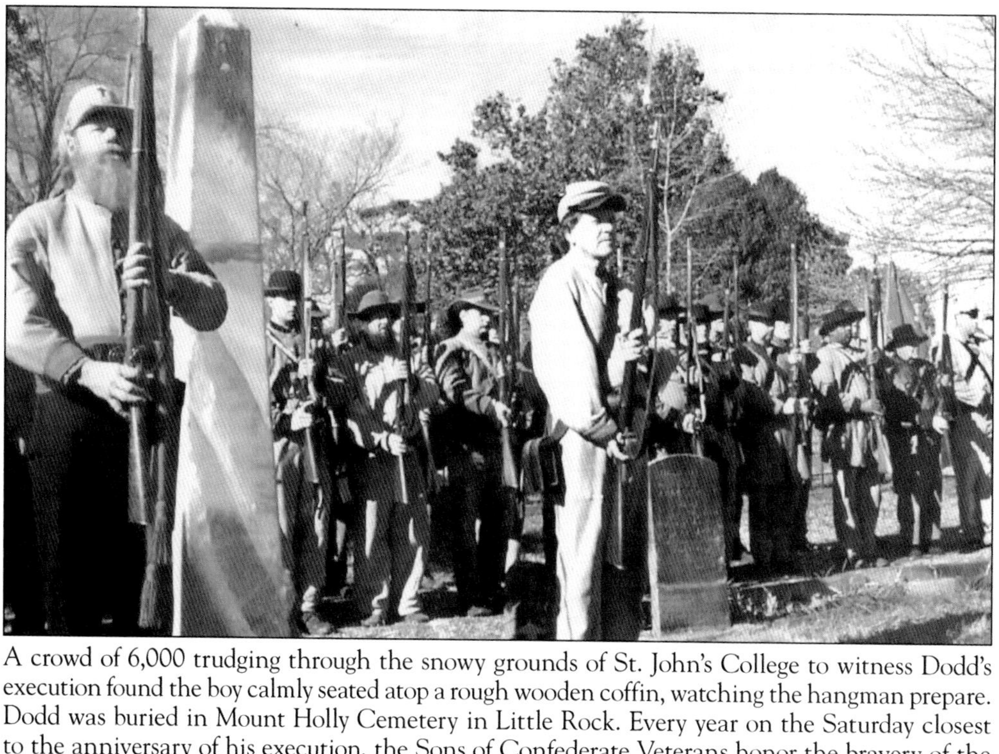

A crowd of 6,000 trudging through the snowy grounds of St. John's College to witness Dodd's execution found the boy calmly seated atop a rough wooden coffin, watching the hangman prepare. Dodd was buried in Mount Holly Cemetery in Little Rock. Every year on the Saturday closest to the anniversary of his execution, the Sons of Confederate Veterans honor the bravery of the teenager who refused to betray a friend. (Courtesy of Arkansas Sons of Confederate Veterans.)

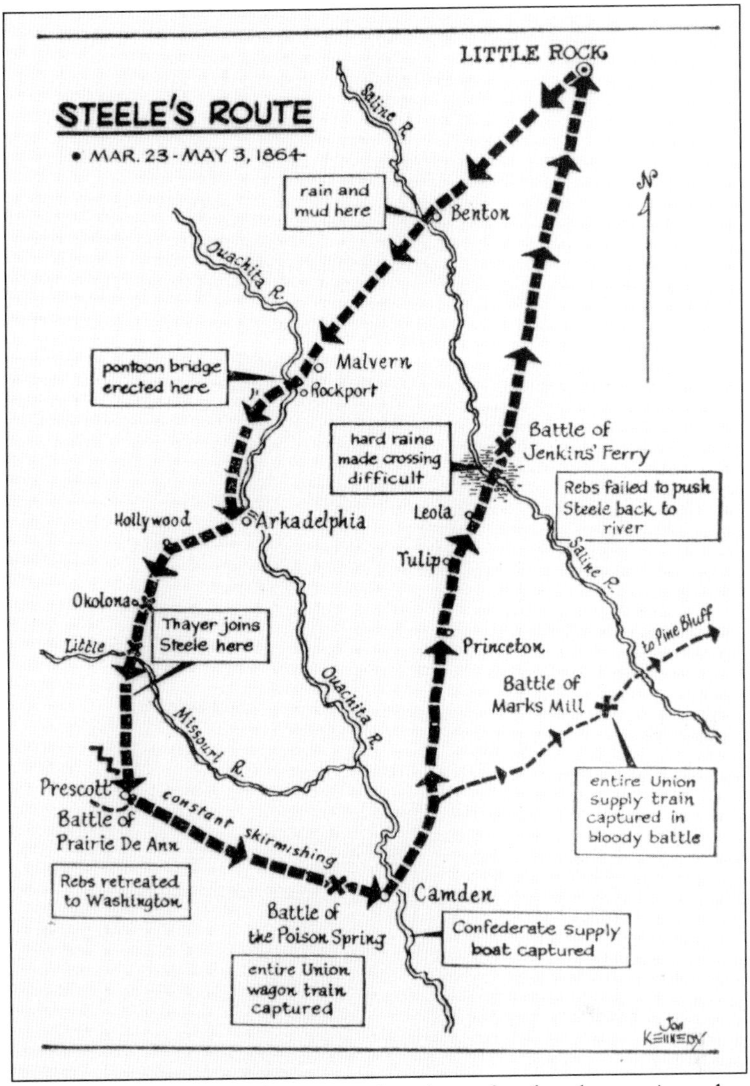

By the spring of 1864, Confederate Arkansas was largely confined to the state's southwest quadrant, with the capital having relocated to Washington, in Hempstead County. General Steele's Union troops moved out of Little Rock intent on squeezing the remaining Confederates as part of a larger effort known as the Red River campaign. Steele's route, shown here, led to three major encounters; Steele was to discover the bitter taste of defeat. Steele's Union army occupied Camden on April 15 and dug in at the Ouachita River port to plan what was intended to be the conquest of the remainder of Confederate Arkansas. However, at Poison Springs, General Marmaduke's cavalry had routed the Union troops bringing supplies to Steele. Marmaduke's men faced the mostly black troops of the 1st Kansas, which suffered heavy losses at the hands of the Confederates. The loss of a second supply train at Mark's Mill when its 240 wagons were taken by Confederate general Fagan's 4,000 troops forced Steele to attempt a retreat back to Little Rock with the Confederates in hot pursuit. In a driving rainstorm, the Confederates, led by Gen. Thomas Churchill, caught up to Steele's forces as they were crossing the Saline River at Jenkins Ferry. "The firing was terrific," reported General Steele, "and the struggle was desperate beyond description." The rugged, muddy terrain kept the Confederates from gaining an advantage; Steele finally got his army over the river and burned the Union pontoon bridge before the Confederates could use it to follow him.

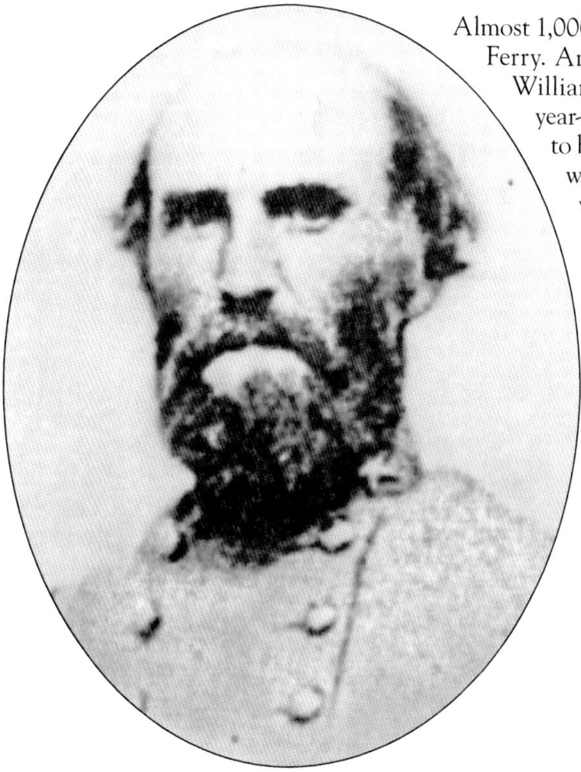

Almost 1,000 men were killed or wounded at Jenkins Ferry. Among the Confederate losses was Gen. William Reed Scurry, pictured here. The 42-year-old Scurry was badly wounded but refused to be removed from the field while the fight was on. Two hours later, he asked, "Have we whipped them yet?" Assured that his men had prevailed, he ordered, "Take me to a house where I can be made comfortable and die easy."

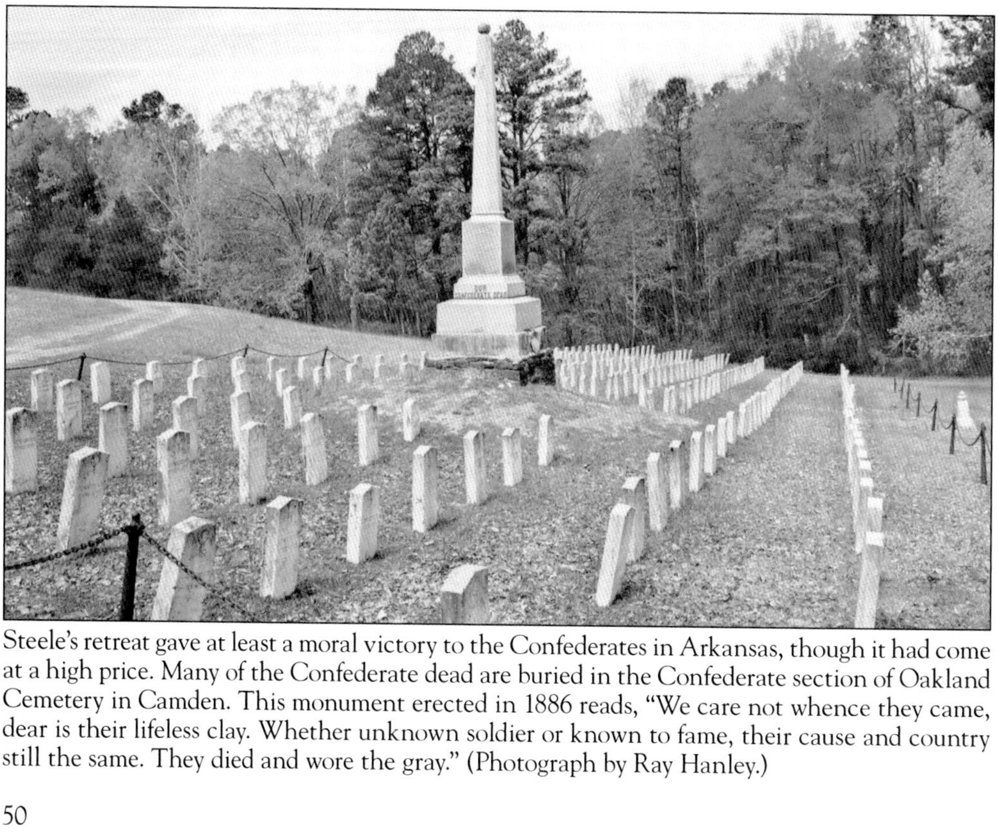

Steele's retreat gave at least a moral victory to the Confederates in Arkansas, though it had come at a high price. Many of the Confederate dead are buried in the Confederate section of Oakland Cemetery in Camden. This monument erected in 1886 reads, "We care not whence they came, dear is their lifeless clay. Whether unknown soldier or known to fame, their cause and country still the same. They died and wore the gray." (Photograph by Ray Hanley.)

Most of the Confederates buried in Camden fell in battle and now lay beneath stones marked "Unknown Confederate Soldier." One exception was Steven S. Stedman of Company G of the 3rd Arkansas Infantry. He survived the war and died in 1918, the year the unified states of the South and the North saw their young men fighting together in Europe. His gravestone proclaims: "He died as he lived, a Christian." (Photograph by Ray Hanley.)

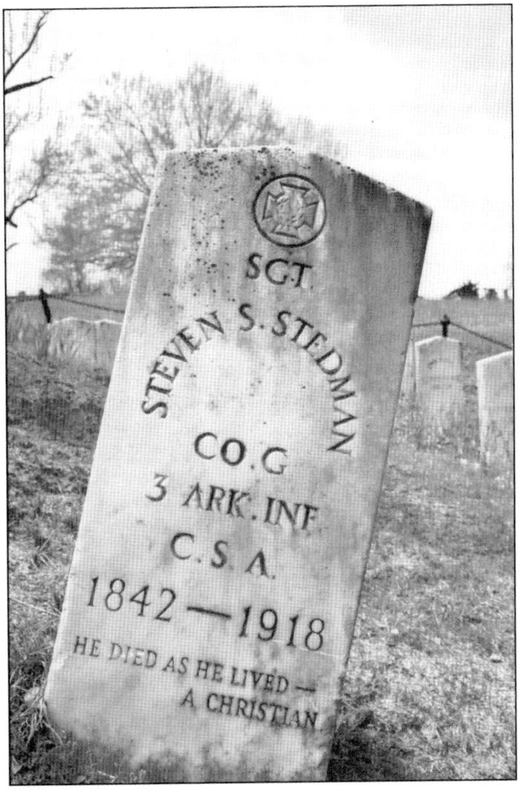

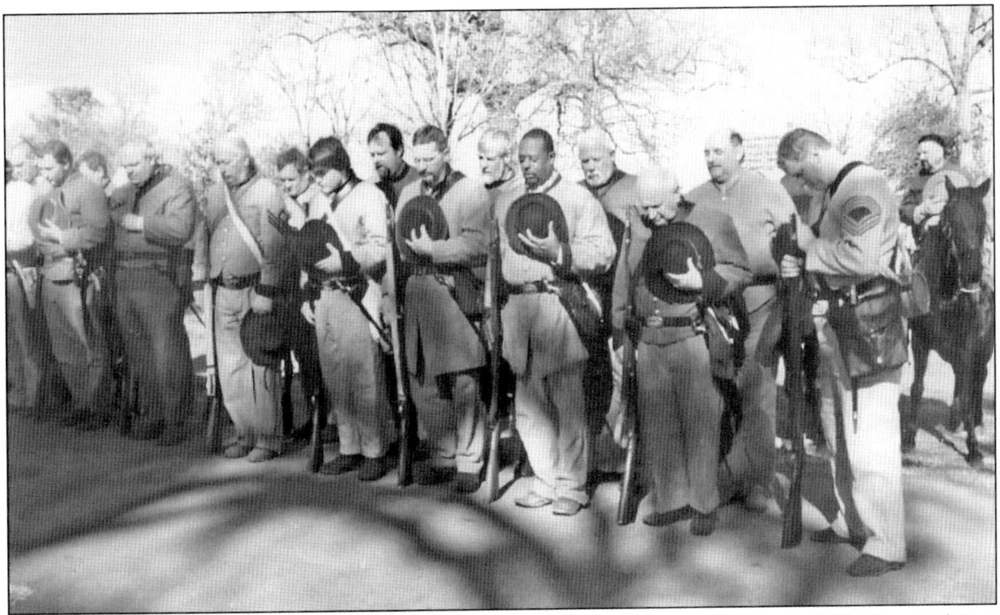

The rest of the war in Arkansas consisted mostly of skirmishes; in April 1865, General Lee surrendered. As in this assembly of SCV members in Mount Holly Cemetery, the surviving Confederate soldiers returned to their homes with heads bowed, some in defeat but many more in sorrow over their comrades who had fallen on the fields of Pea Ridge, Gettysburg, Prairie Grove, Helena, Franklin, and many more scenes of epic warfare.

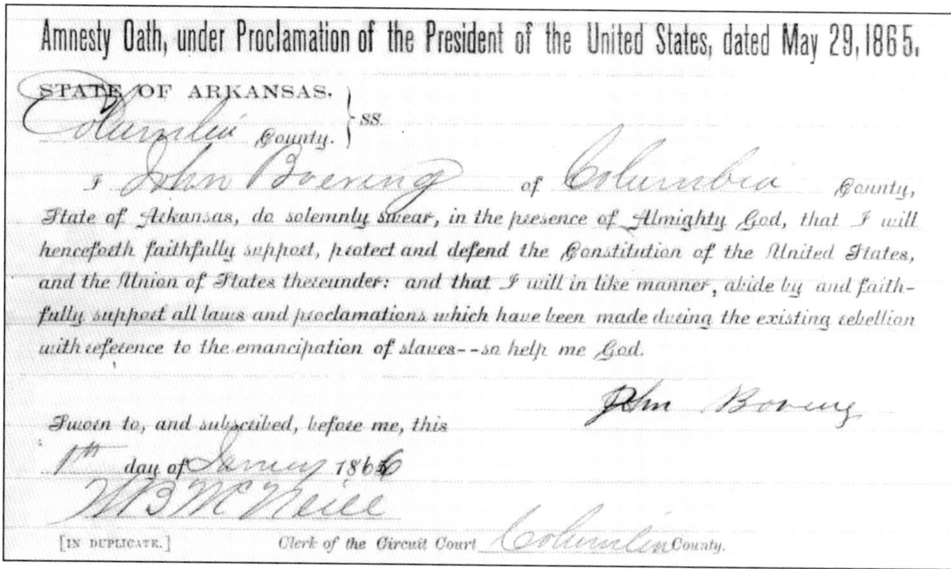

Amnesty Oath, under Proclamation of the President of the United States, dated May 29, 1865.

STATE OF ARKANSAS, }
Columbia County. } SS.

I John Bovening of Columbia County, State of Arkansas, do solemnly swear, in the presence of Almighty God, that I will henceforth faithfully support, protect and defend the Constitution of the United States, and the Union of States thereunder: and that I will in like manner, abide by and faithfully support all laws and proclamations which have been made during the existing rebellion with reference to the emancipation of slaves--so help me God.

John Bovening

Sworn to, and subscribed, before me, this 1st day of January 1866

W B McNeill

[IN DUPLICATE.] Clerk of the Circuit Court Columbia County.

The Arkansas Confederate soldiers who survived the war returned to a state in economic and political ruin. It would take almost a decade to shake off the federally imposed Reconstruction government. Many of the state's veterans, like John Bovening of Columbia County, signed the Amnesty Oath, which was instituted through a proclamation issued by Pres. Andrew Johnson only a few weeks after Lincoln's assassination. (Courtesy of MacArthur Museum of Arkansas Military History.)

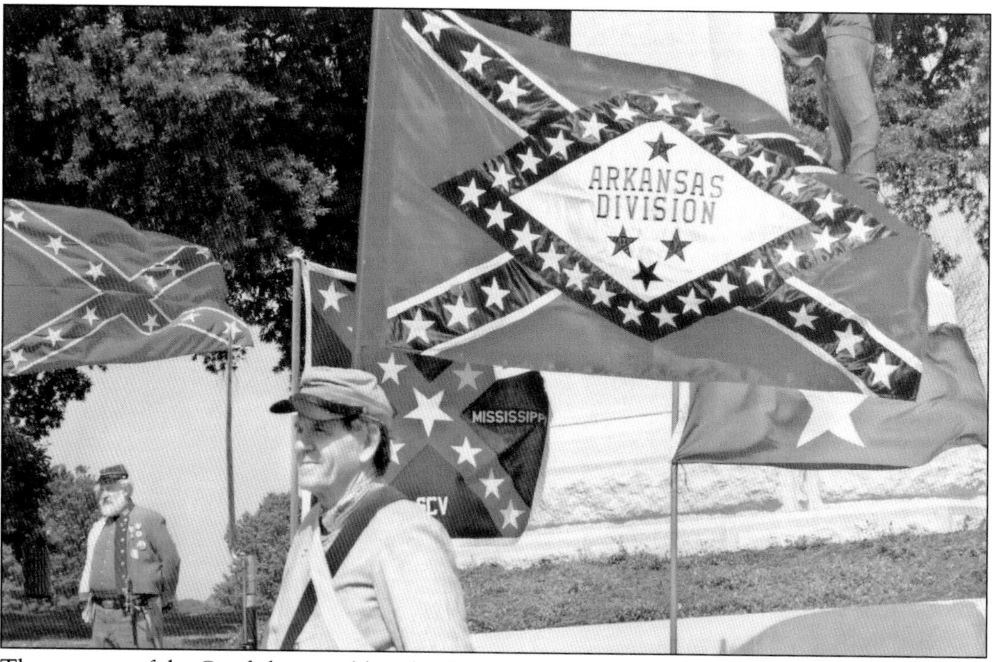

The memory of the Confederate soldiers has been preserved by the Sons of Confederate Veterans, formed in 1896. Pvt. Jimmy Stevens of the Robert Shaver Jonesboro Camp poses at attention before the Arkansas SCV Division flag on Confederate Memorial Day in 2006 at the state capitol's Confederate Monument. Paul Slayton of Dardanelle is to the left. The Arkansas Division flag was created in 2002 by SCV members Terry Bandy and Phillip Priest. (Photograph by Ray Hanley.)

Four

Reconciliation and Honoring Those Who Served

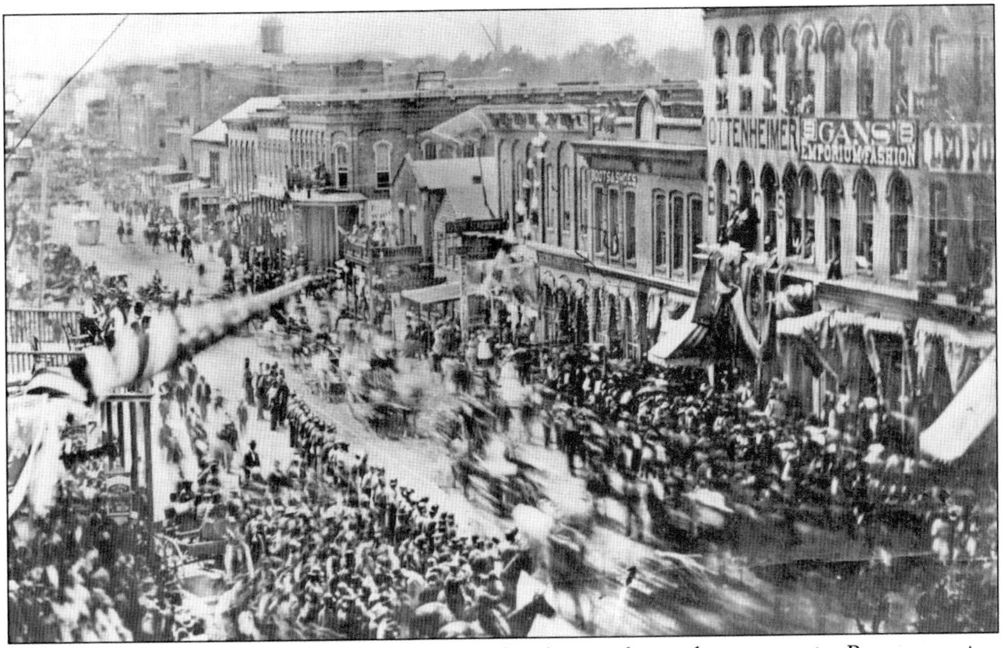

The hardships of Arkansas would linger for years after the war, first with an oppressive Reconstruction government of occupation and the "carpetbaggers" it brought. The conflict even led to the Brooks-Baxter "war," in which some 50 people died to settle who would govern the state. Still reconciliation was coming, and efforts to honor the men who served the Confederacy took hold. Unity between North and South was building in 1880 when former president and Union army commander Ulysses S. Grant visited Little Rock. The parade down Main Street honoring Grant drew the largest crowd ever assembled in the history of the city to that time. While a sense of unity was evident, the South still had its pride and was intent on honoring its Confederate veterans and the version of history it believed most accurate. (Courtesy of Butler Center for Arkansas Studies.)

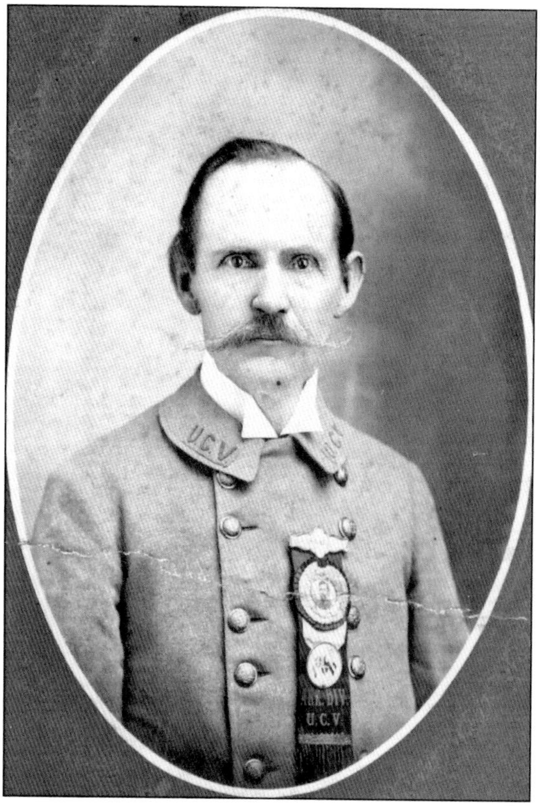

The United Confederate Veterans (UCV) organization was formed in 1889. UCV brigadier general B. H. Crowley of Paragould proudly wore his Arkansas UCV Division medal for a photographer's sitting around 1900. At its height, 160,000 veterans in the United States belonged to the UCV, which lobbied for veterans' pensions, raised money for monuments, and worked to tell what the veterans considered the true history of the Civil War. (Courtesy of Butler Center for Arkansas Studies, Paul Dolle Civil War Collection.)

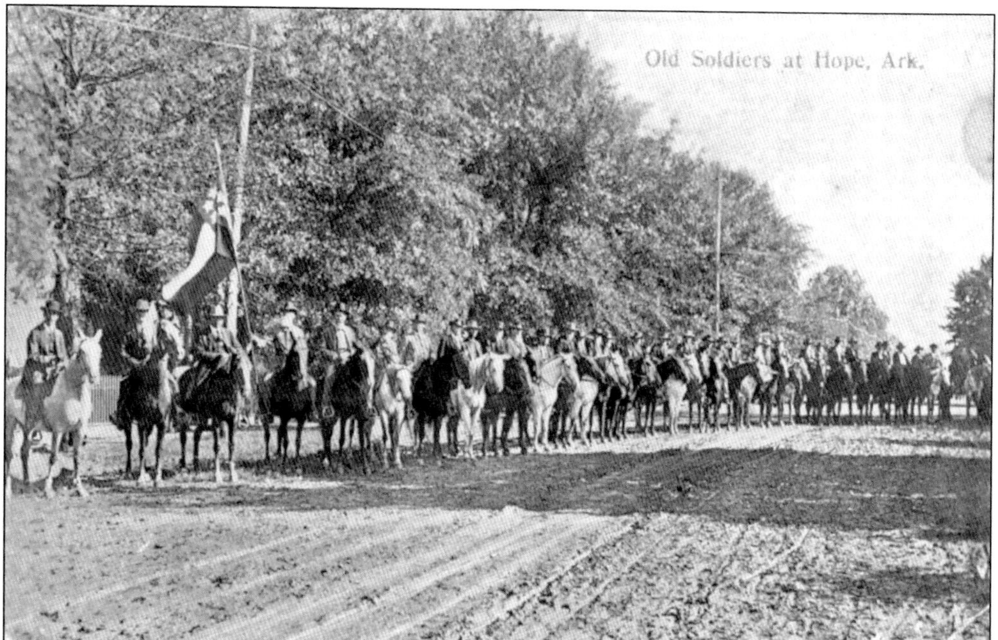

Among the veterans whom the monuments were erected to honor, the survivors were aging rapidly. However, as seen here in Hope's wagon-rutted street around 1910, many could still mount a horse almost a half-century after going off to battle the Union forces.

The counter organization to the UCV was the Grand Army of the Republic (GAR), formed in 1886 to work for the benefit of those who had worn Union blue. One in five Arkansans who died in the war fought for the Union, and Arkansas became the first former Confederate state to form a GAR post. Among the 2,200 members in Arkansas was I. A. Church, photographed here in Texarkana around 1900. (Courtesy of Butler Center for Arkansas Studies, Paul Dolle Civil War Collection.)

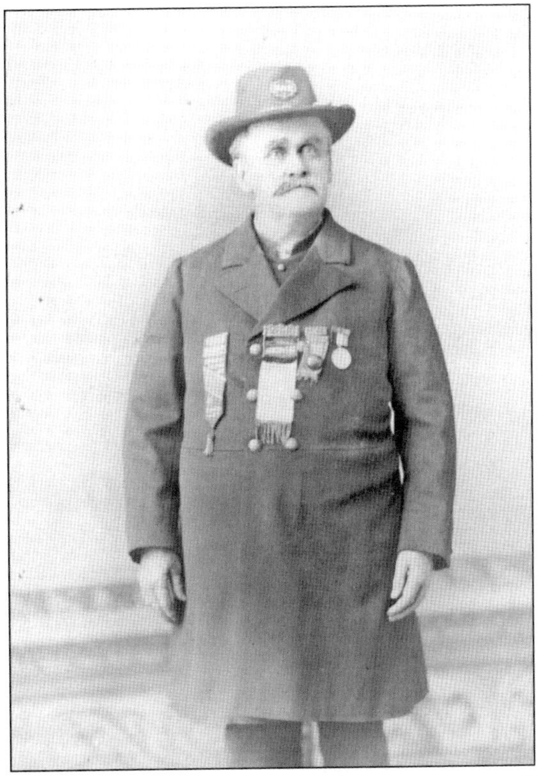

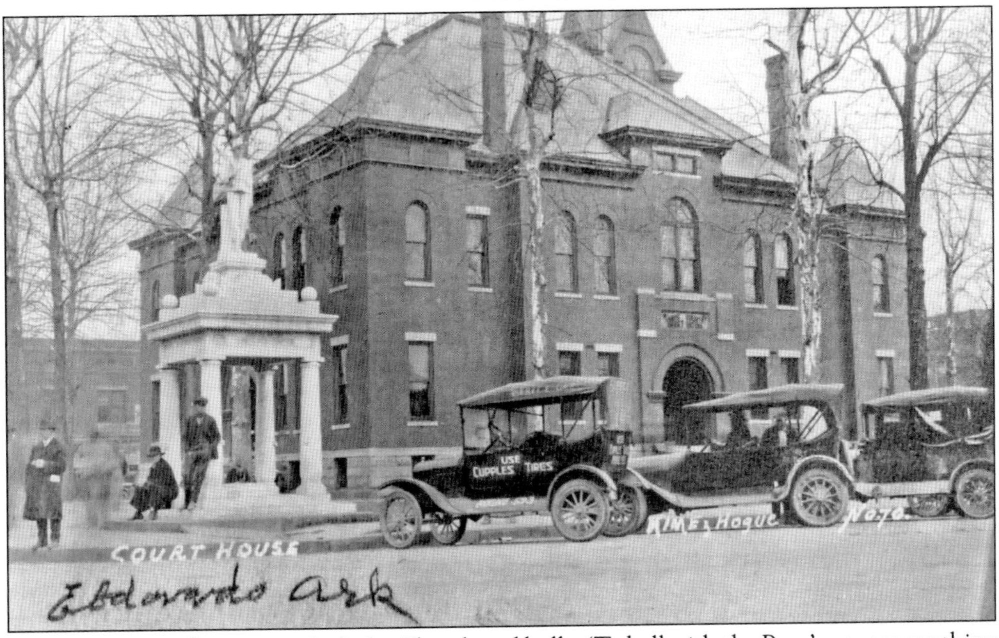

"One might as well get into a Catholic Church and holler 'To hell with the Pope' as to say anything against the Gray in this county," was the message penned on a postcard of the Confederate monument in El Dorado. More than 30 Civil War monuments were erected in Arkansas—three to the Union troops, the rest to the Confederates. This legacy in stone remains today scattered across Arkansas.

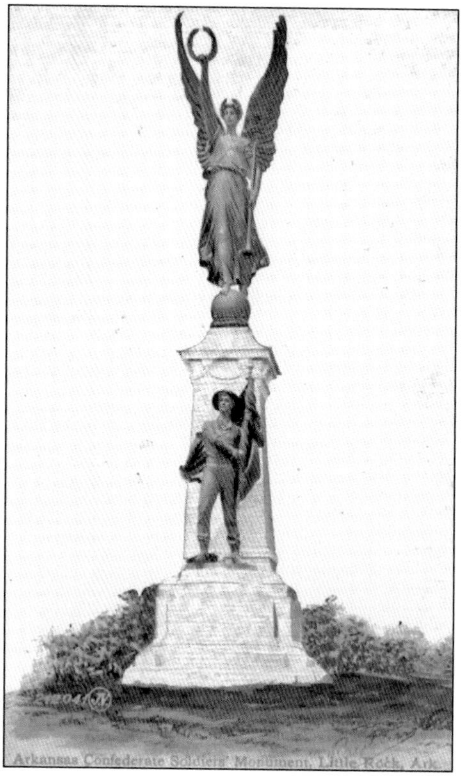

Col. J. N. Smithee, editor of the *Arkansas Gazette*, succeeded in raising $5,000 for a monument "that the children of veterans can feel proud of." With an additional $5,000 from the Arkansas legislature, the work of sculptor Frederick Ruckstuhl was unveiled in front of the new State Capitol building. Today the monument sits on the northeast corner of the capitol's front lawn, having been moved from its original, more prominent spot seen in the postcard.

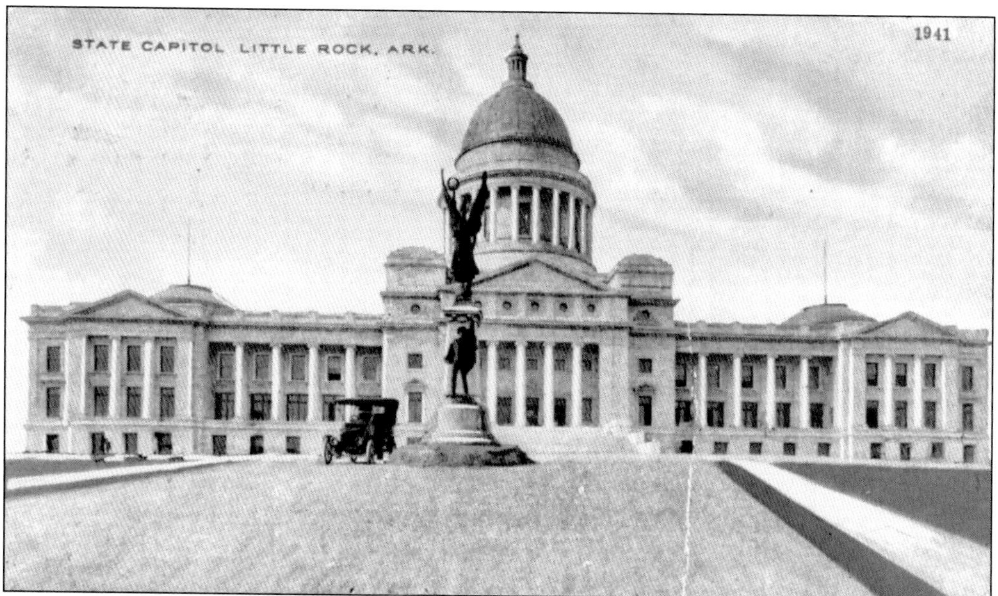

As described by its sculptor, the statue depicts "A young Arkansas soldier grasping the butt end of a flagstaff while the flag flutters back and about him. With his feet firmly planted, he holds his ground in the midst of the din of battle and wreck and ruin, apparently unmindful of everything but the holding of the half-destroyed banner in the face of overpowering numbers. On his face are expressed that profound devotion to the cause of his people and that indomitable grit and courage which have immortalized the Confederate soldier."

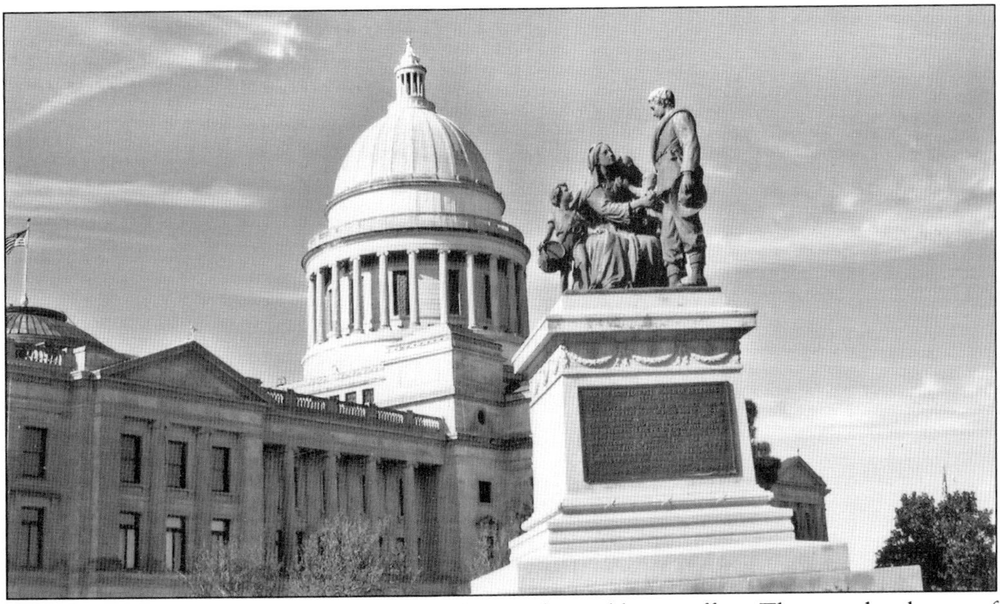

One Confederate monument on the capitol grounds would not suffice. The grandest legacy of the Arkansas Chapter of the United Confederate Veterans is the Monument to Confederate Women, which was referred to by some as "Mother of the South." Swiss sculptor J. Otto Schweizer created in bronze the image of a mother and daughter bidding farewell to their 16-year-old son and brother, who is leaving to join his battle-weary father fighting the Union troops. Gov. J. M. Futrell unveiled the monument in 1913 before 3,000 onlookers. The *Arkansas Gazette* wrote at the time that the monument "will serve to remind future generations of the patient bravery and silent sufferings of those who stayed at home through four long years of civil strife and gave courage and inspiration to the men who wore the gray." (Photographs by Ray Hanley.)

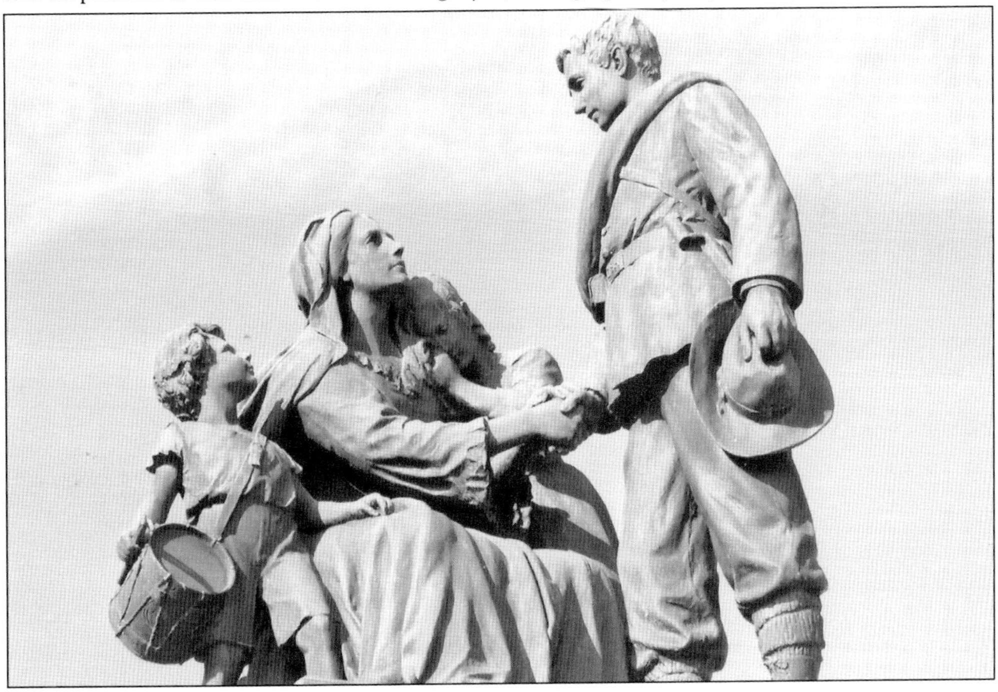

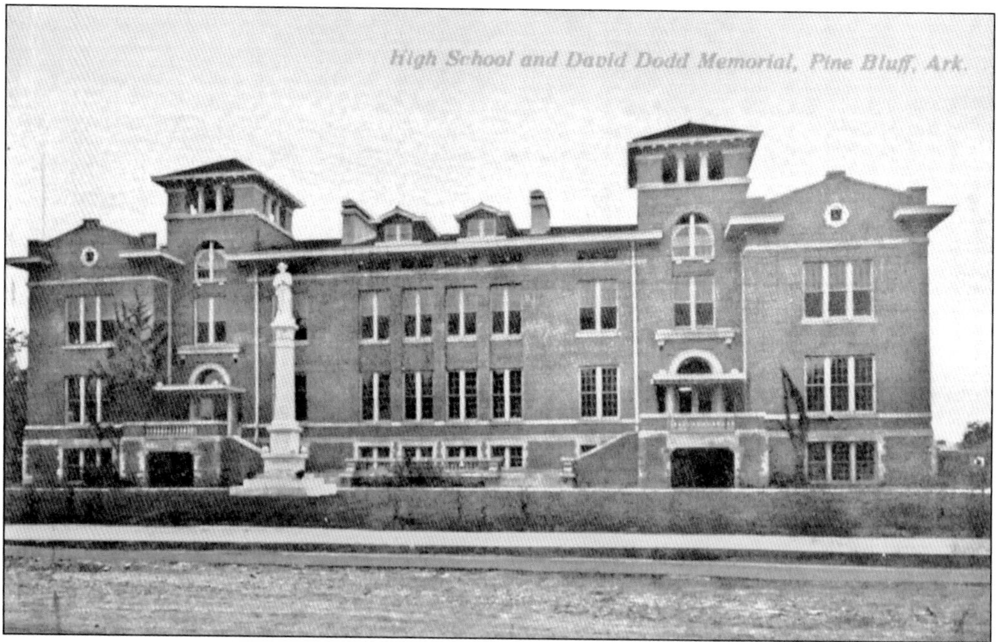

The David O. Dodd Chapter of the United Daughters of the Confederacy (UDC) erected its monument on the grounds of the Pine Bluff High School, the only such placement in the state. In 1974, the school building was razed to make way for a new one, and the rebel soldier today has been relocated to the rear lawn of the Jefferson County Courthouse.

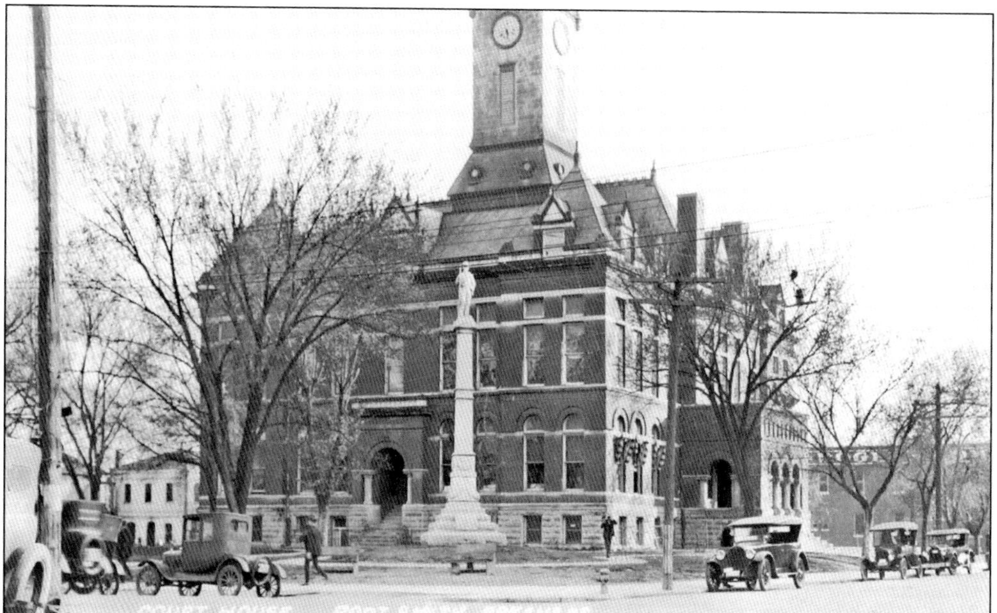

In Fort Smith, the Jefferson Davis Chapter of the Daughters of the Confederacy planned to place their memorial monument in that city's U.S. National Cemetery. However, when the governing quartermaster of the U.S. Army learned that the words "Lest We Forget" were inscribed on the base, he perceived an attitude of Southern defiance and refused the site. The statue was instead dedicated in 1903 on the Sebastian County Courthouse lawn.

"Their Names Are Borne On Honor's Shield. Their Record Is With God. They Fought for Home and Fatherland," reads the base of the monument on the square in Bentonville. The 1908 dedication by the James H. Berry Chapter of the Daughters of the Confederacy came complete with a parade of veterans and a float with 11 pretty girls representing the number of states that seceded from the Union.

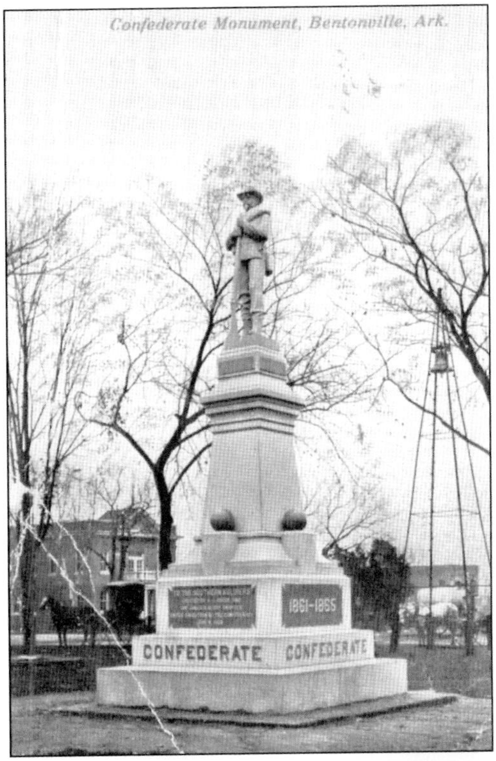

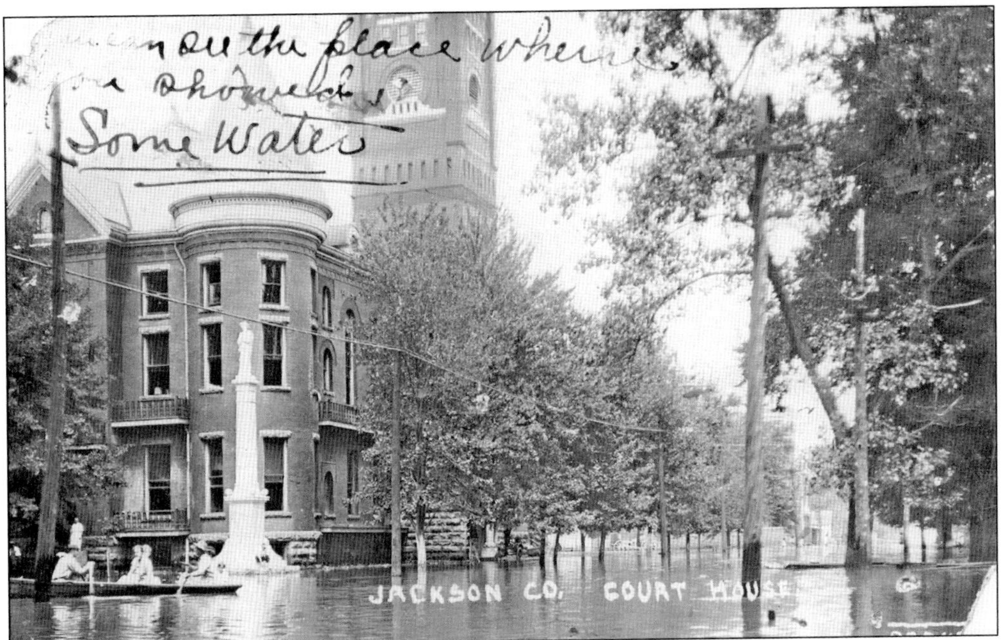

Most Confederate war monuments were made by the McNeel Marble Company, which almost mass-produced them and flooded the South with sales pitches to local government officials. The Jackson County Courthouse in Newport was home to a McNeel sculpted monument that was placed on its lawn around 1910. Seen here in 1915, the lone soldier looks over the floodwaters of the White River.

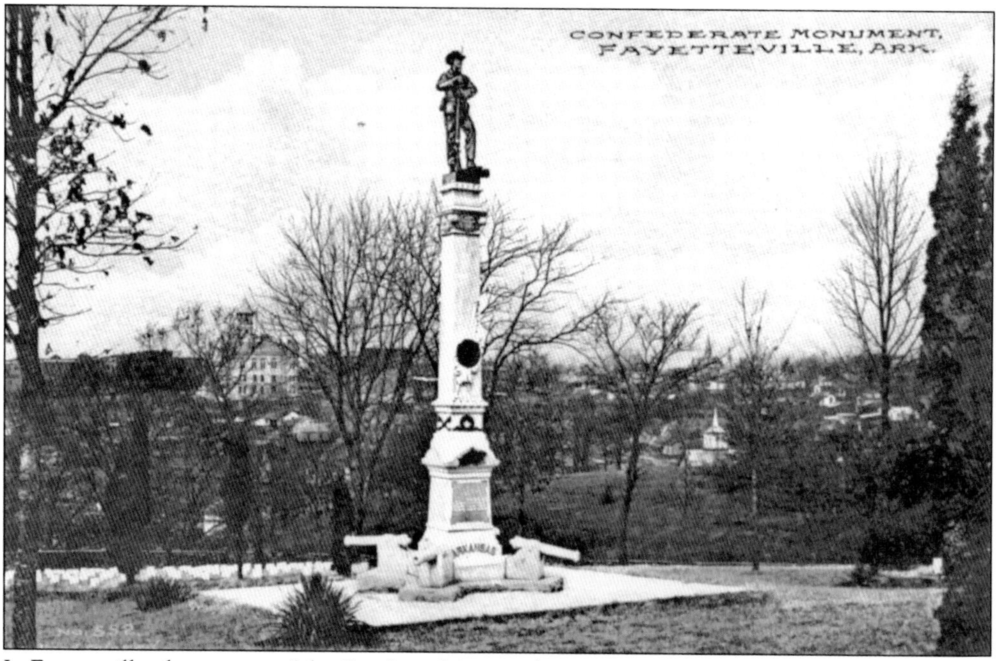

In Fayetteville, the women of the Southern Memorial Association purchased three acres atop East Mountain as a cemetery for the 500 Confederate soldiers who had fallen in Northwest Arkansas at the battles of Pea Ridge, Prairie Grove, and Fayetteville. In 1897, a crowd of several thousand, complete with 350 University of Arkansas cadets, dedicated the monument overlooking the last resting places of the fallen.

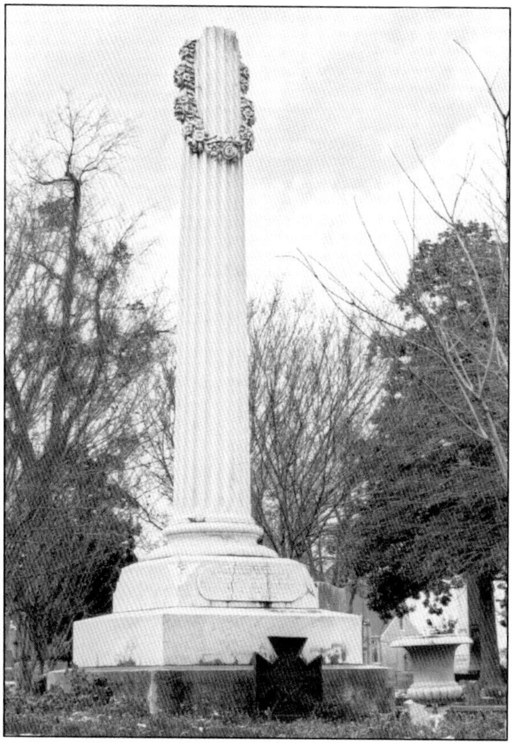

Some Confederates whose families were of means obtained a personal monument to stand over their earthly remains. Lt. Col. Anderson Watkins had been born in Little Rock in 1818 and fell upon the field of battle in Atlanta on July 22, 1864. His family erected this imposing wreathed marble column over his grave, marked with the Confederate Cross of Honor, in Little Rock's Mount Holly Cemetery. (Photograph by Ray Hanley.)

Col. James H. Fletcher of the 20th Arkansas Regiment, Confederate States of America, was the cousin of Gen. John Gould Fletcher, who commanded the Capitol Guards. Colonel Fletcher fought in a number of battles and had his horse shot from beneath him at Corinth, Mississippi. Fletcher died in 1906; his imposing monument in Little Rock's Oakland Cemetery bears the inscription, "An upright man, a brave and gallant soldier, he died trusting in the Lord." (Photograph by Ray Hanley.)

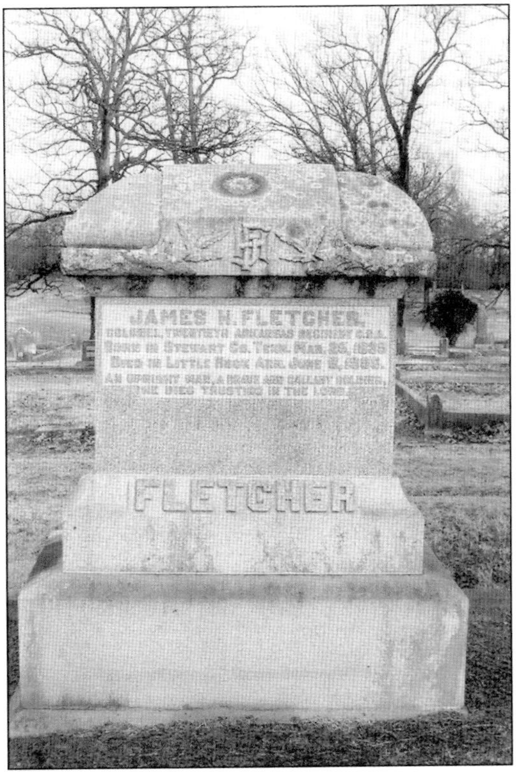

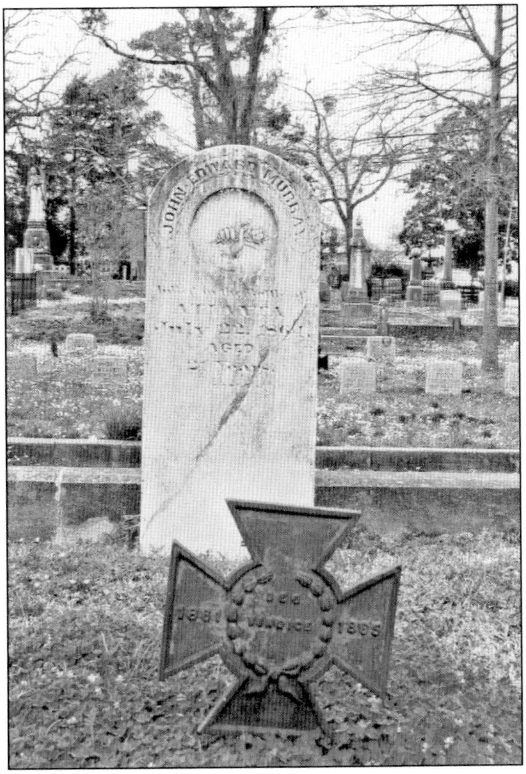

Some cemetery monuments contain surprising history lessons that can be found with a bit of effort. John Edward Murray, at the age of 21, was the youngest general in the Confederacy. He died in the battle of Atlanta, Georgia, on the day his commission was effective but before he received the notification of his promotion. His grave is in Little Rock's historic Mount Holly Cemetery. (Photograph by Ray Hanley.)

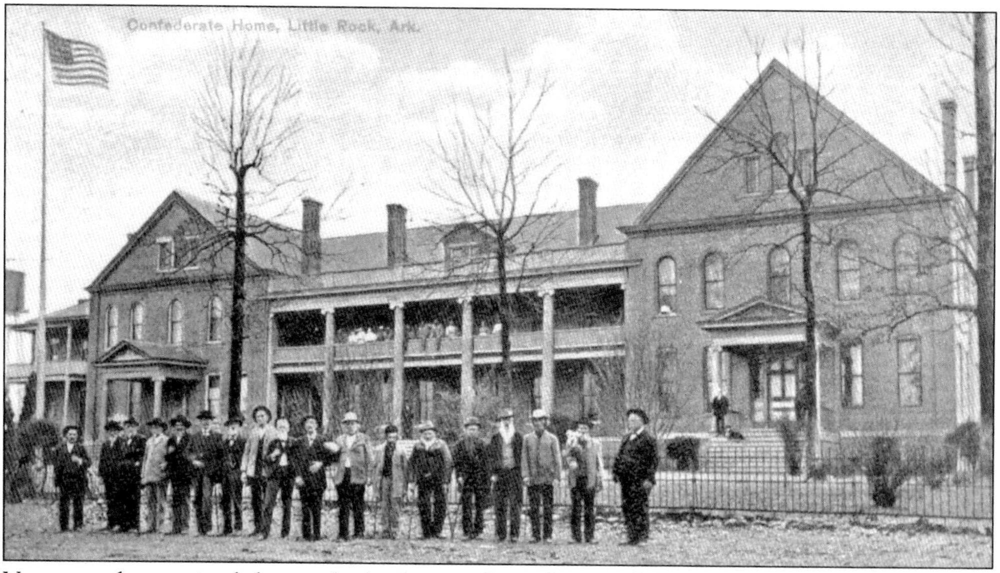

Veterans who survived the war had other needs as they aged, for they often carried the effects of their wounds and impoverishment. The Ex-Confederate Association purchased, for $3,000, a stately home located in Sweet Home, southeast of Little Rock, and by 1892, it had become the state-owned Confederate Soldier's Home. In September 1943, readers of the Sunday *Arkansas Democrat* read that the Confederate Home was "doomed." A large quantity of bauxite ore, sorely needed in World War II, lay beneath the structure. Of the 82 remaining residents, only 4 were actual veterans, with the remainder being widows; all were relocated to Camp Robinson. The article ended acknowledging that "none are more willing than the boys in gray and their women folk to make, just as they did almost a century ago, whatever sacrifice seems necessary to meet their country's needs." (Below image courtesy of the *Arkansas Democrat*.)

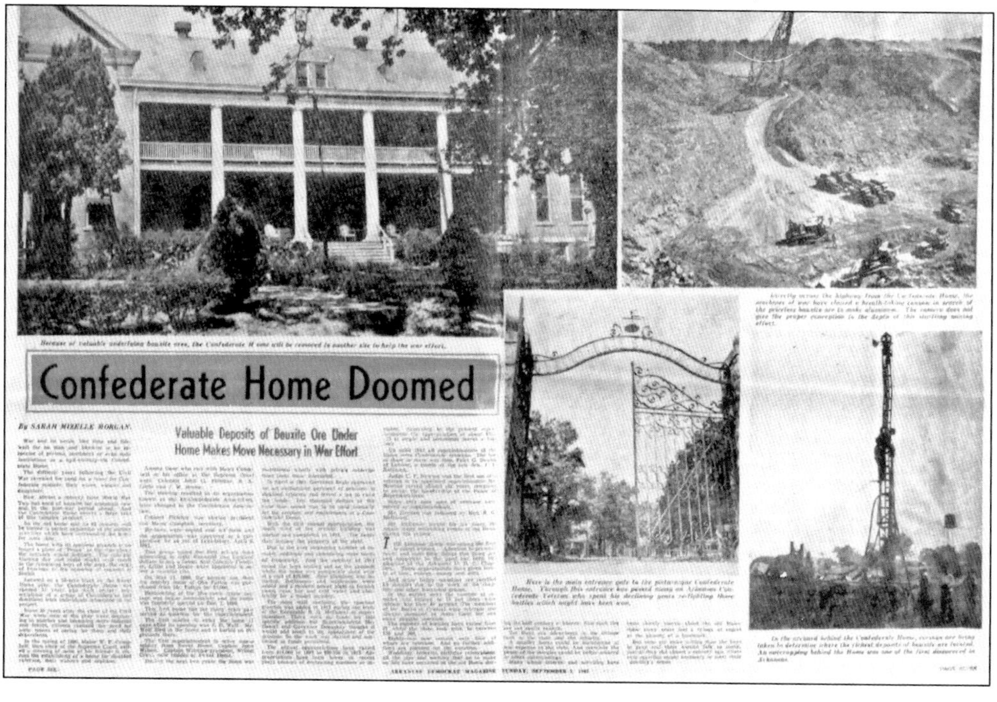

Confederate Home Doomed

Valuable Deposits of Bauxite Ore Under Home Makes Move Necessary in War Effort

Five

The United Confederate Veterans Reunion of 1911

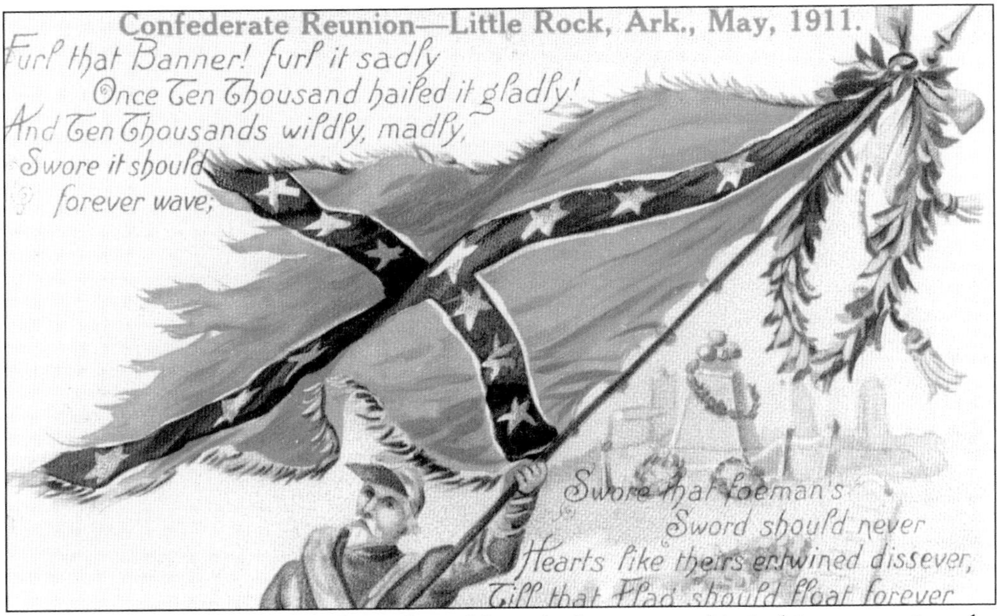

For three days in May 1911, Little Rock would see the largest crowd in its history pour into the city. From May 16 through 18, the capital city pulled together in a tremendous effort to celebrate its Confederate history and welcome thousands of honored veterans and guests. The logistical details included feeding, lodging, and entertaining the veterans at no charge, as well as arranging for smooth transportation, decorating the city for a proper welcome, and staging dozens of meetings and parties for 100,000 guests. Not until 1992, when Arkansas governor Bill Clinton won the presidency, would a larger crowd come to town. The United Confederate Veterans (UCV) was formed in 1890 to generate assistance, and honor, for the aging soldiers. The highlight of the UCV was its annual reunion, and in 1911, Little Rock was the host city for the 21st Annual Reunion of the UCV. The population of the city at the time, 50 years after the start of the war, was 45,000; preparing to host perhaps 100,000 visitors would be a daunting challenge.

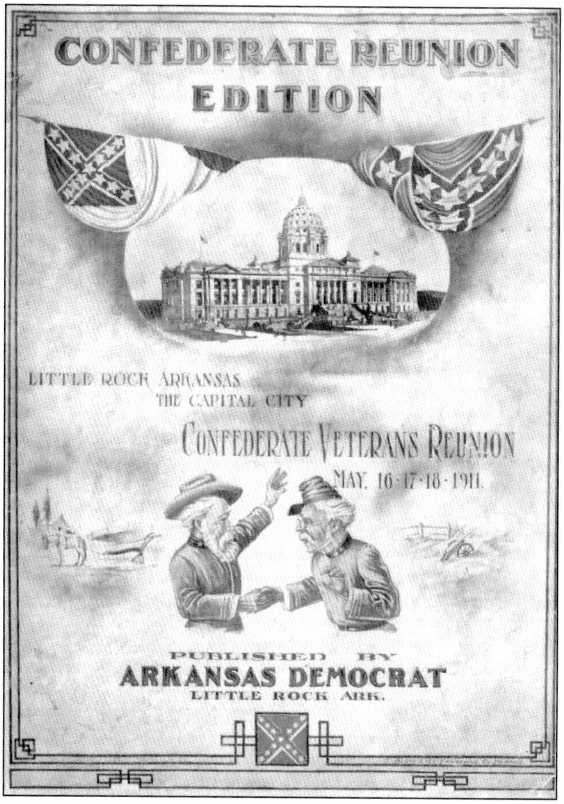

The *Arkansas Democrat*, in an effort to promote the state of Arkansas, put out a 95-page *Confederate Reunion Edition* prior to the event. The publication was filled with advertisements, messages from city leaders, and photographs paying tribute to the UCV organization. The centerpiece photograph on the newspaper's cover, over the two reunited old rebs, was of the state's brand-new $2-million State Capitol building.

Little Rock's leaders were on display in the *Democrat*'s feature, including Mayor Charles Taylor (top left) and Police Chief Frank McMahon (bottom center); the men are framed around the city hall. At the opening ceremonies, Mayor Taylor would proclaim, "It is the Stars and Stripes interwoven and intertwined and interwreathed with the Stars and Bars—the conscious strength of the present united with the hallowed memories of the past."

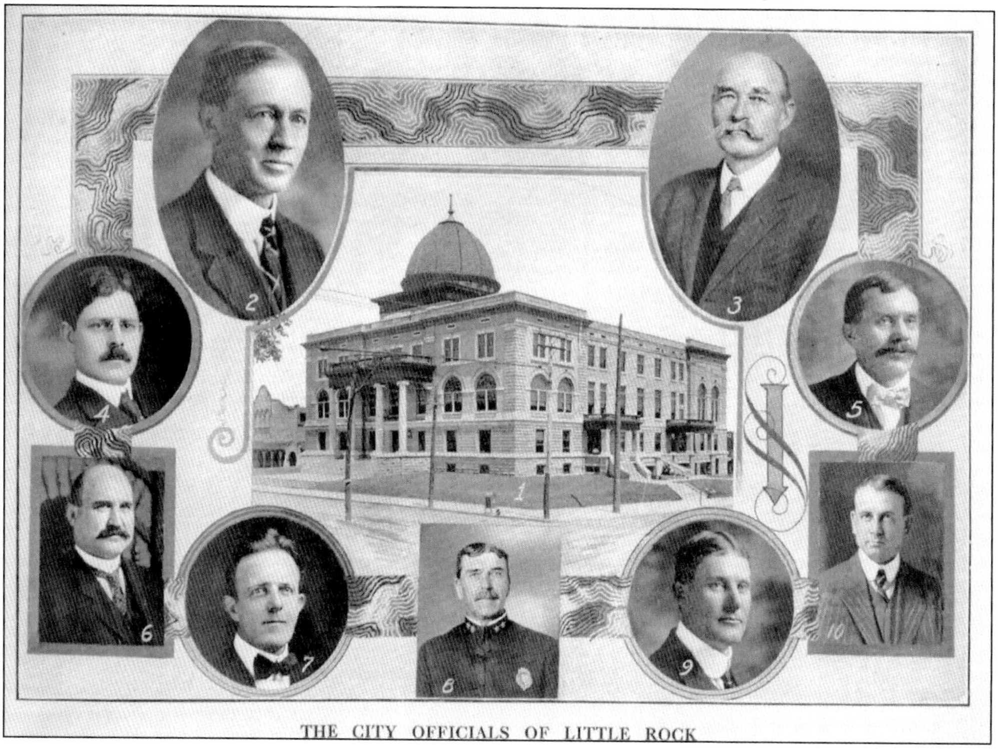

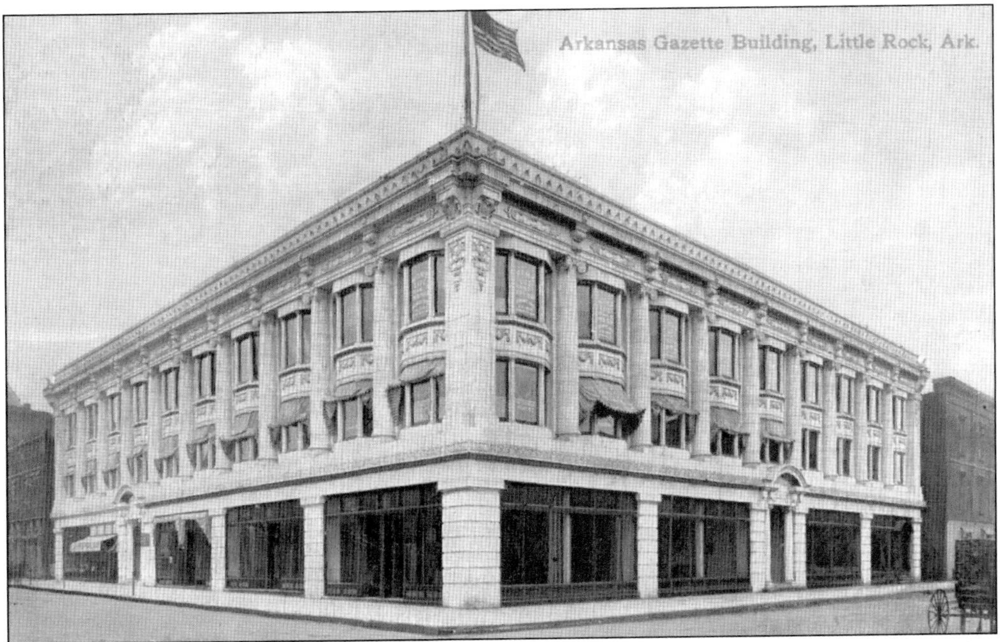

In advance of the UCV reunion, the *Arkansas Gazette* penned from its offices, seen here, that the event should "be in accord with the dignity and importance of the occasion." A week before the arrival of the old soldiers, the paper proclaimed: "The chances are, a piece called 'Dixie' will be heard in Little Rock this week." The paper set up a bureau in the veterans' encampment in City Park.

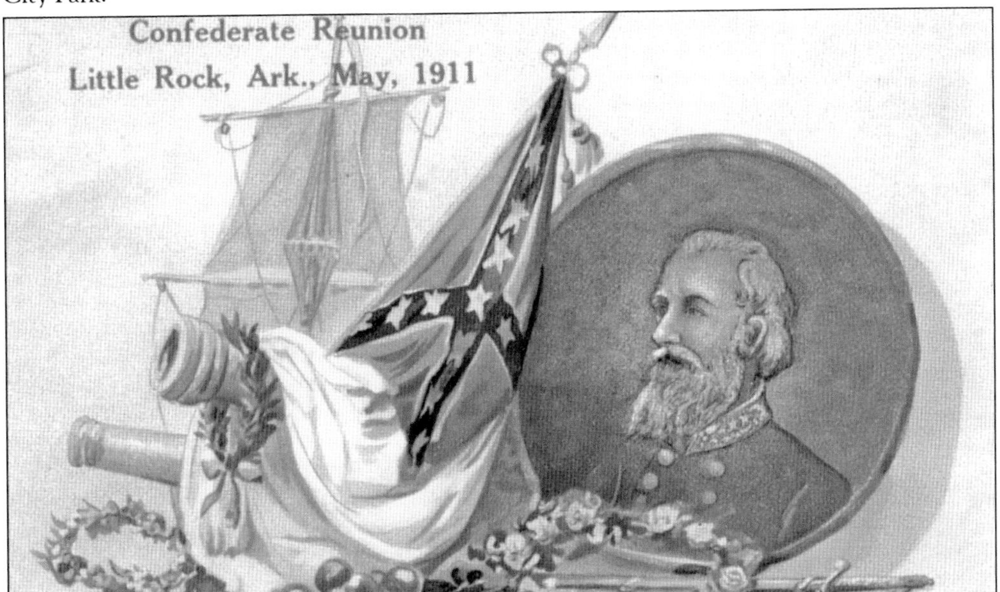

Souvenir postcards, like this one bearing the image of Stonewall Jackson, were easily made to mark the event. However, raising the large sums of money the city needed to keep its commitments to the old soldiers was far more difficult. In wooing the UCV at the previous year's event in Mobile, Little Rock's city fathers had promised to house, feed, and entertain the old soldiers without charge. Raising the money would be a challenge.

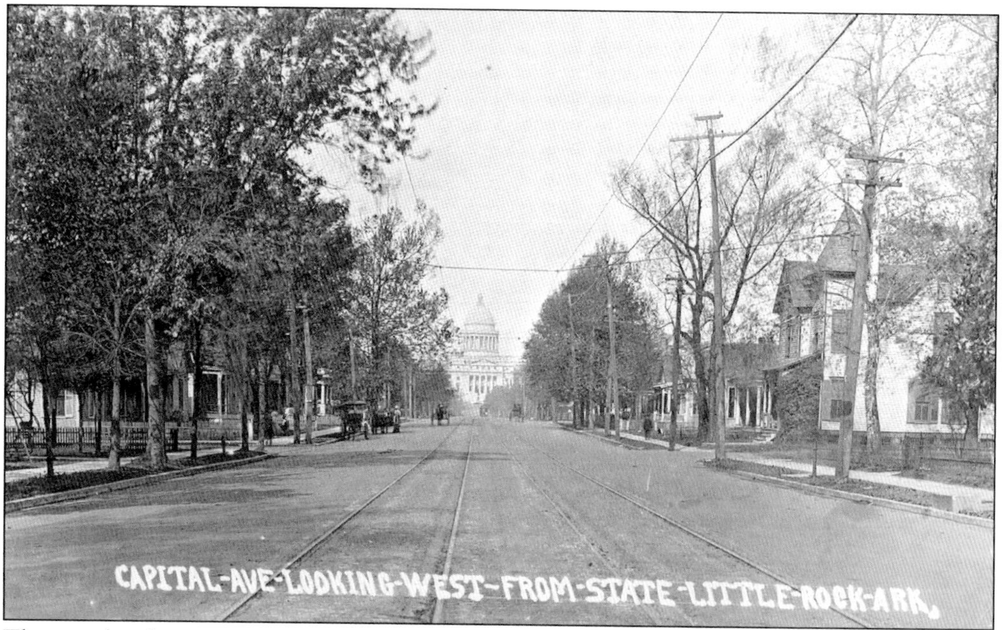

The state legislature was in session at the head of Capitol Avenue, where the new capitol building neared completion. Little Rock's reunion organizers requested an appropriation of state funds to help pay for the reunion. The legislature refused, contending that the citizens of Little Rock had not contributed enough for an event that would greatly enhance the local economy. The United Daughters of the Confederacy began selling $1 "tribute buttons" to raise funds.

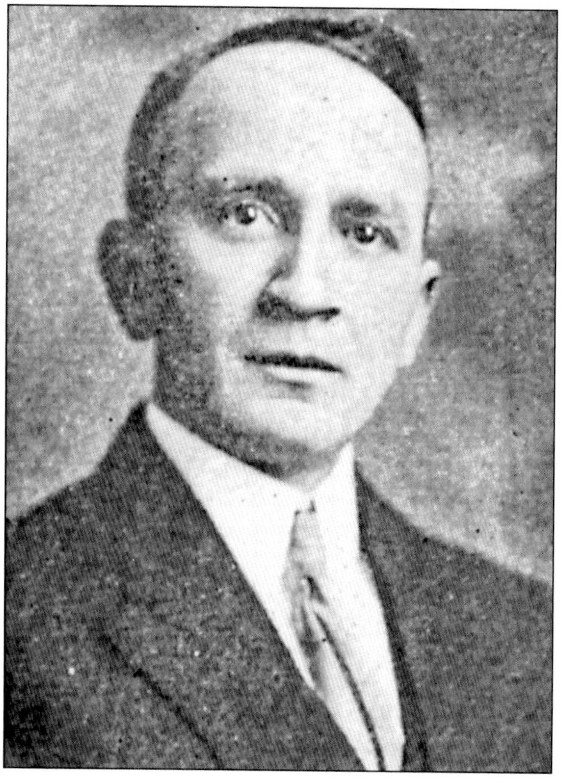

Hal Norwood, the Arkansas attorney general who led fund-raising efforts, took offense at what he considered the "paltry" donations of the Little Rock saloon owners, who expected to profit during the three-day UCV event. He urged the city council to return their $600 donation and close the saloons during the reunion unless the donations were substantially increased. The council declined the suggestion, and the saloon owners did not ante up any more money.

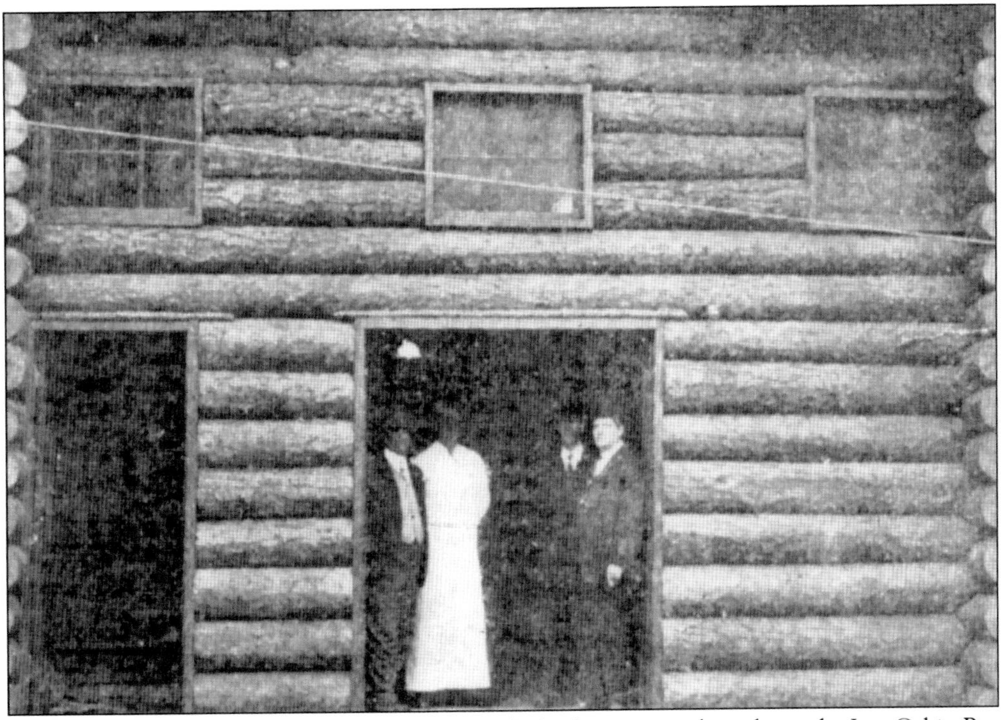

One of the targets of Attorney General Norwood's displeasure may have been the Log Cabin Bar at 119 Main Street. Advertisements described it as "one of the most unique places of interest in Little Rock . . . inviting Reunion visitors to visit this bar and note the many interesting souvenirs of the Civil War, the 'old timey' fire-place, chimney, and partake of juleps, toddies, etc., as made 'Befo de Wah.' "

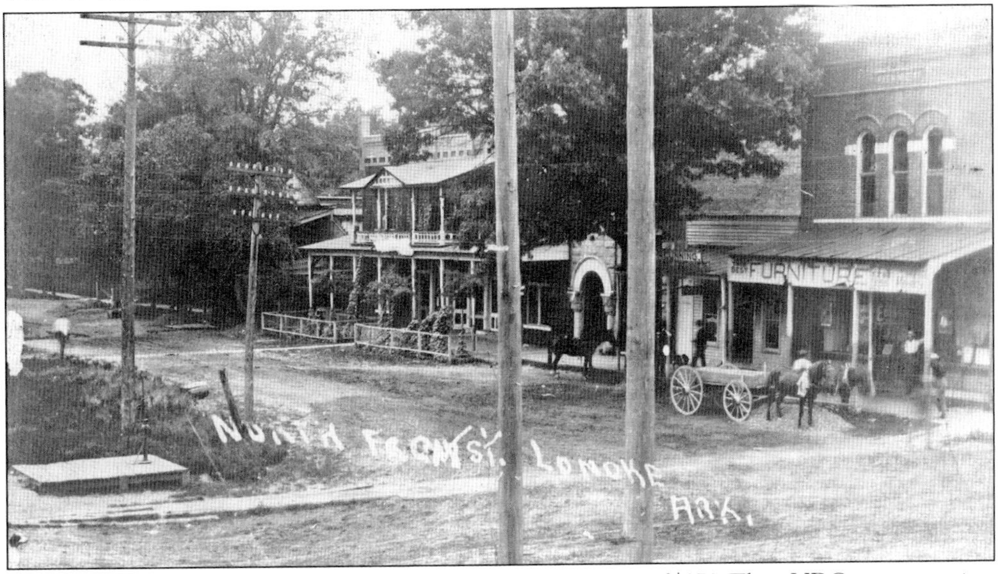

The small farming town of Lonoke's UDC group sent a donation of $279. Their UDC representative, Mattie Trimble, said of the Confederate flag that it was "a flag dear to every Southern heart. Many a Confederate flag during the dark days of '61 had been stained with the blood of the South and softened by the tears of weeping mothers and wives."

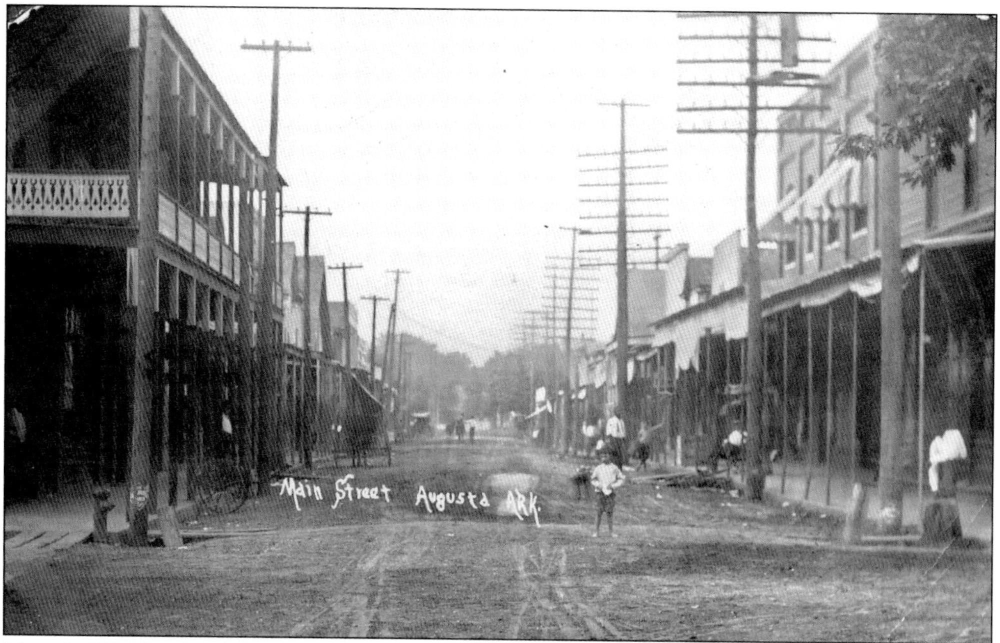

Mrs. G. W. Hatch of the Eastern Arkansas town of Augusta, seen above, wrote the reunion fund-raising committee a letter describing a tale of the biblical "widow's mite." She stated that she wanted to contribute cash, but was only a poor widow of a Confederate veteran. Instead of money, she offered 3,000 lilies from her garden to pin on visiting veterans, whom she described as "noble heroes of the South."

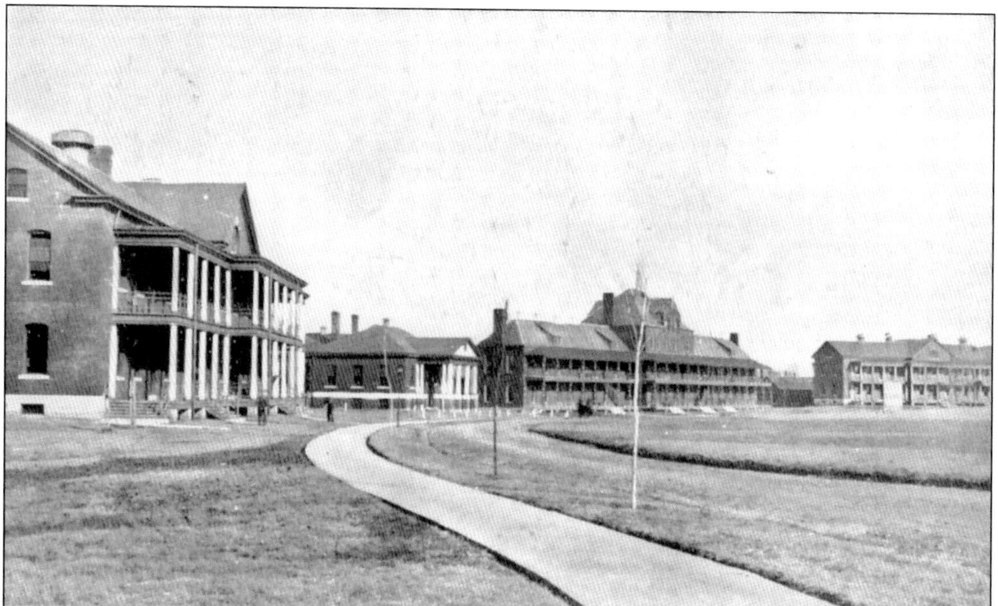

City fathers knew the numbers of veterans were going to be larger than initially forecast. Arkansas senator James P. Clarke passed a bill for the U.S. Army to supply 1,333 tents, along with 40 soldiers to erect them in Little Rock's City Park. The tents and soldiers came from Fort Logan H. Roots, located across the Arkansas River; its parade ground is seen on this postcard.

Logan H. Roots ran all the supply lines for General Sherman's vast army on its march through Georgia. After the Civil War, Roots settled in Arkansas and led the civic effort to secure funding for the army fort across the Arkansas River from Little Rock that bears his name. He died in 1893 and is buried in Little Rock's Oakland Cemetery, under this monument bearing the words, "A servant unto the Lord, faithful unto death." (Photograph by Ray Hanley.)

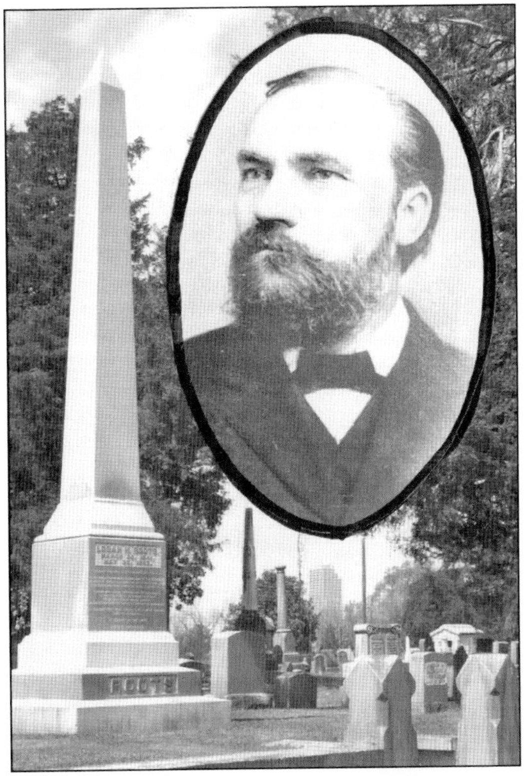

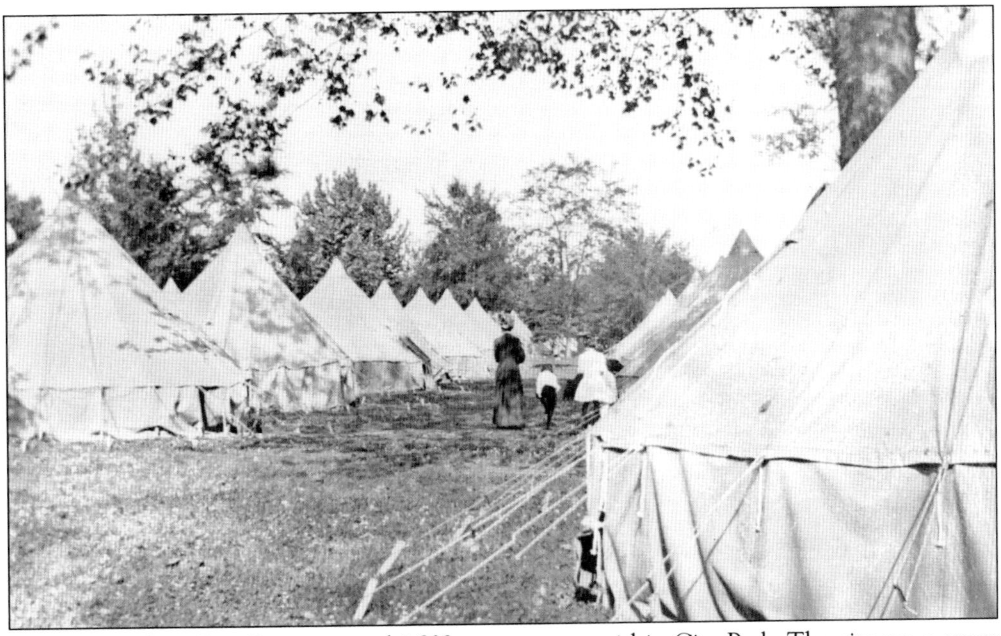

The soldiers from Fort Roots erected 1,333 canvas tents within City Park. The city ran a sewer line to the camp, while the public works superintendent worried about the capacity of the town's systems, publicly stating, "I wish to caution all property owners to get after their cooks and instruct them not to allow slops, vegetable peelings, old bread and many things to get into the sanitary sewer next week. With thousands of visitors in our city, our sewers will be greatly overtaxed."

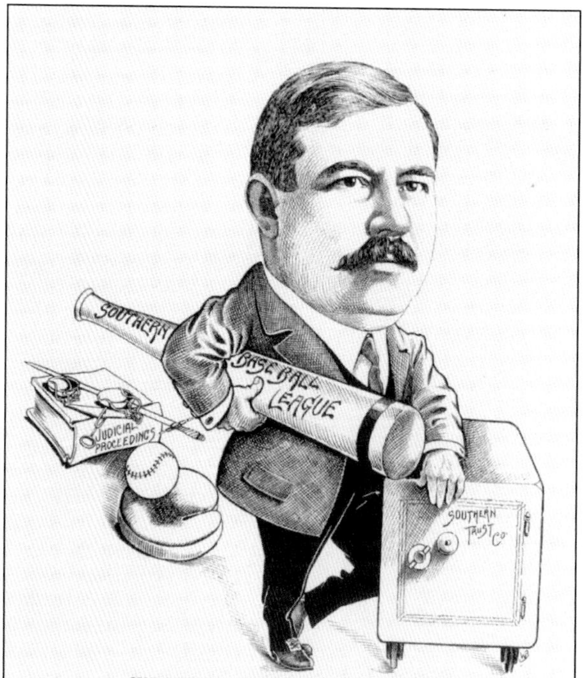

JUDGE W. M. KAVANAUGH, Little Rock
President Southern Trust Company

Judge W. M. Kavanaugh, chairman of the reunion's executive committee, stated: "We are literally swamped. We expected 1,500, we prepared for 5,500, we now have 11,000 to house and entertain." Kavanaugh, a prominent figure in Pulaski County, had been the president of Little Rock's semi-professional baseball team and in 1913 would be appointed a U.S. senator by the Arkansas legislature. By the time the reunion opened, Kavanaugh declared Camp Shaver, the veterans' City Park encampment, filled to "bursting at the seams."

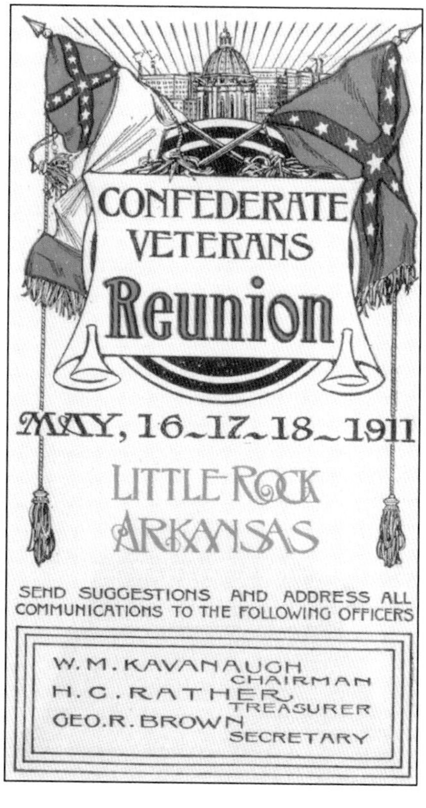

This promotional pamphlet made many bold claims: "Plans are being wrought out on a larger scale than ever before attempted. . . . 'The Thinning Line of Gray' will be the honored guests of Arkansas and Little Rock, and every one of our beloved Heroes who visits 'The City of Roses' will find thoughtful preparation for his comfort; and watchful, loving care assuring his safety and pleasure during the Reunion. . . . Nothing will be stinted in equipping quarters for the Veterans."

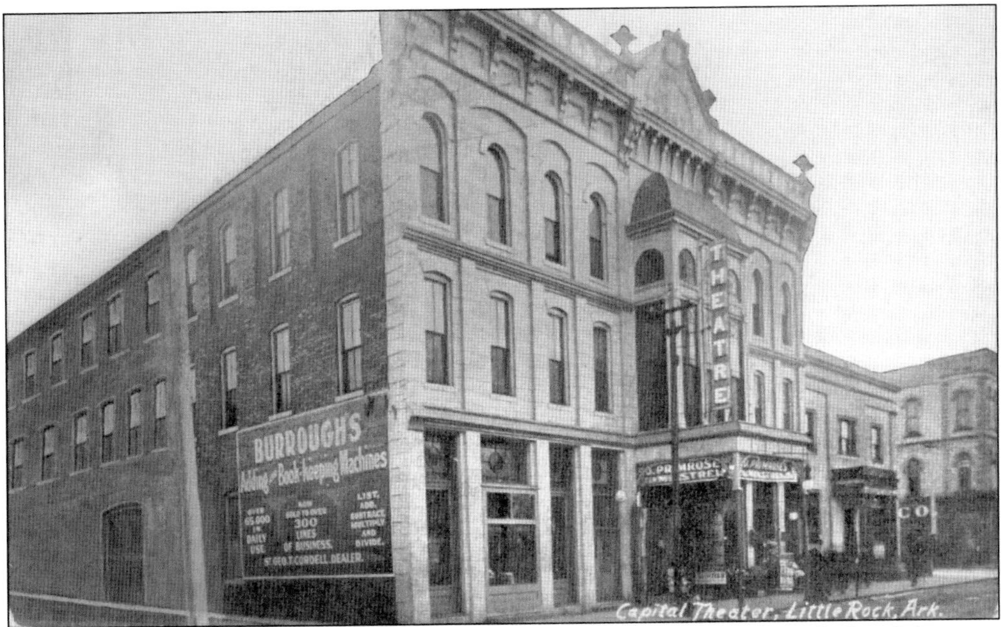

Judge Kavanaugh not only led the effort to house the old soldiers, but also worked with business leaders to keep the promise of providing entertainment for the veterans while in Little Rock. One venue was the Capitol Theater, located on Markham Street across from the Old State House, where the secession vote had occurred in 1861. The Fraternal Order of Eagles was performing, with blackface artists doing three performances of a minstrel show at the theater.

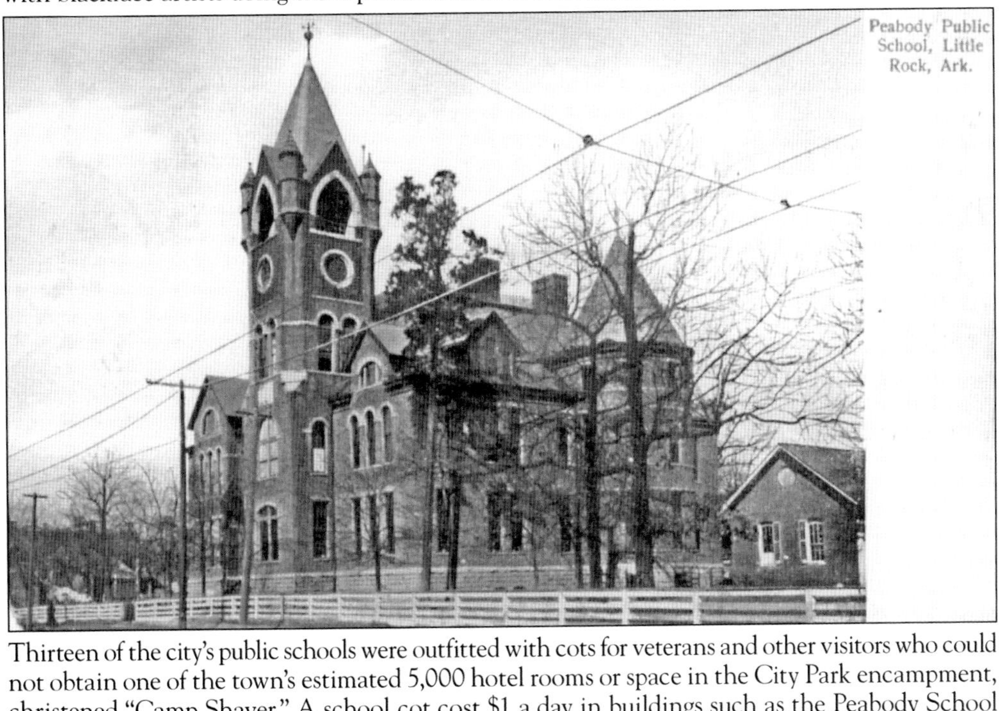

Thirteen of the city's public schools were outfitted with cots for veterans and other visitors who could not obtain one of the town's estimated 5,000 hotel rooms or space in the City Park encampment, christened "Camp Shaver." A school cot cost $1 a day in buildings such as the Peabody School located on Capitol Avenue. During the reunion, W. L. Gallaway, an elderly veteran from Paris, Texas, fell from a second-story window of the school and died.

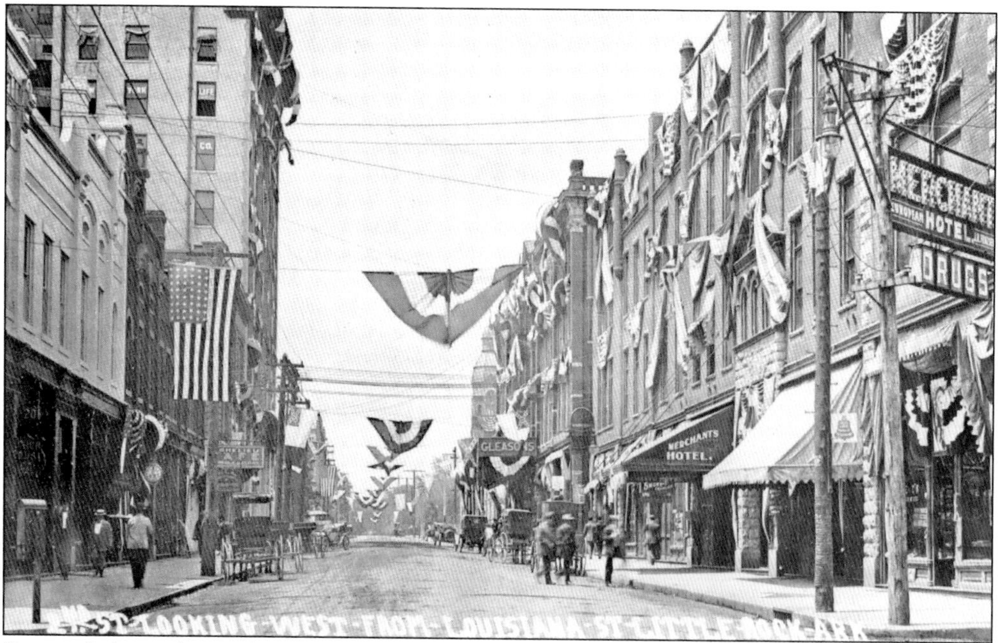

Bargain lodging choices for visitors during the reunion on well-decorated Louisiana Street included the Merchants Hotel to the immediate right and Gleason's Hotel farther down the block. Each advertised rooms at rates running from $1.50 to $2 a night. Thousands of beds in private homes and schools were offered at prices not to exceed $1 a night, a rule of the reunion's "Lodging and Eating Committee," which registered homes offering the beds.

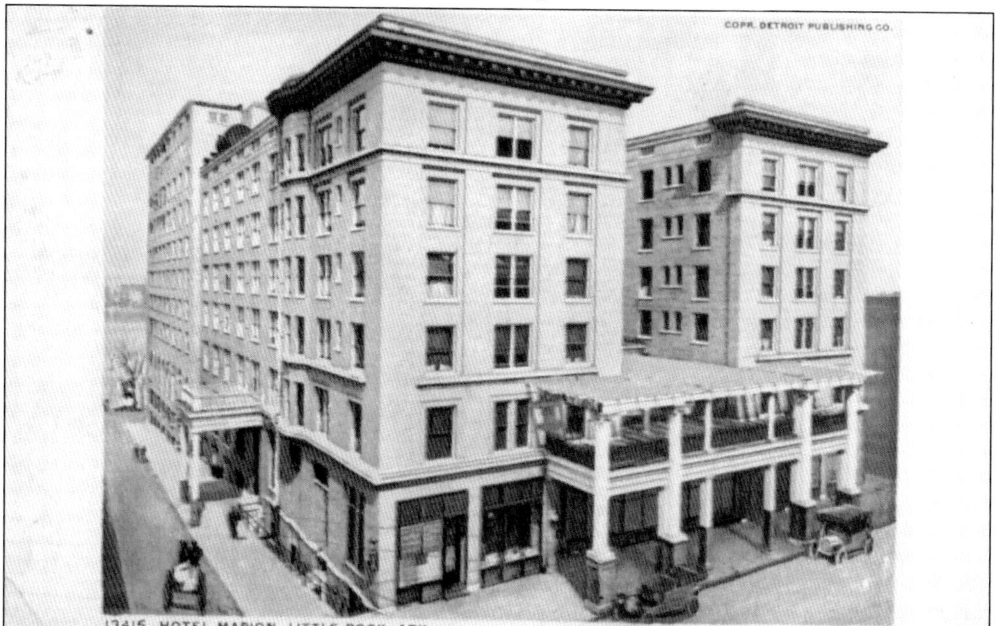

For those with means who also had reservations made well in advance, the finest lodging during reunion week was at the Marion Hotel, which had opened in 1906 and was given the first name of its owner's daughter. Lodging at the Marion ranged from $2 to $5 for a room with a private bath, while rooms went for $1 to $2 if a bath down the hall would suffice.

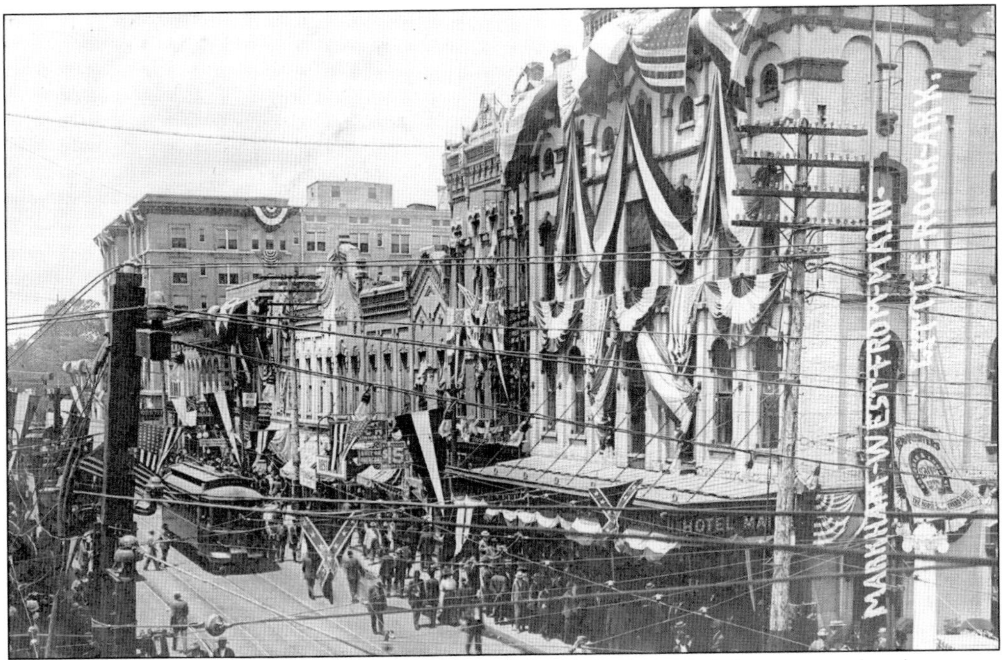

The Marion Hotel (the large building just past the trolley) housed the reunion headquarters, and as seen in this photograph, it was in the hub of activity. A room at the well-decorated Hotel Main, seen to the right, could be had for less. There were at least two saloons located in the block between these two hotels; both did a booming business during the reunion.

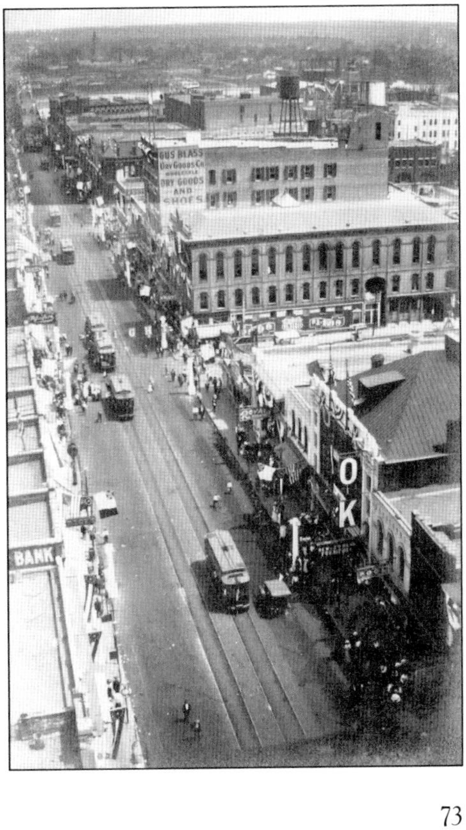

The State National Bank, the city's tallest building, provided a photographer's platform in all directions. This view looked north up Main Street toward the Arkansas River, seen just past the Gus Blass Dry Goods store. Along the street are seen some of the plaster columns erected for the coming event, along with lines of north- and southbound streetcars whose drivers were surely bracing for the largest crowds in the city's history.

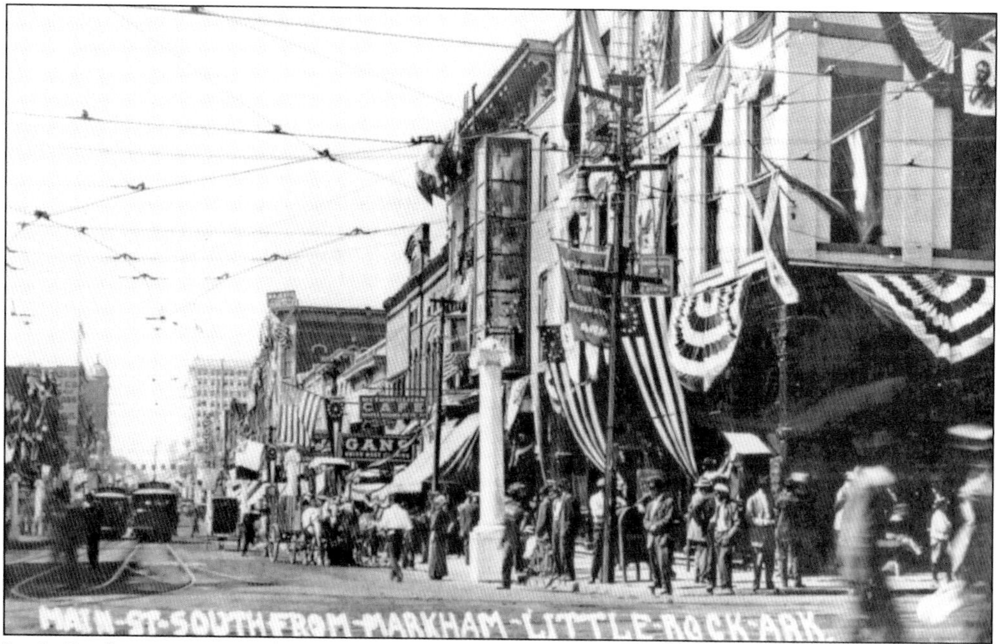

Little Rock went agog with decorating two weeks before the reunion, draping at least 100 city streets with banners and flags. Gan's Clothing store, in the middle of the block, had a well-decorated reunion window. Two wax figures, described as "the most lifelike ever seen," were dressed as Confederate and Union generals posed to be shaking hands. The city's most striking features were the 60 plaster columns that stood 12 feet high, each crowned with a lighted globe of red and white lights, as seen in both these photographs. The columns, marching down Main Street beneath garlands of lights, led from Markham Street (top photograph), down to Ninth Street (below), then to the City Park and Camp Shaver. Seen between the columns to the right in the lower photograph is the Airdrome Summer Theater, an open-air playhouse that staged *A Gilded Fool* during the reunion.

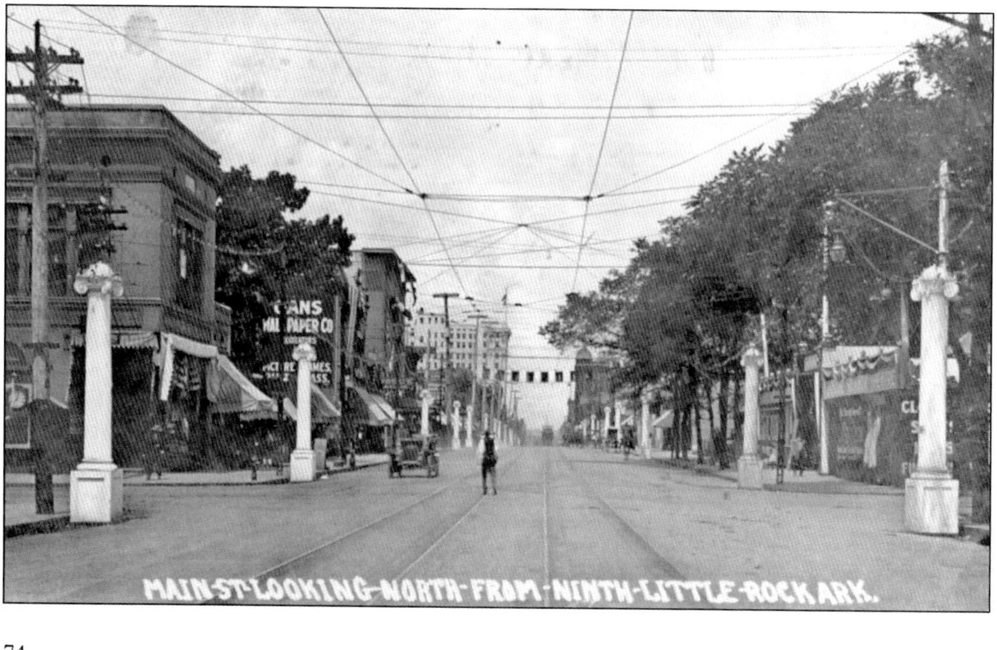

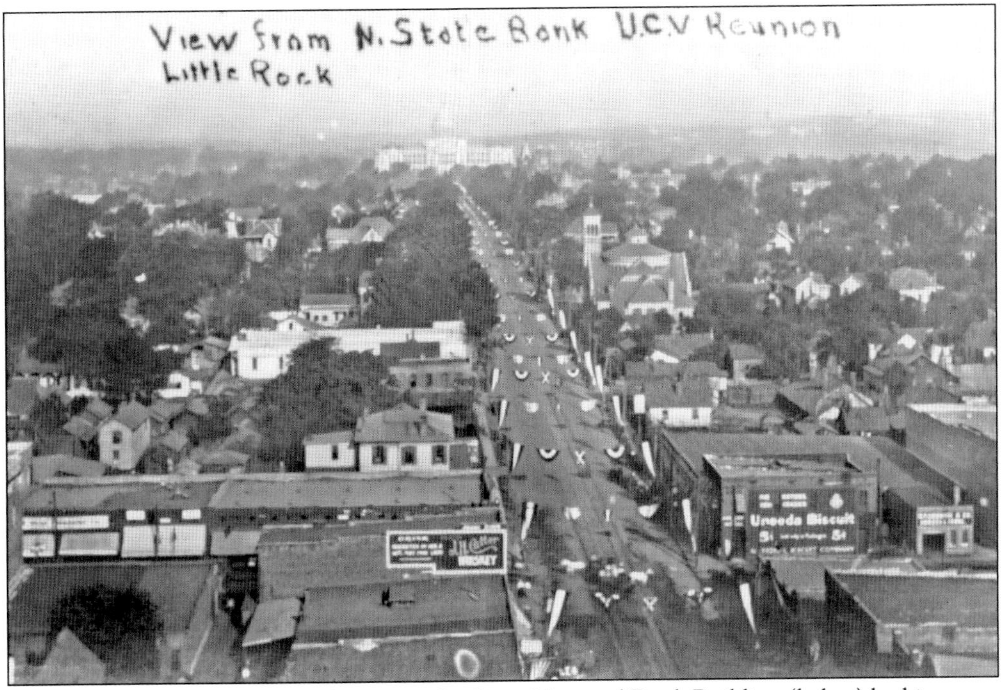

A photographer took this shot from atop the State National Bank Building (below) looking west down Capitol Avenue toward the capitol dome. The bird's-eye view (above) of Main Street's intersection with Capitol Avenue was taken a week or so before the opening of the reunion, while below is the same intersection from street level during the event. Perhaps any Confederate veterans who arrived with a toothache would have been struck by the irony of being able to seek relief at the Union Painless Dentist to the right, promising "Teeth Extracted Without Pain."

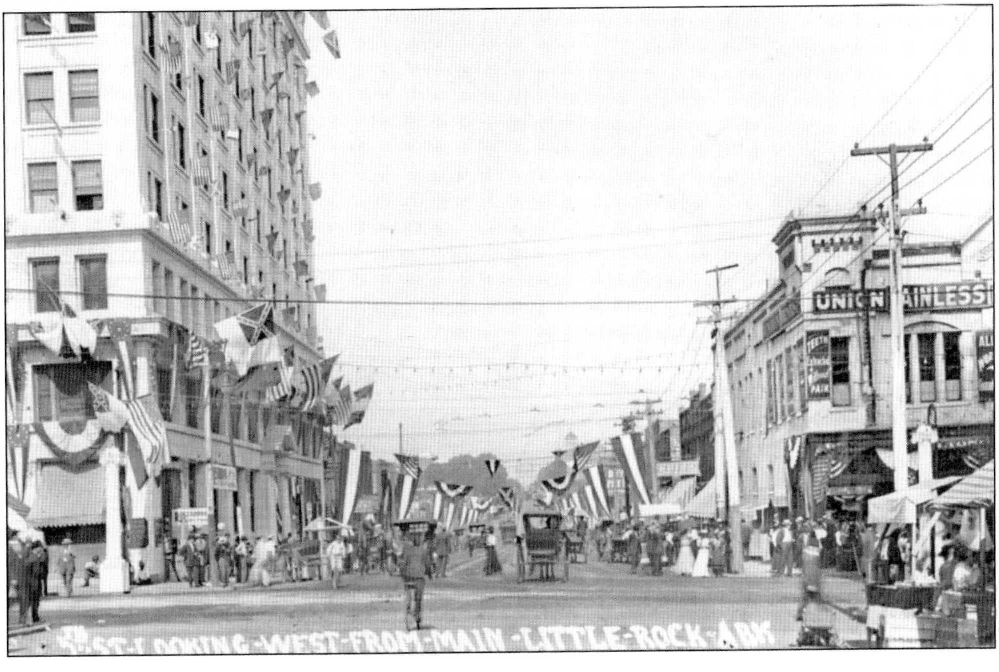

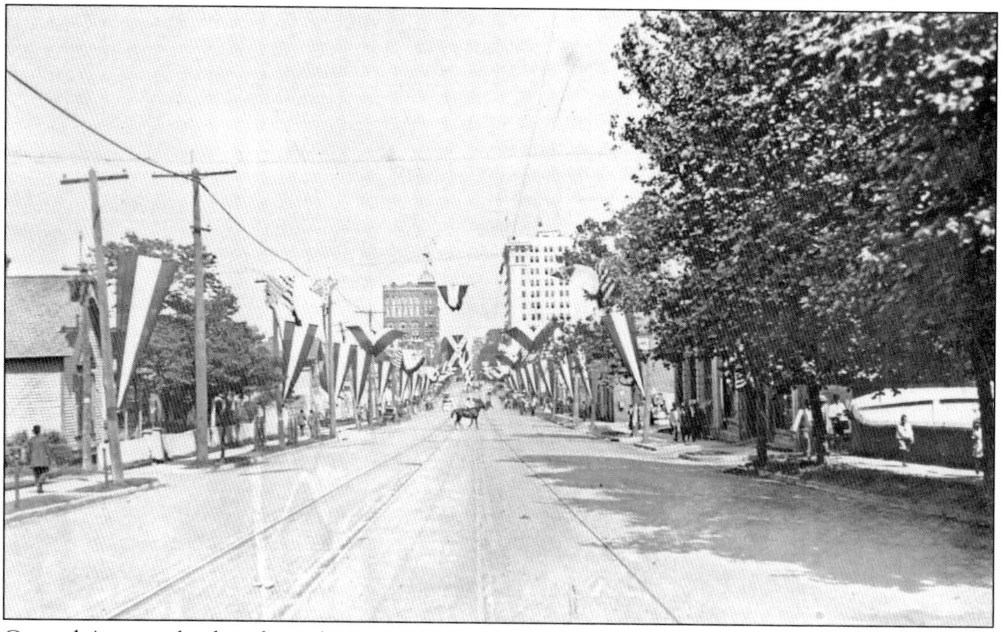

Capitol Avenue, leading from the State Capitol building east to its intersection with Main Street in the distance, was lined with Confederate flags and banners. In the distance on Main Street are the towering State National Bank on the right and the Masonic Temple on the left. During the reunion, streetcars ran constantly back and forth between Main Street and the capitol building, site of two Confederate monuments. (Courtesy of Arkansas History Commission.)

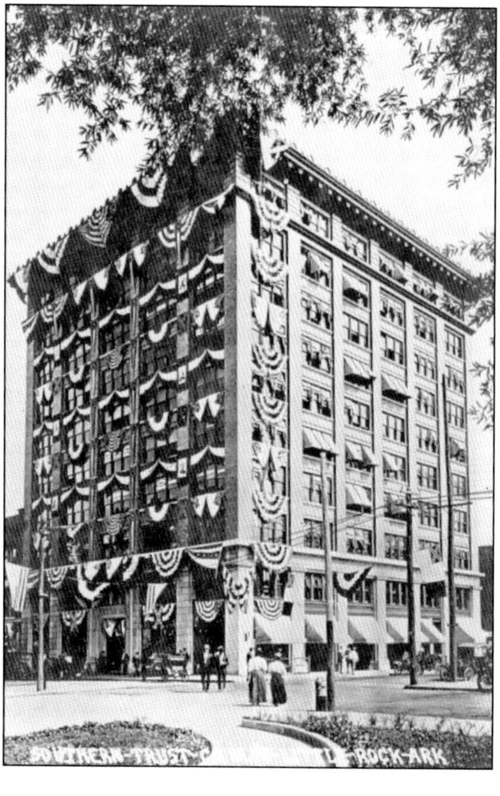

The city's business community's support of the UCV reunion was very evident, seen here on the well-decorated Southern Trust Company building at Second and Center Streets. On the second day of the reunion, a part of the bunting hanging from the Southern Trust building caught fire but was extinguished by a passerby.

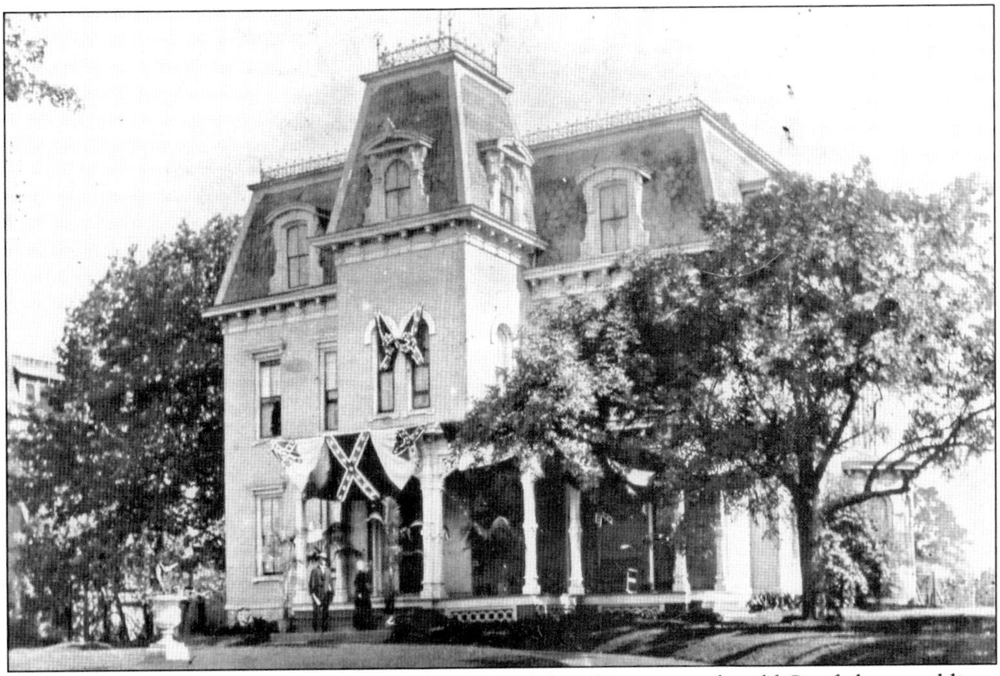

Owners of prominent homes in the city also showed their homage to the old Confederate soldiers. The 22-room Packet House mansion (still standing) was erected in the late 1860s by Alexander MacDonald, a former Union soldier who had helped occupy Little Rock during the Civil War. He returned during Reconstruction to erect the home on Lincoln Avenue, or "Carpetbagger Row" as it was sometimes called. (Courtesy of Quapaw Quarter Association.)

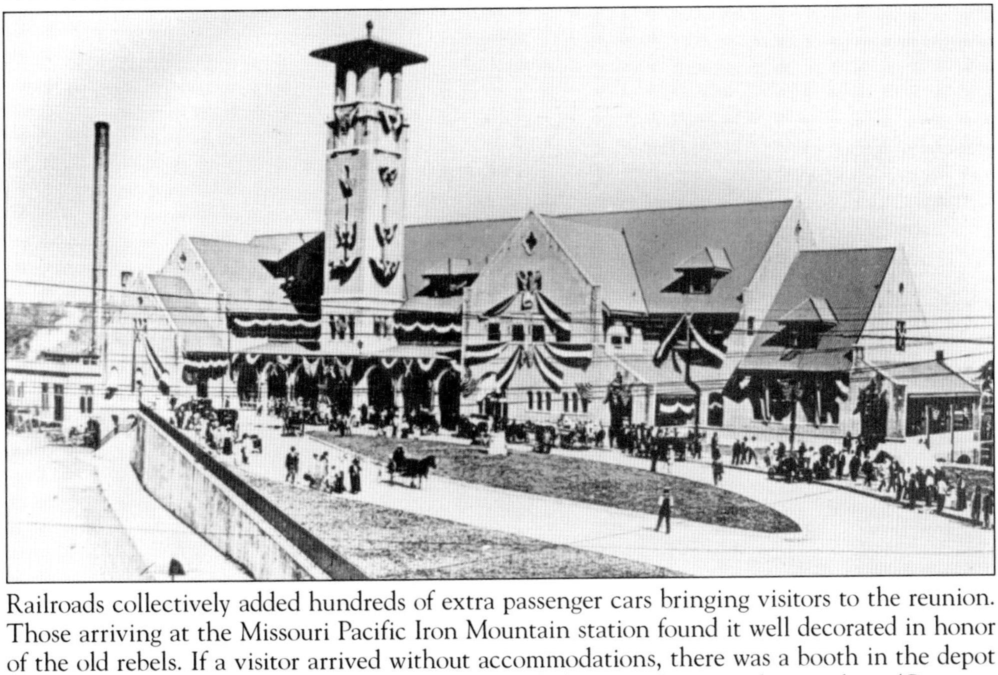

Railroads collectively added hundreds of extra passenger cars bringing visitors to the reunion. Those arriving at the Missouri Pacific Iron Mountain station found it well decorated in honor of the old rebels. If a visitor arrived without accommodations, there was a booth in the depot manned by a member of the reunion committee to help guests locate a place to sleep. (Courtesy of Butler Center for Arkansas Studies.)

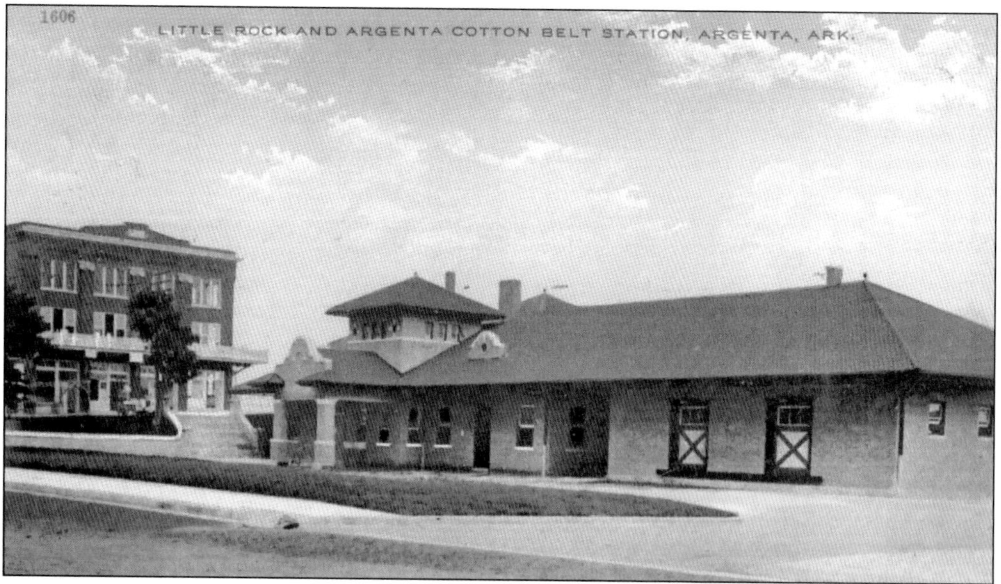

"Three Veterans Robbed," read a newspaper headline. The Cotton Belt Railroad brought its share of visitors to the reunion, arriving at the Argenta depot just across the Arkansas River from Little Rock. Three of the elderly veterans arriving at the depot were victims of pickpockets aboard a darkened train coming from Pine Bluff. The three elderly men, aboard a special reunion train, lost $14, $18, and $30, surely representing all the money they had for their visit. Cotton Belt officer J. C. Cheek promised to make every effort to apprehend the thief.

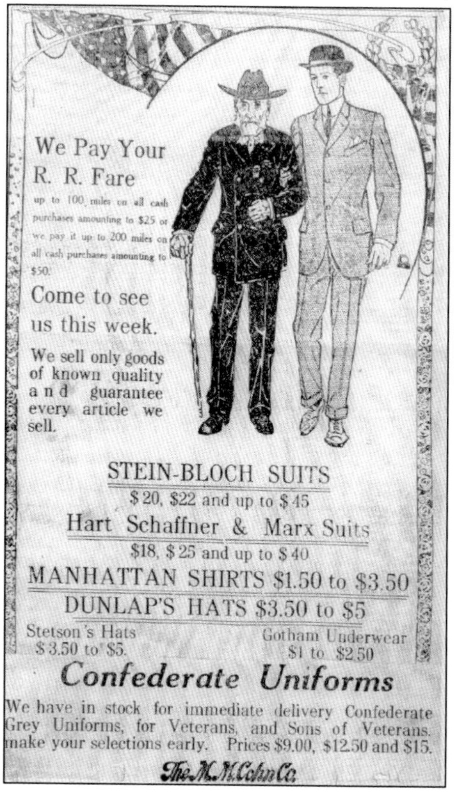

M. M. Cohn's, most likely the city's finest department store, ran the advertisement at left. Railroad fare would be free depending on how far the visitor had traveled to be at the reunion. Stetson hats went for $5 or less, Hart Schaffner, and Marx suits from $18 to $40, and "Gotham underwear for as little as $1." Veterans and sons of veterans could purchase Confederate gray uniforms for prices ranging from $9 to $15.

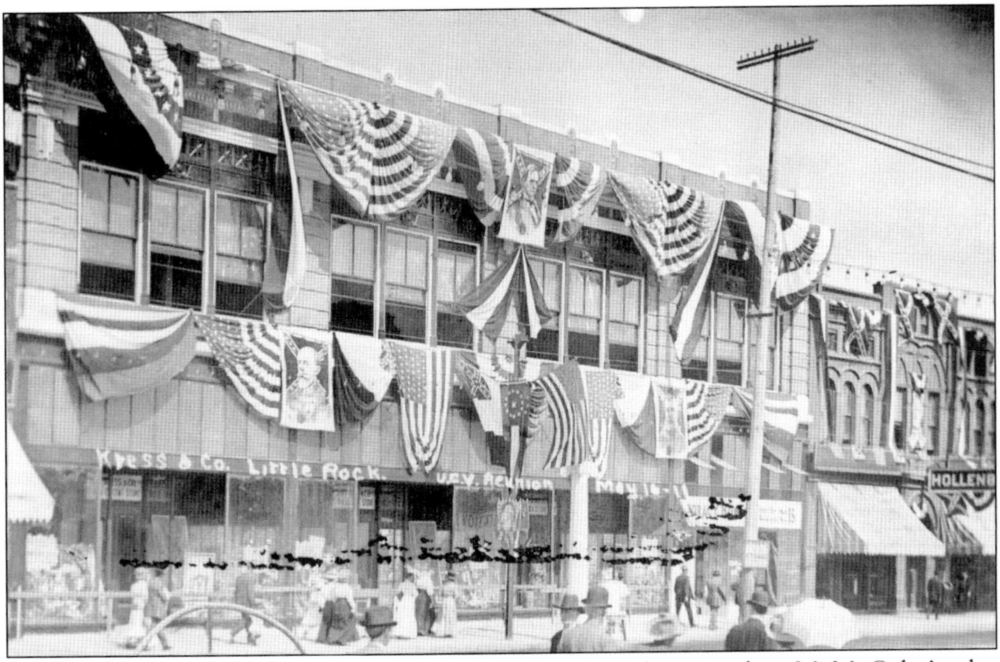

Kress and Company, appealing to more bargain-conscious shoppers than M. M. Cohn's, also prepared the exterior of its Main Street store for the arrival of the old soldiers and visitors. Amid the bunting and American flags are portraits of revered Confederate generals. Hollenberg's Music store next door likewise adorned its storefront with the Stars and Bars. (Courtesy of Arkansas History Commission.)

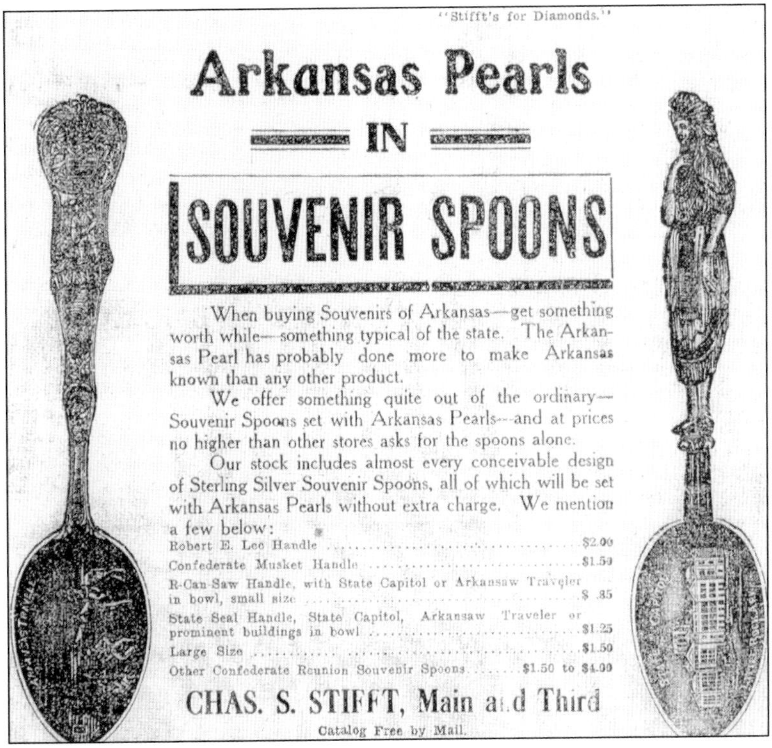

Stifft's Jewelry store ran this advertisement promoting souvenir spoons of Arkansas and the reunion. Two dollars would buy a spoon with the Robert E. Lee handle, while $1.50 would obtain the Confederate Musket handle; for only 85¢ one could purchase a spoon with the "R Can Saw" handle showing the letter R, an oil can, and a handsaw, forming a rebus image for Arkansas.

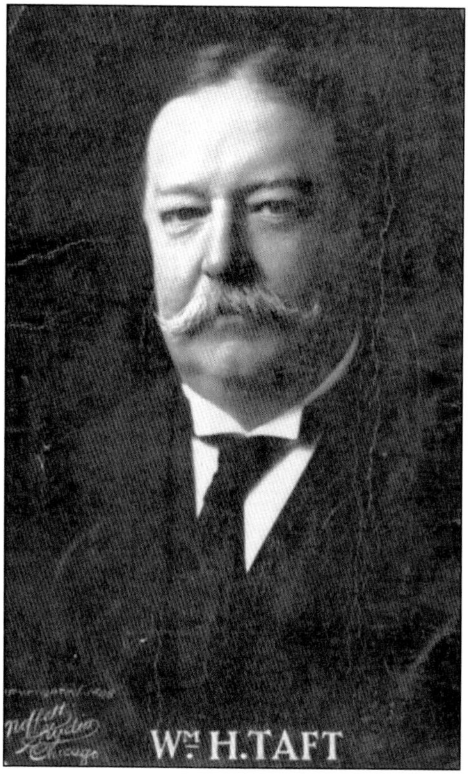

Pres. William H. Taft sent greetings to the veterans: "The men of the Confederate army fought for a principle which they believed to be right, and for which they were willing to sacrifice their lives, their homes—in fact all those things which men hold most dear. . . . The contending forces of half a century ago have given way to a united North and South, and to an enduring union. I congratulate the South and the wonderful progress it is now making."

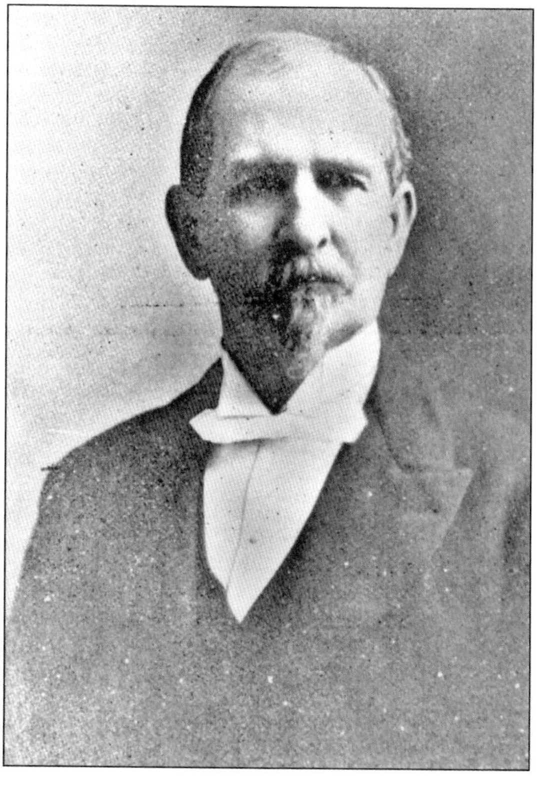

Daniel Webster Jones, Arkansas's last governor (1896–1900) to serve in the Civil War, spoke to an SCV gathering the day before the reunion opened. Jones had been shot in the chest at the battle of Corinth, Mississippi, in 1862; he was taken prisoner, later exchanged and made a colonel, and returned to the 20th Arkansas Infantry. "Never let it be said that your fathers fought for a cause they believed to be right: rather that they knew was right; nor never say that cause was lost. It was the Civil War that made possible the present Union; without the war the existing scheme of things could not have been. We fought for the constitution and now we have a Union which I am proud of, but which I was not proud of when the war broke." (Courtesy of Butler Center for Arkansas Studies.)

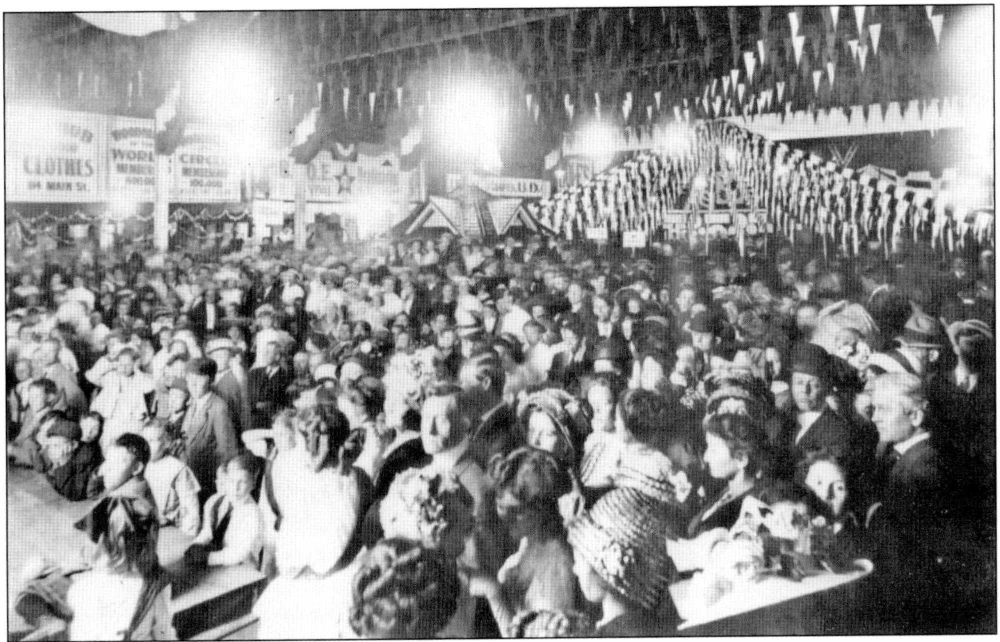

At the YMCA auditorium's event where former governor Jones spoke, the crowd seen here also heard the Sons of Confederate Veterans commander Henry Hartzog proclaim in his remarks: "Arkansas is a great state to live in and a great state to die in, because the state was so near heaven the transmission after death was less abrupt than in any other state in the union." (Courtesy of Arkansas History Commission.)

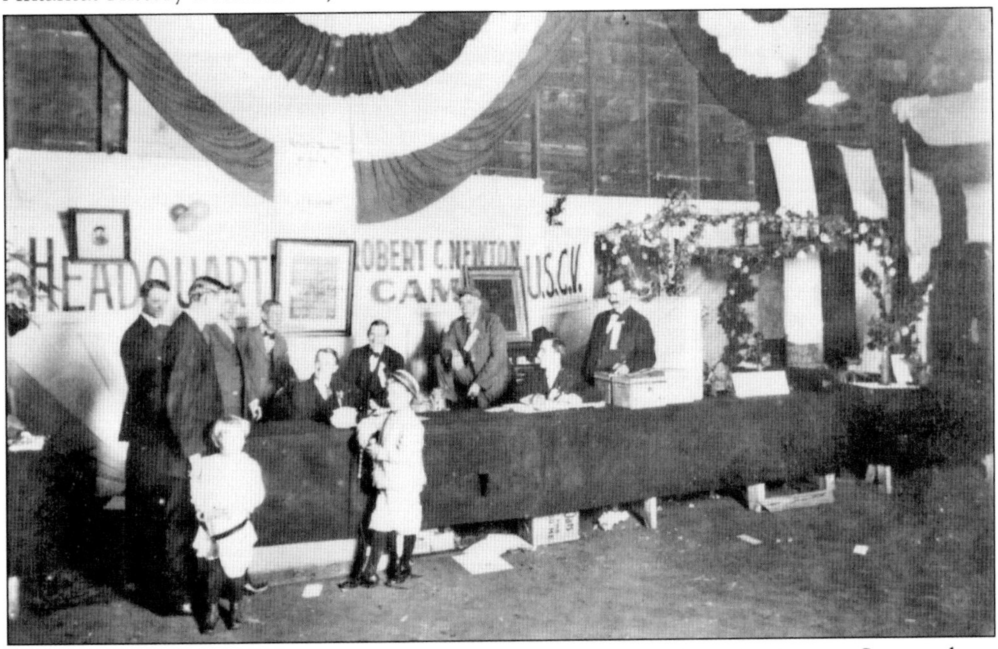

The host UCV camp for the 1911 reunion was Little Rock's Robert C. Newton Camp, whose temporary headquarters in the auditorium is seen here. The camp, named for Confederate cavalry commander Newton, has had its work carried on to the present day by the Robert C. Newton Chapter of the Sons of Confederate Veterans. (Courtesy of Arkansas History Commission.)

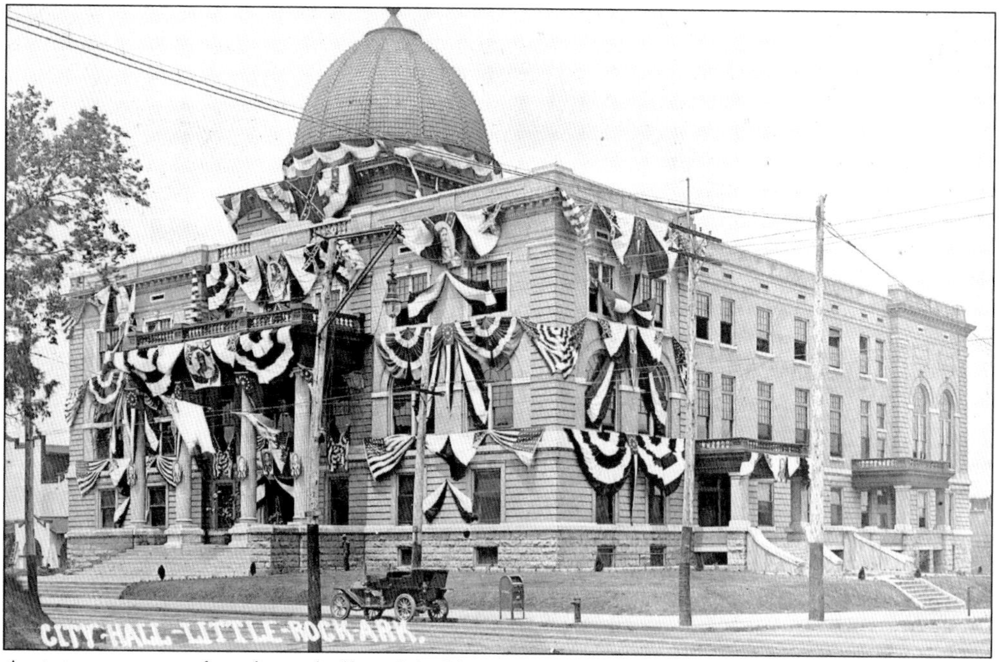

Arriving veterans found city hall, at Markham Street and Broadway, adorned with banners, Confederate flags, and portraits of Southern generals. Dashing young Confederate cavalry general J. E. B. Stuart's image hangs over the front entrance. To accommodate the overflow crowds, 130 cots were set up on the third floor of this building. A newspaper account reported that someone had walked away with two brass drinking cups, valued at $5 each, affixed to the building's drinking fountain.

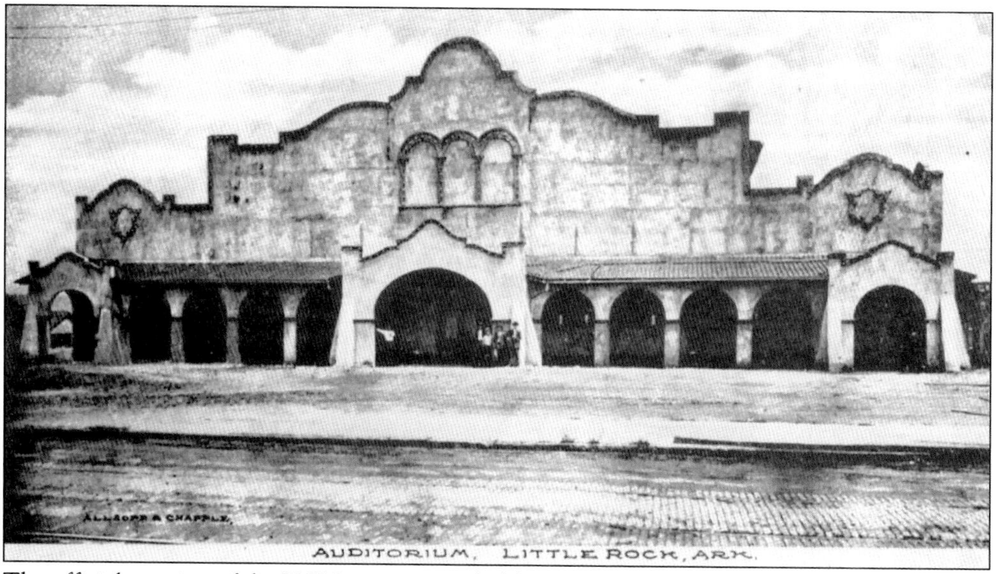

The official opening of the UCV reunion was held at 8:30 a.m. on May 16 in the city auditorium seen here, located adjacent to city hall. Speeches came from Arkansas governor George Donaghey and Little Rock mayor Charles Taylor. Attorney General Norwood, who had headed up reunion fund-raising, referred to the South as a "Land of martyrs and memories." The elaborately decorated hall had on the ceiling what was described as "the largest Confederate flag ever made."

Gen. J. F. Smith, in his position as the commander of the Arkansas Division of the UCV, helped open the reunion in the auditorium. Smith had entered the service of the Confederacy in Fayetteville in June 1861 and served throughout the war. He fought at Pea Ridge and later in Missouri and Mississippi. He was within the breastworks of Vicksburg for 48 days during U. S. Grant's siege of that city. (Courtesy of *Arkansas Democrat*.)

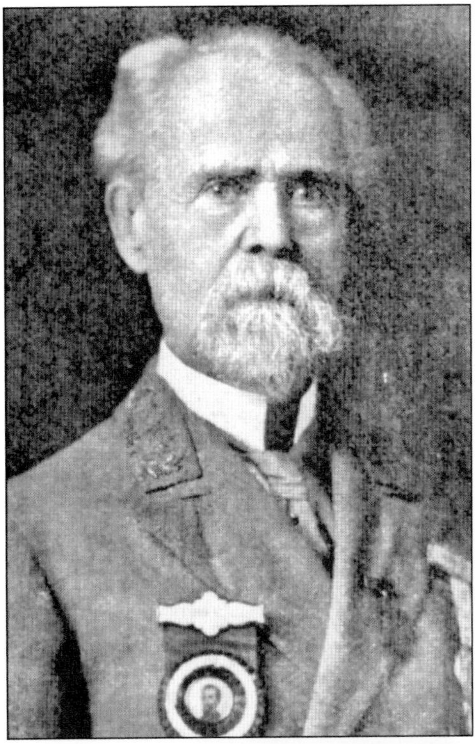

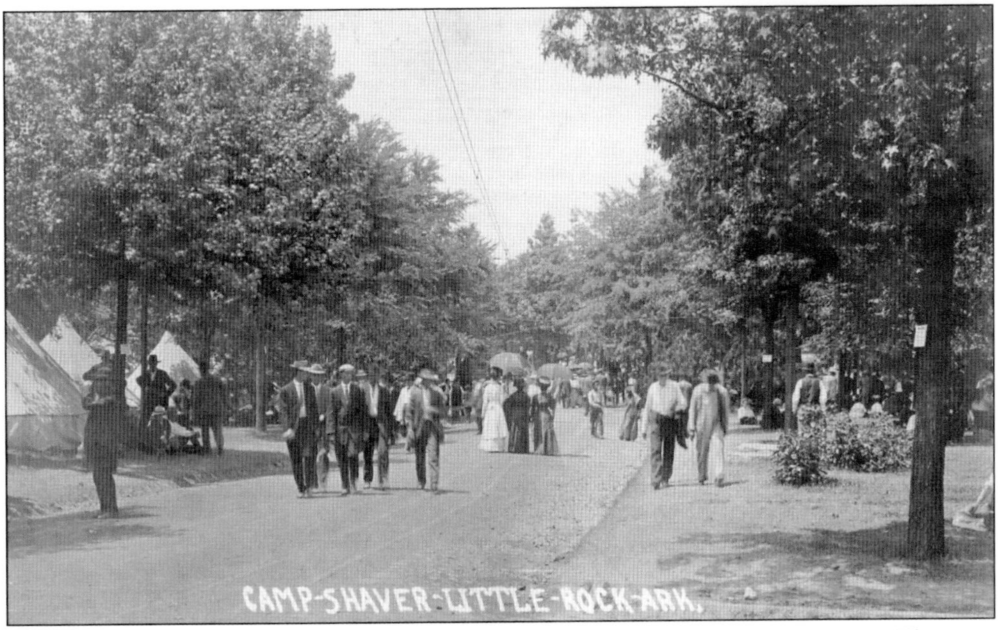

"Early Throngs Cause Surprise: Veterans Pour Into Camp Shaver," said one newspaper. The more than 1,300 U.S. Army tents were erected and filled to capacity in the City Park encampment called Camp Shaver. As veterans arrived by train, reunion committee representatives met them and arranged transportation to the park, where the tents were arranged by state groupings. At certain times of the day, the general public was allowed into the camp, as was the case here with the strolling women on the park roadway.

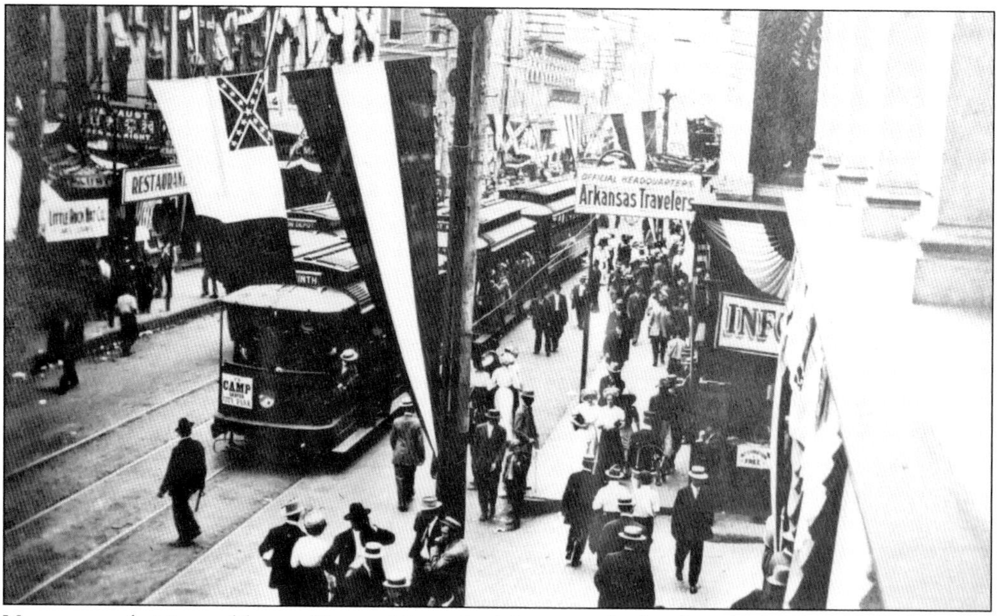

Veterans and visitors alike could travel from the Marion and other hotels to Camp Shaver aboard specially marked streetcars like this one. To handle the great passenger load, the city brought in some 40 experienced "car men" from other cities.

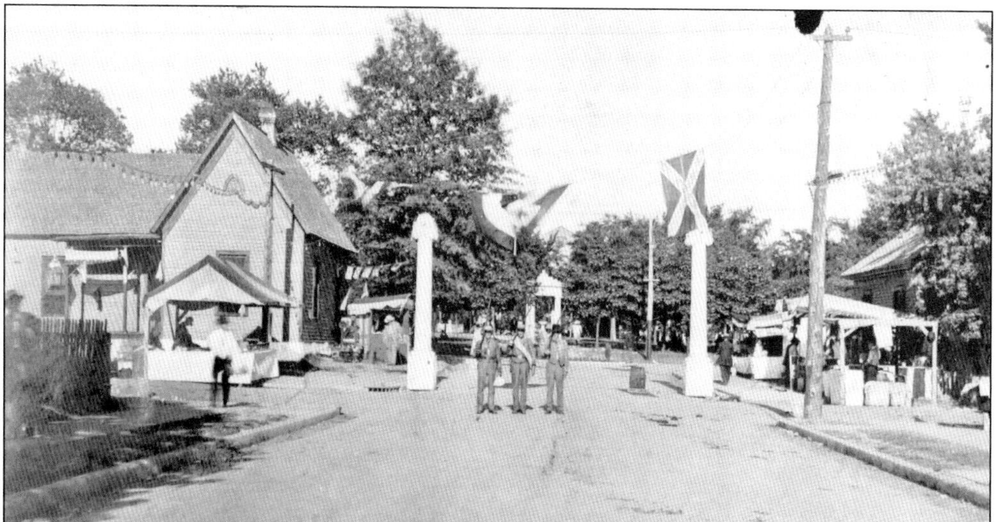

Entrance into Camp Shaver necessitated clearance at the gate, guarded here by Confederates, all with rifles on their shoulders for the photographer's benefit. The camp was opened for part of the day to allow visitors and local people into the camp to visit and walk through the park. It must have been a unique sight indeed to see the thousands of elderly soldiers encamped among the tree-shaded lanes of City Park.

Robert G. Shaver, commander of the reunion camp that bore his name, was a lawyer in the tiny Lawrence County town of Smithville when the Civil War started. He joined the Confederacy and organized a regiment of 1,200 men from North Arkansas. He fought at the Battle of Shiloh, in which he reportedly had four horses shot from beneath him. Though critically wounded, he survived to continue his service and earn the nickname "Fighting Bob." (Courtesy of Rhodes Collection.)

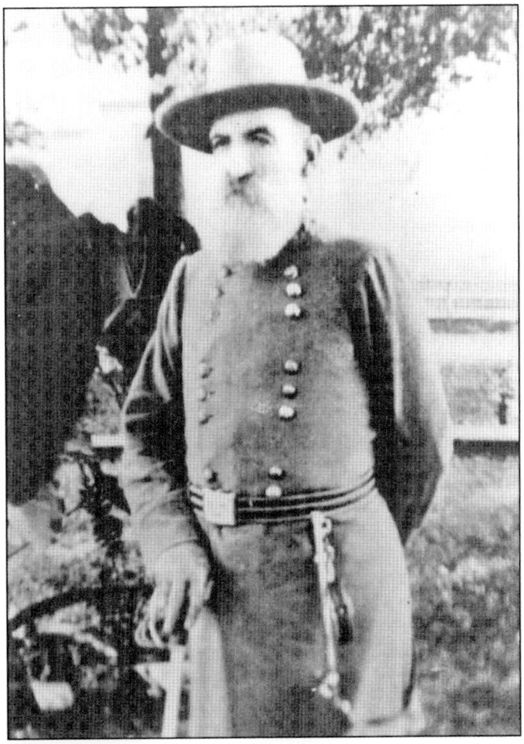

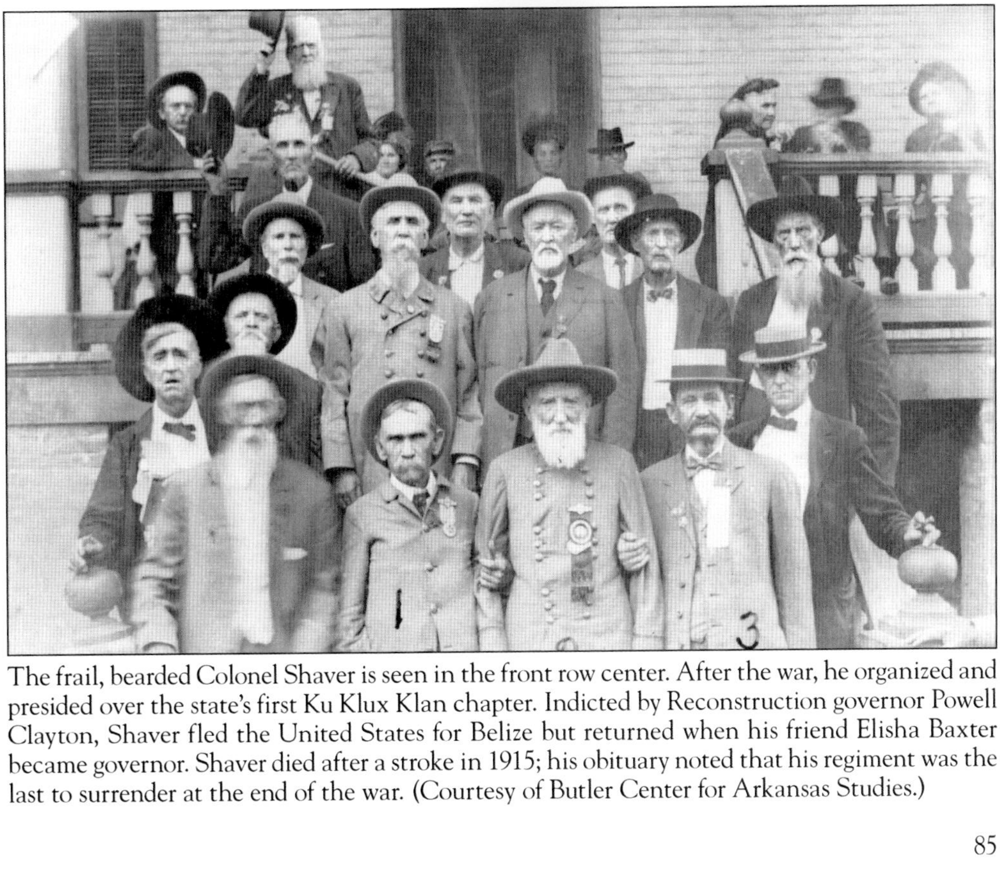

The frail, bearded Colonel Shaver is seen in the front row center. After the war, he organized and presided over the state's first Ku Klux Klan chapter. Indicted by Reconstruction governor Powell Clayton, Shaver fled the United States for Belize but returned when his friend Elisha Baxter became governor. Shaver died after a stroke in 1915; his obituary noted that his regiment was the last to surrender at the end of the war. (Courtesy of Butler Center for Arkansas Studies.)

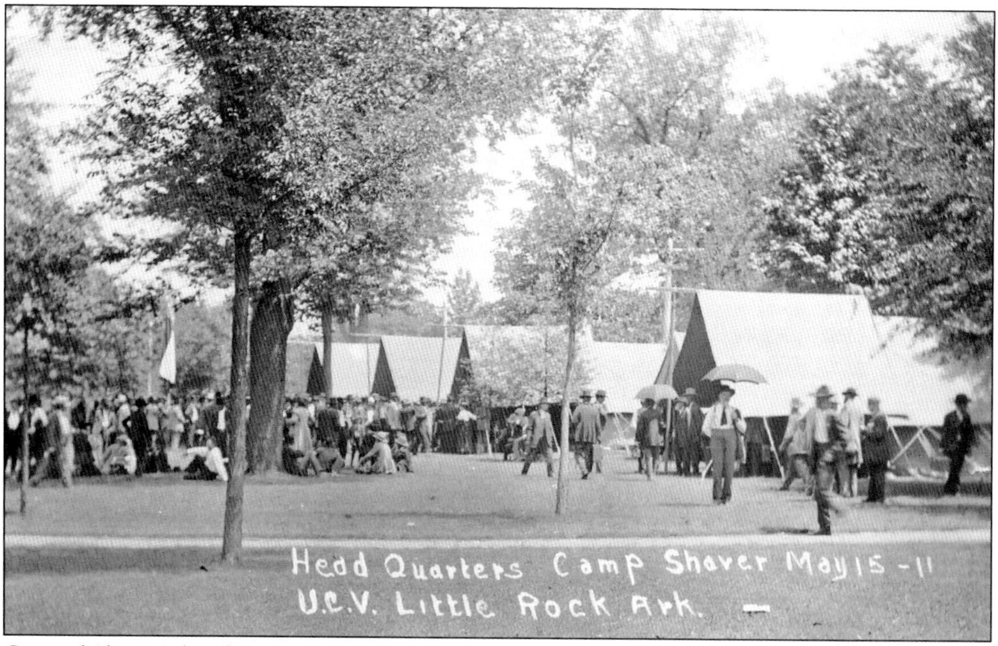

General Shaver's headquarters and the central mess tent were in this cluster. At the initial camp meal, Shaver became upset when the veterans made a mad rush to the meal tent when the bell rang: "This will not be done anymore because there is no necessity for it. We have made ample provisions for all veterans to be fed wholesome food. If there is any more of this rushing and shoving I will place the State Guards at the entrance to enforce order."

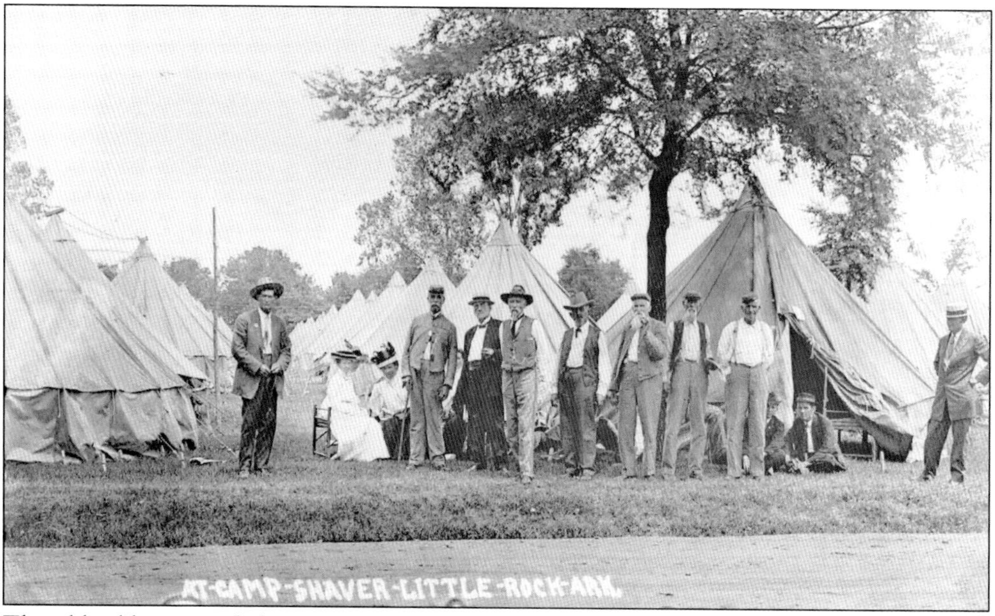

The old soldiers taxed the city's reunion committee pledge to feed them at no charge. The provisions consumed included 16,000 loaves of bread, 8,000 pounds of steak, 3,000 pounds of roast beef, 110 cases of eggs, and 1,700 pounds of coffee. The old soldiers also enjoyed 350 bushels of potatoes, 124 gallons of canned corn, and 600 pounds of navy beans. (Courtesy of Butler Center for Arkansas Studies, Paul Dolle Civil War Collection.)

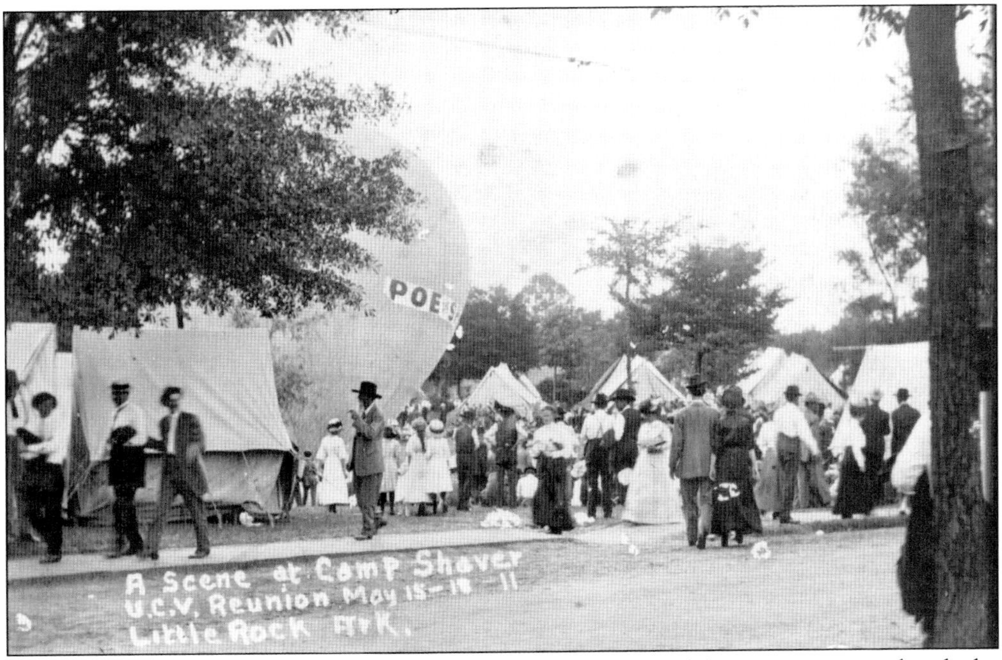

Reunion sponsors had promised to entertain the veterans. One of the activities, staged with the assistance of the Fraternal Order of Eagles, was to be free rides in the "world's largest" helium balloon. A defective supply of gas reportedly rendered the balloon unable to rise enough to lift the gondola from the ground, disappointing many old soldiers who told tales of seeing Union forces use such balloons for observation platforms during the war.

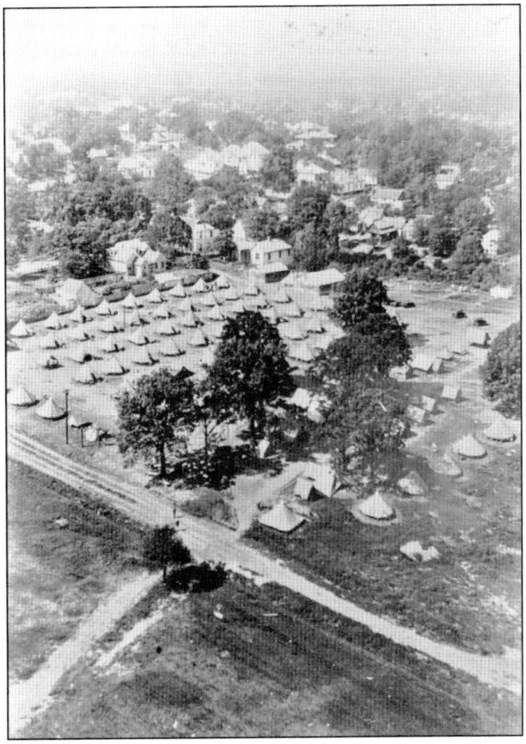

A smaller balloon apparently had been able to lift off in a practice tethered flight a few days before the veterans began to arrive for the reunion. The camp tents were already erected and standing empty on the grounds when a photographer looked down through his lens at the tents spread across a back section of City Park. (Courtesy of Butler Center for Arkansas Studies.)

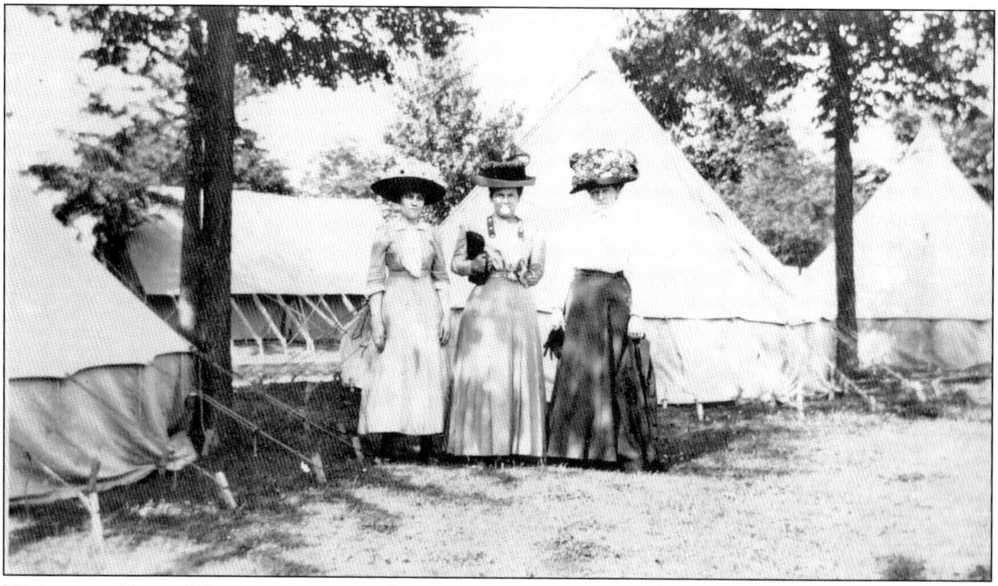

Visitors to Camp Shaver were treated to some entertainment by two North Carolina brothers who both wore artificial legs made of cork as a result of wounds received at Gettysburg. Each had lost his lower left leg, and their prosthetic limbs were interchangeable, so that they could make a show out of swapping legs. Young boys were amused, but reportedly some of the ladies, like those seen here, were less so.

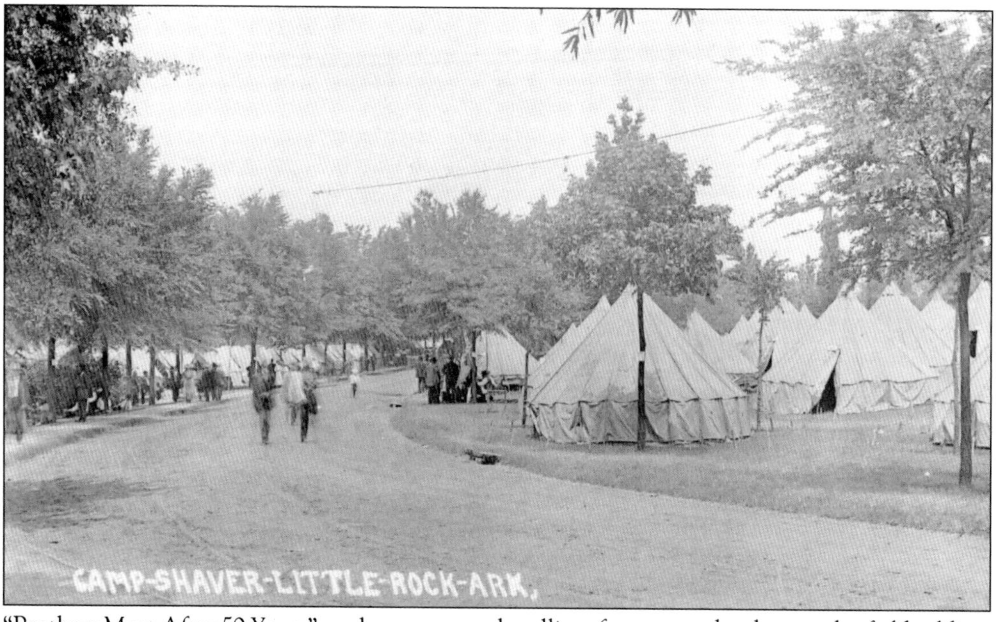

"Brothers Meet After 50 Years," read a newspaper headline, for among the thousands of old soldiers gathered at the camp, there was a reunion within the reunion. Gus and Willis Thompson were brothers who had been separated 50 years earlier, and neither had known that the other still lived. Willis was at war, and Gus, then only age eight, had left besieged Atlanta with Texas-bound emigrants. When Willis returned to the ruins of Atlanta after the war, he found his parents dead and no trace of Gus. Arriving at the camp, Gus decided on a whim to check the roster for Georgia veterans; he found his older brother's name among those registered.

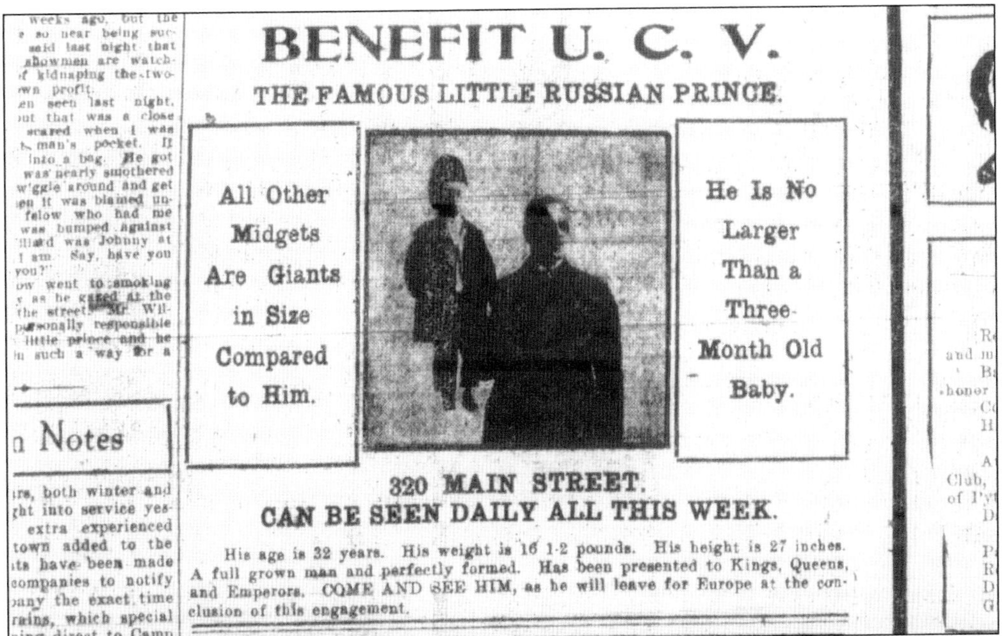

BENEFIT U. C. V.

THE FAMOUS LITTLE RUSSIAN PRINCE.

All Other Midgets Are Giants in Size Compared to Him.

He Is No Larger Than a Three-Month Old Baby.

320 MAIN STREET.

CAN BE SEEN DAILY ALL THIS WEEK.

His age is 32 years. His weight is 16 1-2 pounds. His height is 27 inches. A full grown man and perfectly formed. Has been presented to Kings, Queens, and Emperors. COME AND SEE HIM, as he will leave for Europe at the conclusion of this engagement.

The strangest of all entertainments, in a fund-raising benefit for the UCV, was the showing of Nicholai, "the famous little Russian Prince," 32 years old, weighing 16-and-a-half pounds, and standing 27 inches tall. "Come and see him before he leaves for Europe," the advertisements insisted. At an appearance on Main Street, a man grabbed Nicholai and stuffed him under a coat. After a chase, the prince's manager caught hold of the would-be kidnapper and freed the tiny man, while the kidnapper fled.

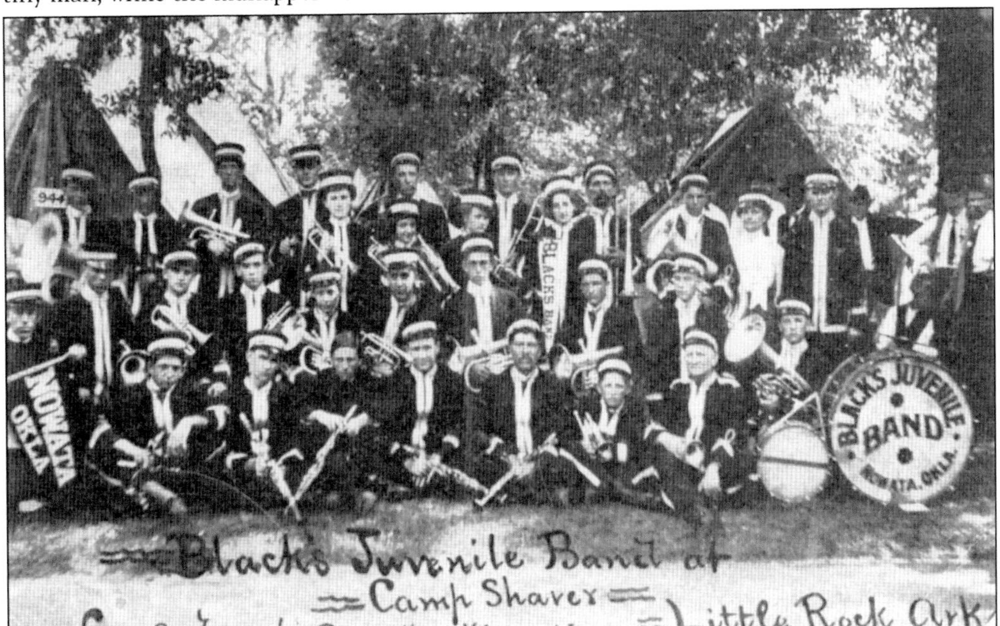

The veterans in Camp Shaver were entertained by Black's Juvenile Band of Nowata, Oklahoma. The young men's drums, horns, and flutes sent the tune "Dixie" reverberating throughout the camp and generated vigorous singing by thousands of old men.

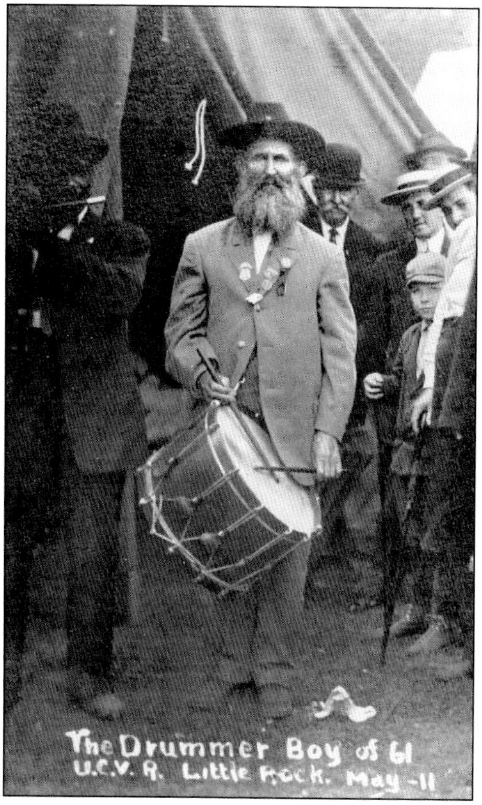

A popular postcard subject of the reunion was "The Drummer Boy of '61," posed before his tent in Camp Shaver. The drummer marched in the closing parade but could not finish the 22 long blocks of the parade route in the May heat. As he fell into the arms of a policeman, he reportedly cried out, "Just fan me a little and help me along, and I will finish this march or die in the attempt." (Courtesy of Tom Mertens.)

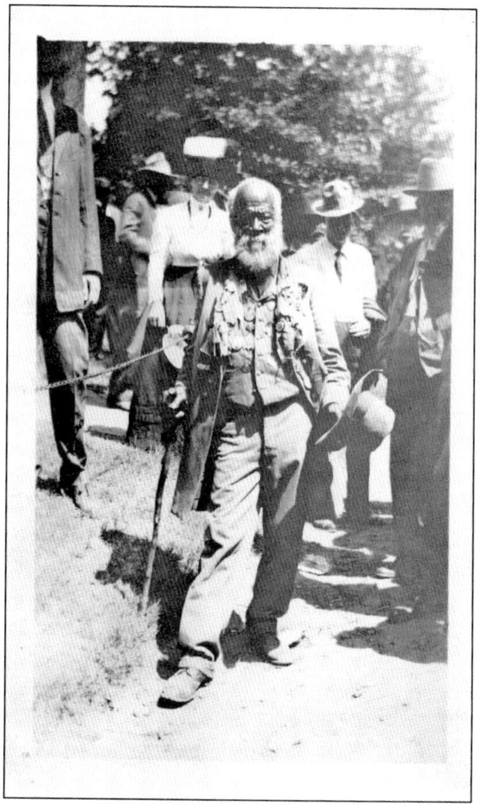

The "Negro Body Servants" who once cared for Confederate officers were also meeting in Little Rock. The group's leader stated, "We give thanks to the good people of the City for their kind treatment of the Negro veterans. . . . We have met with many reunions but we would like to say the Lord lives in Little Rock. If I were permitted to do so I would change the name of Little Rock to 'Little Rock Paradise' or I would call it the 'Paradisiacal City.' "

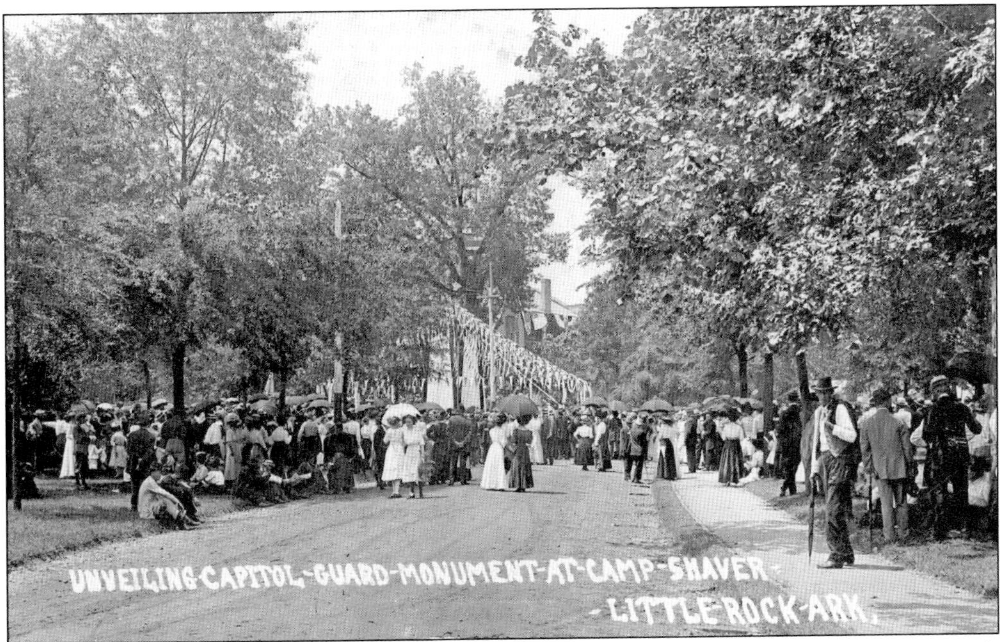

A highlight of the reunion was a dedication to the memory of the Capital Guards, Company A of the 6th Arkansas Regiment. The crowds are shown gathering for the unveiling of the statue honoring the "Flower of Little Rock," the 67 young men who helped capture the arsenal in 1861 and then marched off to war east of the Mississippi River. Only a handful survived the conflict to return home, and only three survivors of the regiment were present in 1911 for the monument's dedication. One of these, Judge W. C. Ratcliffe, a first lieutenant in the guard, spoke: "We were gay then—all gay, we did not appreciate what was before us when we marched off to war." Dr. Charles Hyde offered a prayer for the unveiling: "We are proud of the legacy of the heroic deeds of those who died for us, and with loving hearts dedicate this monument today."

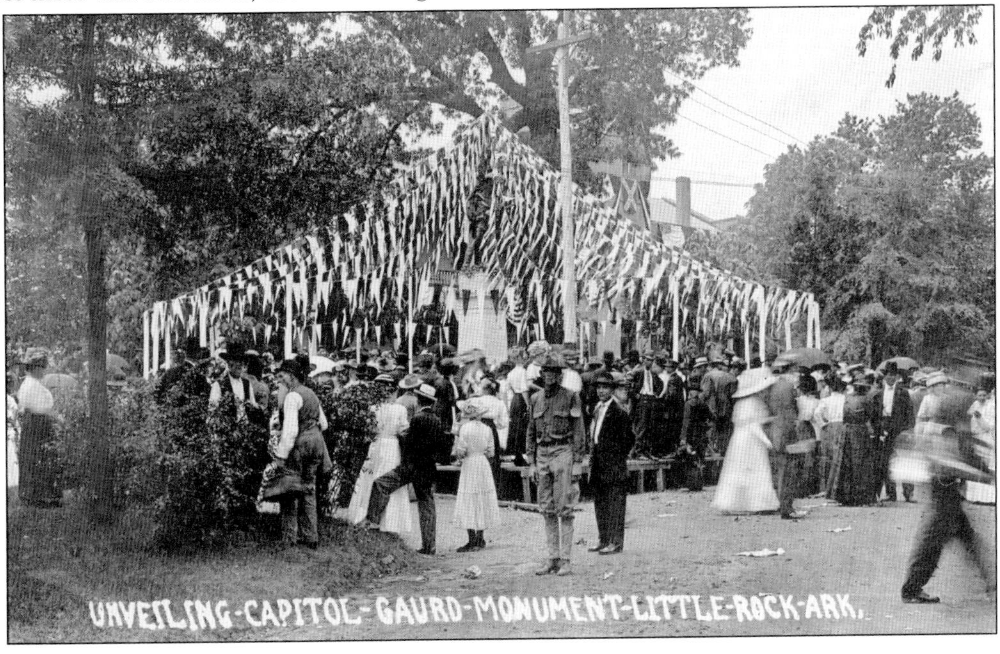

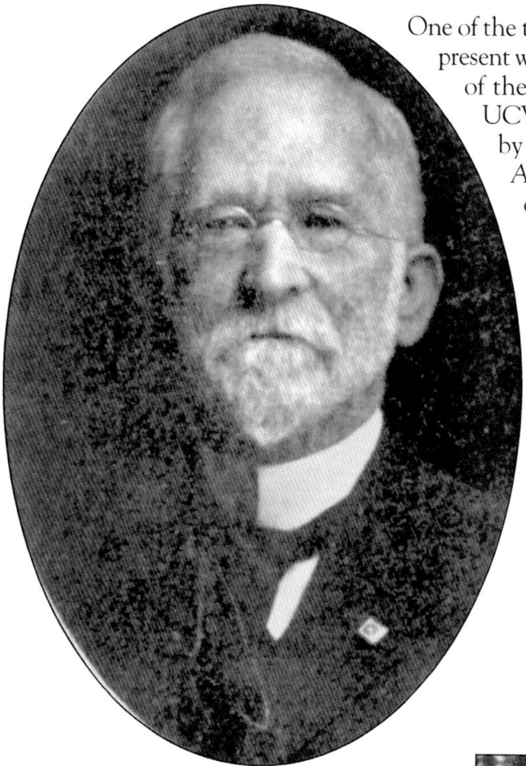

One of the three surviving members of the Capital Guards present was Brig. Gen. Jonathan Kellogg, the commander of the 1st Brigade of the Arkansas Division of the UCV. After the war, Kellogg wrote a book, assisted by the UDC, entitled *Confederate Women of Arkansas*, telling of the sufferings and sacrifices of the heroic women of the state while their husbands and sons were "in the ranks."

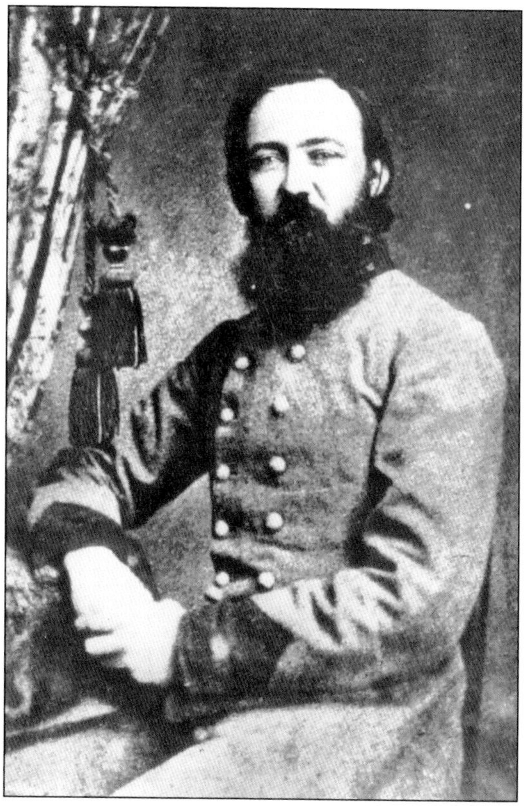

John Gould Fletcher was a captain with the Capital Guards who assumed command of the regiment at the 1862 Battle of Shiloh. Severely wounded and left on the battlefield, Fletcher was a Union prisoner for almost a year. After the war, he served as Little Rock's mayor. He died in 1907. His daughter was present for the 1911 dedication; she pulled the ribbon that unveiled the monument and simultaneously showered the crowd with 20,000 rose petals. (Courtesy of MacArthur Museum of Arkansas Military History.)

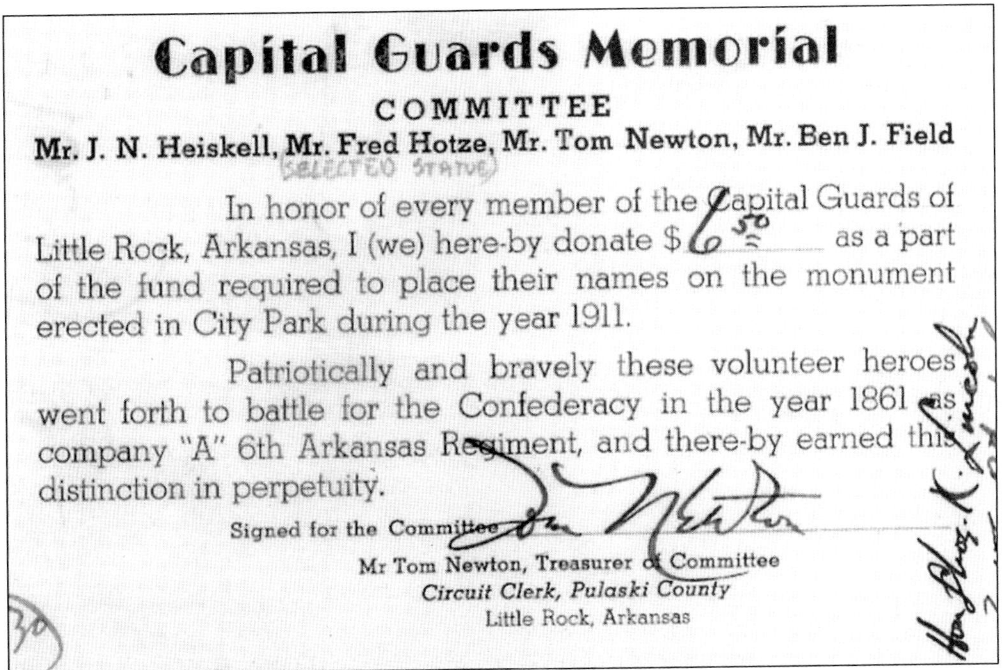

Capital Guards Memorial

COMMITTEE

Mr. J. N. Heiskell, Mr. Fred Hotze, Mr. Tom Newton, Mr. Ben J. Field

(SELECTED STATUE)

In honor of every member of the Capital Guards of Little Rock, Arkansas, I (we) here-by donate $6 50 as a part of the fund required to place their names on the monument erected in City Park during the year 1911.

Patriotically and bravely these volunteer heroes went forth to battle for the Confederacy in the year 1861 as company "A" 6th Arkansas Regiment, and there-by earned this distinction in perpetuity.

Signed for the Committee Tom Newton

Mr Tom Newton, Treasurer of Committee
Circuit Clerk, Pulaski County
Little Rock, Arkansas

The Robert C. Newton Camp of the SCV had led the effort to erect the memorial statue, in part through fund-raising cards like this, by which one donor gave $6.50 to the cause. The prominent committeemen listed include J. N. Heiskell, editor of the *Arkansas Gazette*. The penciled note under the name of businessman Fred Hotze suggests that he selected the design of the statue.

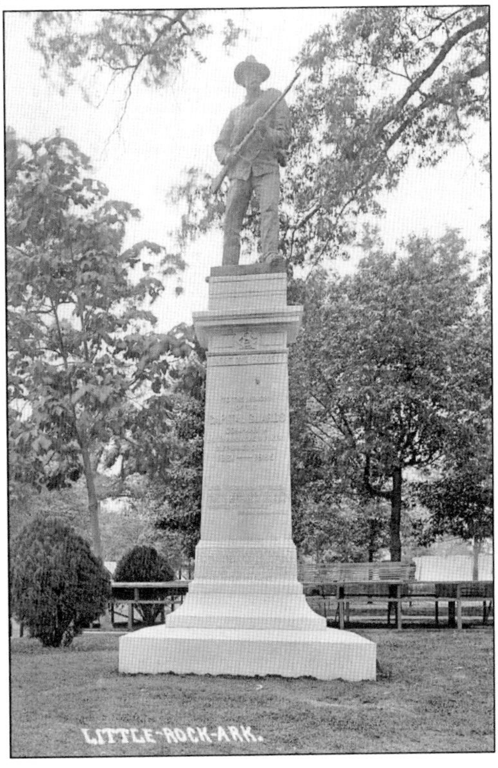

The monument, created by German sculptor Rudolph Schwarz, was topped by a bronze figure of a Confederate solider holding his rifle at the ready. The Capital Guard was attached to the command of Gen. Patrick Cleburne, and the memorial's base bore the slogan of his command: "When his division defended, no odds could break its lines; when it attacked no numbers resisted its onslaught."

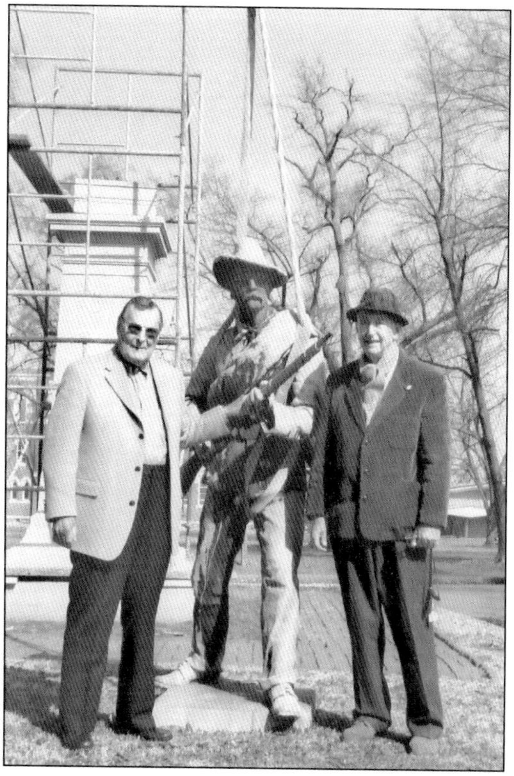

By 2004, the Capital Guards monument was showing the effects of the elements. The MacArthur Museum of Arkansas Military History raised money for restoration. On the day the statue was taken down for shipment to the restoration studio, the last surviving grandsons of the original members of the guards posed. Bill Terry, right, is the grandson of guards captain John Gould Fletcher; Charles Lincoln, left, is the grandson and namesake of regiment member Charles Lincoln. (Courtesy of MacArthur Museum of Arkansas Military History.)

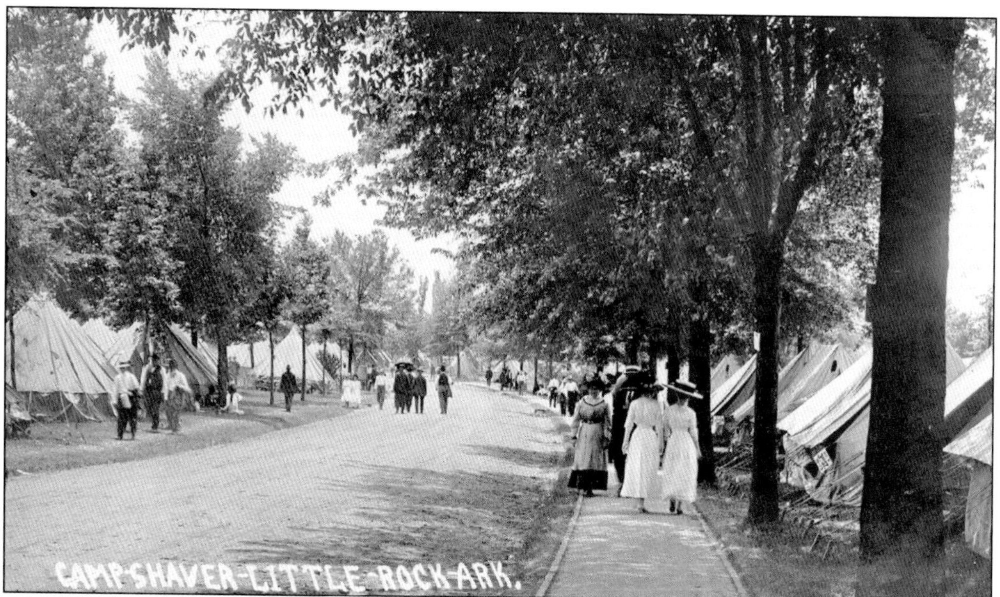

One Texas veteran hoped to find someone to claim a relic he had picked up off the battlefield in Peach Tree Creek, Georgia, in 1864. The Bible was inscribed: "The gift of a sister to her brother going to war. Read a portion of this holy book everyday. Don't forget the prayer our mother taught us. Fear and trust in God, obey your officers, be true to your country." Written by the soldier was, "If I ever fall on the battlefield among the glorious dead I want my Bible to accompany me to my grave."

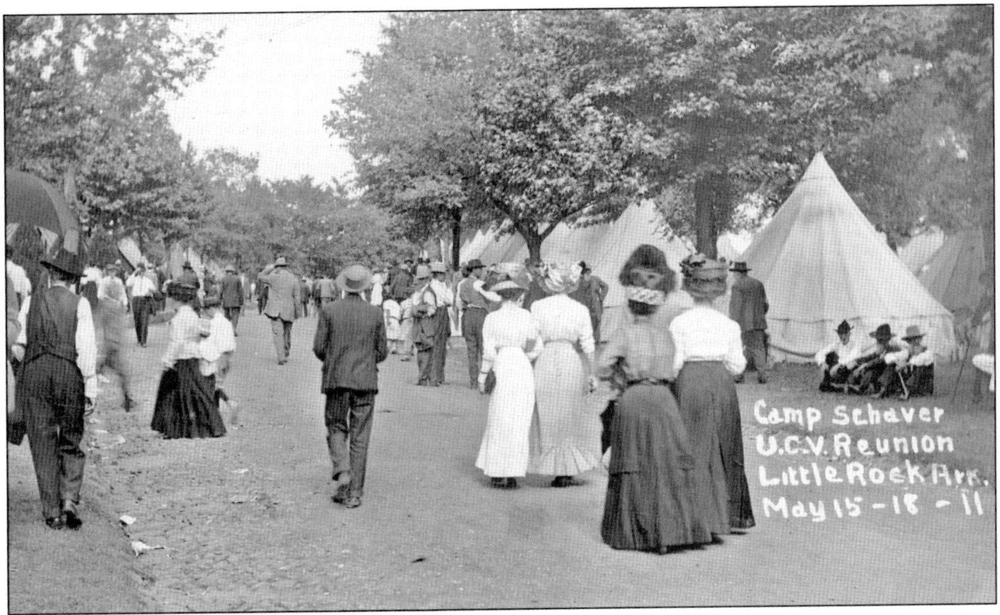

C. B. Graham, a 75-year-old South Carolina veteran, tried to impress a group of women visiting Camp Shaver, proclaiming, "I own a large plantation, have money in the bank, and am looking for a wife." He supposedly promised would-be brides that "anything you want is yours." An observer reported that an older widow expressed interest, but upon looking her over, the old man apparently declined in favor of taking several young ladies to lunch in a café outside the park.

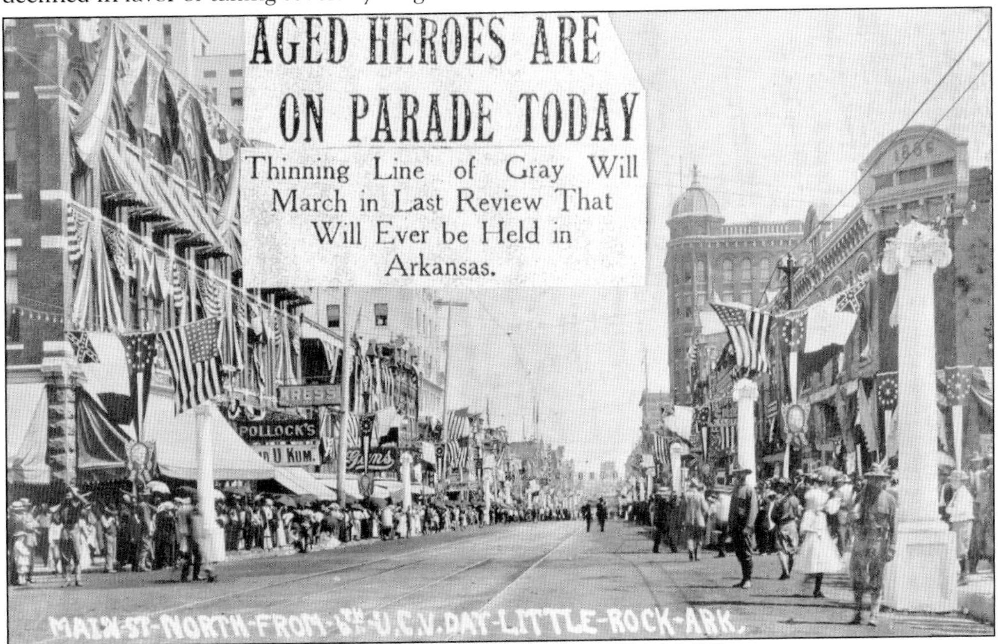
AGED HEROES ARE ON PARADE TODAY

Thinning Line of Gray Will March in Last Review That Will Ever be Held in Arkansas.

May 18, 1911, was the third and final day of the UCV reunion. It was highlighted by a parade of the old soldiers that started at State and Markham Streets, went up Main Street to Tenth Street, then to Camp Shaver, and came back again by the same route, some 22 blocks in all. The photograph above was taken hours before the parade's start, but already people were staking out choice viewing positions.

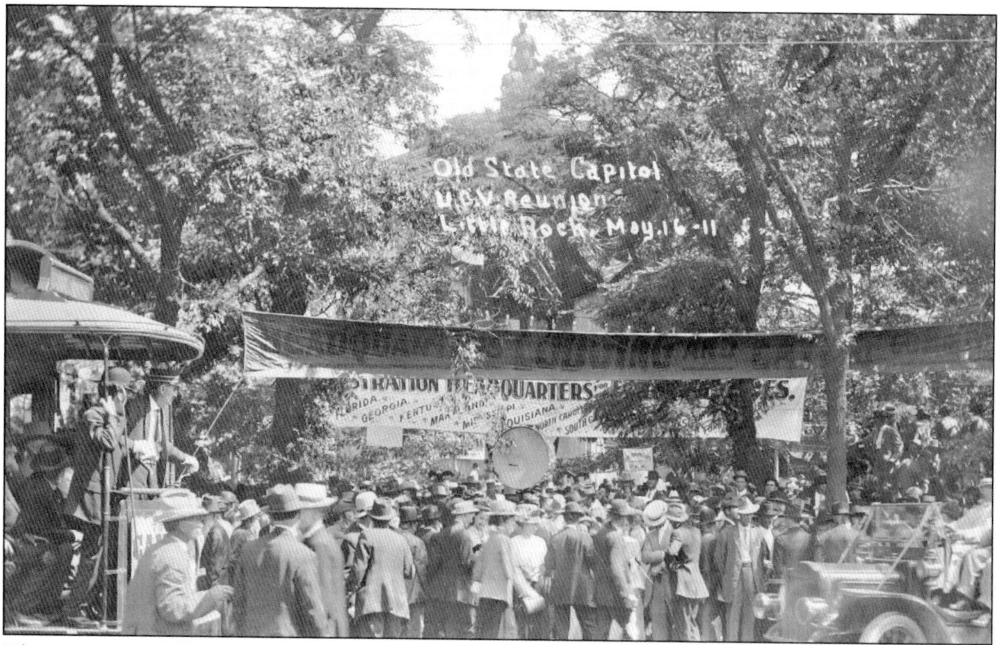

The staging area for the parade was the lawn of the Old State House, next to reunion headquarters in the Marion Hotel. In honor of the UCV, the Confederate flag flew over what had been the Arkansas State Capitol at the time of the Civil War for the first time in some 50 years. The 1861 vote to secede from the Union had been taken in this same building.

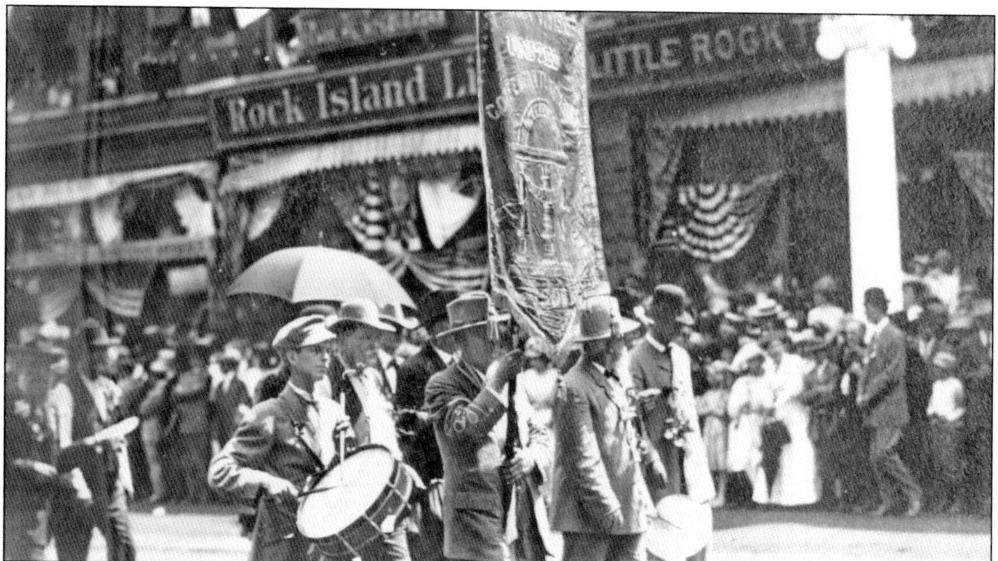

The *Arkansas Gazette* described the scene: "It was noticed that a score of aged men in the line were barely able to hobble along with the quick moving parade. But they would not be denied. As the inspiring strains of 'Dixie' would roll forth from the bands, the gray haired defenders of the South would gather themselves together and make another spurt. It was a sublime spectacle and called forth cheers and tears from onlookers."

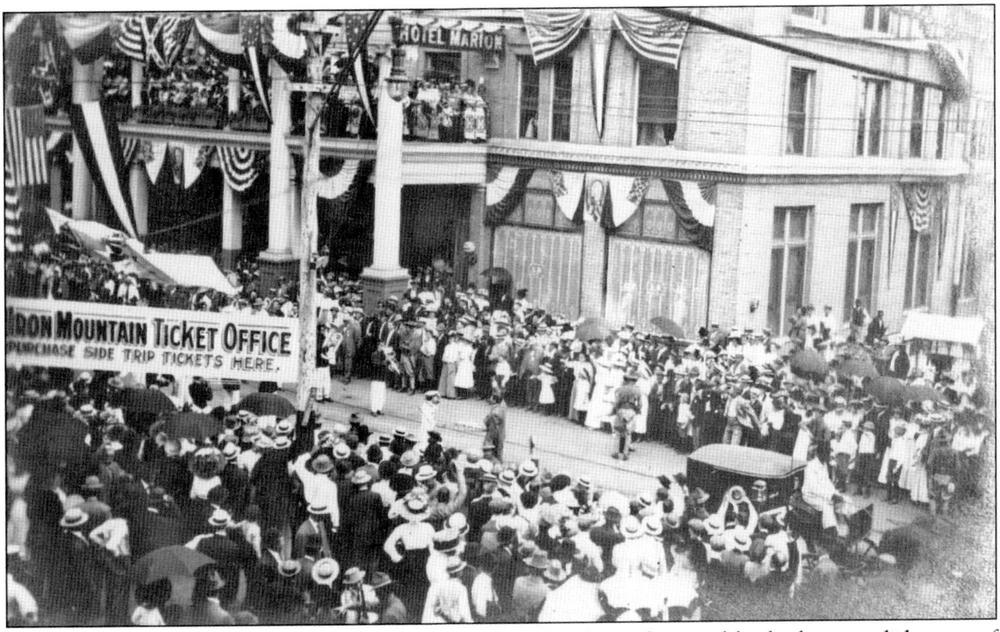

"From any vantage point, the spectator could see nothing for ten blocks but a solid mass of humanity. Men, women and children were packed on the pavements, in the windows, in the doorways, on the ledges and copings of the business buildings and even on the roofs," reported the *Arkansas Gazette* the day after the parade. The crowd here is watching a band passing the Marion Hotel. (Courtesy of *Arkansas Democrat*.)

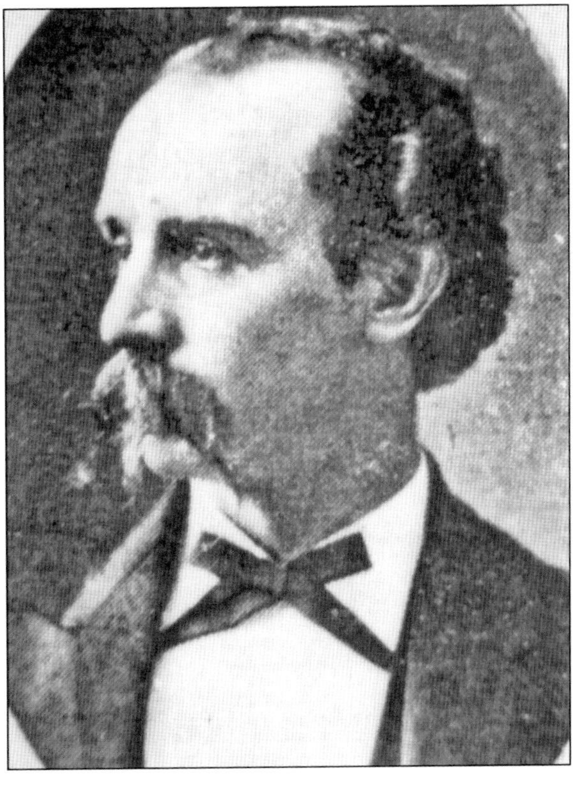

As the veterans passed the Marion Hotel headquarters, they turned and saluted to honor UCV commander in chief Gen. George Washington Gordon, who was ill and confined to the hotel, unable to march. Gordon had fought at Stone's River, Chickamauga, Kennesaw Mountain, Atlanta, and finally Franklin, Tennessee, where he was wounded, captured, and shipped to a Boston prison for the balance of the war. He died in August 1911, two months after the Little Rock reunion.

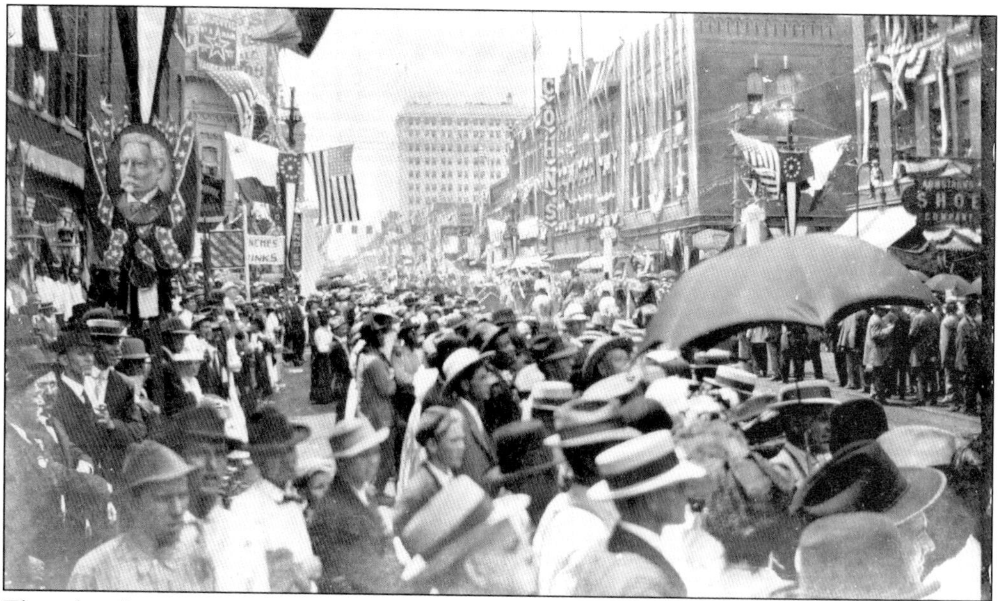

The sidewalks were jammed at the corner of Main and Markham Streets as the parade turned to head up Main Street. According to the *Arkansas Gazette*, "For five or six feet from the edge of the pavement on each side of the street was crowded to the walls of the buildings. Those in the rear utilized boxes and chairs to stand on and thus elevate themselves above the heads of the crowd in front."

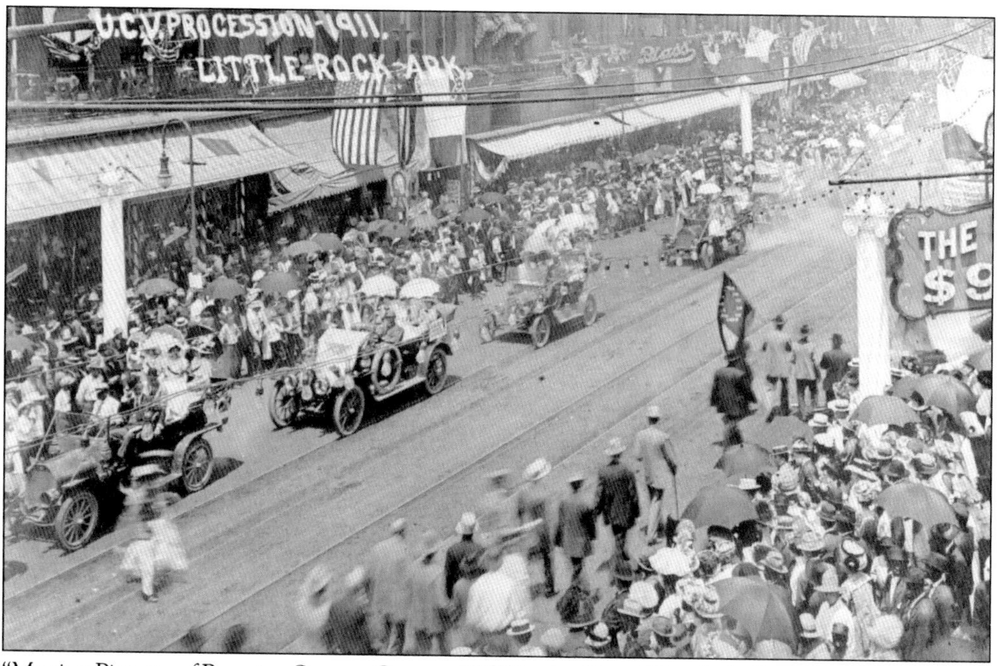

"Moving Pictures of Reunion Scenes: Camera Will Depict Grand Parade." This newspaper headline story reported a contract between the reunion committee and the Industrial Moving Picture Company of Chicago. It was thought for decades that the fragile film had failed to survive, but apparently a portion of it remains today in a private Civil War museum in Pennsylvania. Efforts are underway to obtain a copy for the MacArthur Museum of Arkansas Military History.

The *Arkansas Gazette* reported, "Roofs were favorite places for observing the parade. In many cases awnings and small booths had been constructed on the roofs to protect the spectators assembled from the burning heat of the sun. The more adventuresome climbed telegraph poles and occupied dangerous positions on window ledges, risking falls that would have meant death." To the right can be seen a young man in a straw hat on a risky perch.

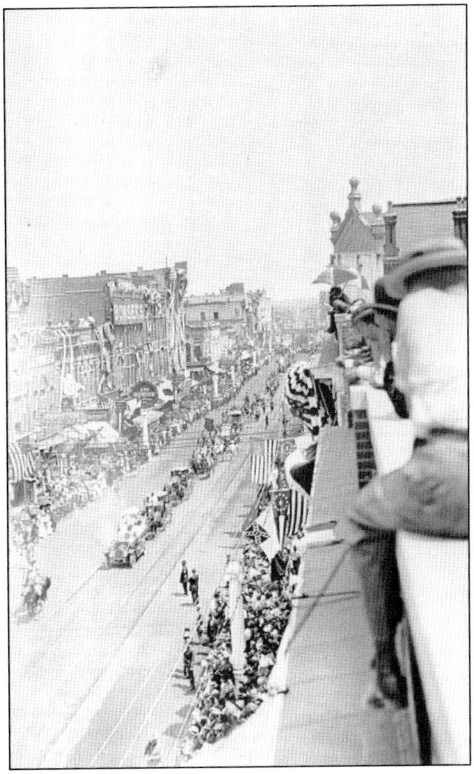

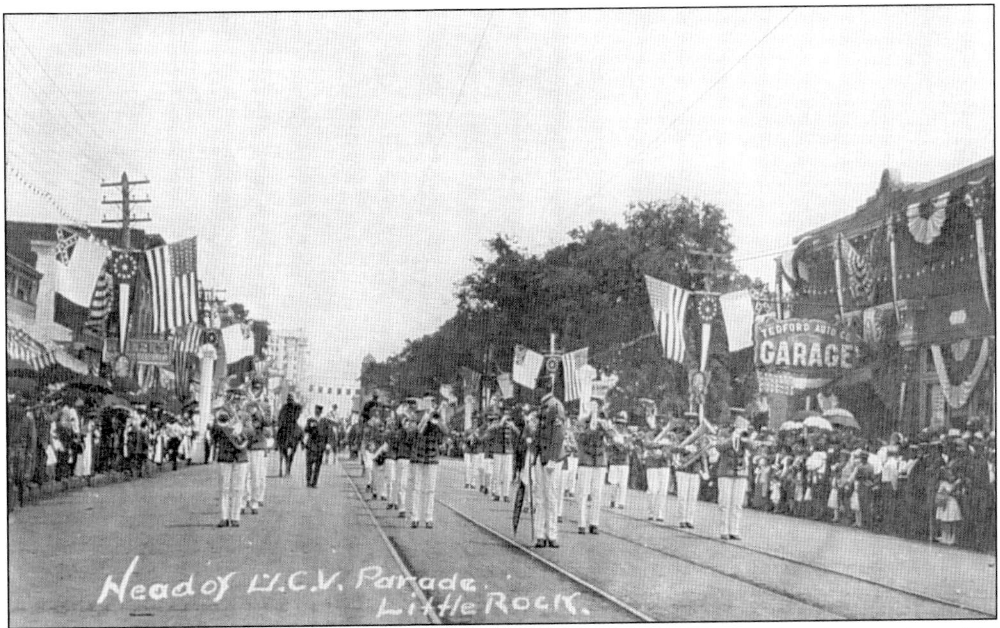

One headline read, "Veterans File through City to War Music." Fourteen bands participated in the parade of 15,000 people, by far the largest in the history of Little Rock. Reportedly all 14 bands were playing different songs but ended each number with stirring renditions of "Dixie." The crowd to the right watched from in front of the well-decorated Tedford's Auto Garage on South Main Street.

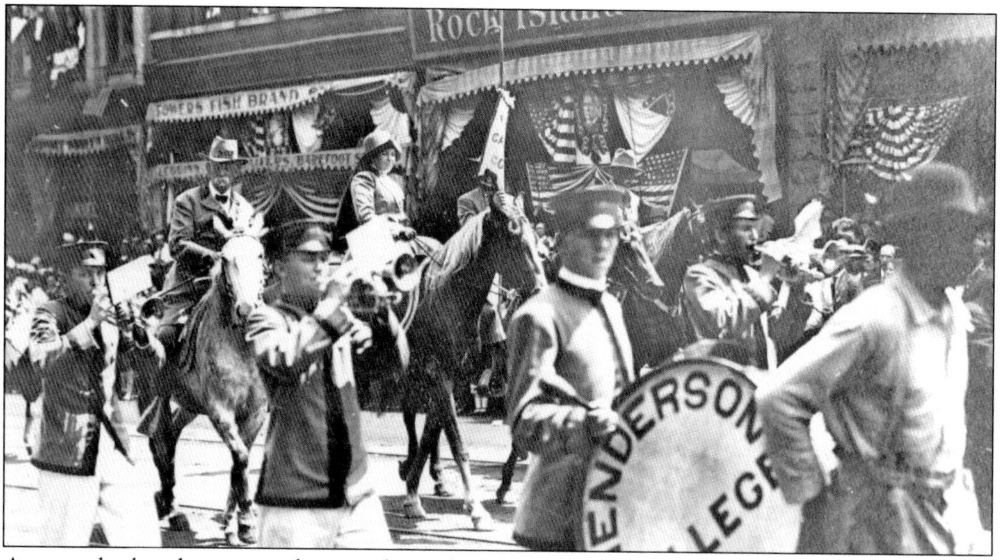

Among the bands serving the grand parade, which reportedly took almost two hours to pass any given point, was this band from Henderson College of Arkadelphia, Arkansas. The bugle players in the center had to step smartly lest they be trod upon by the mounted veterans and young ladies behind them.

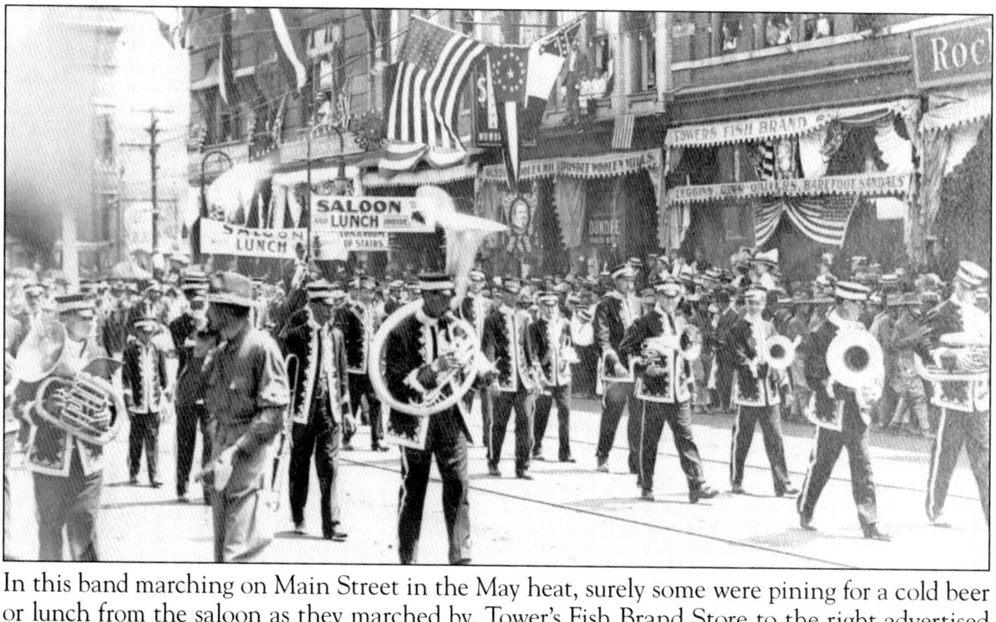

In this band marching on Main Street in the May heat, surely some were pining for a cold beer or lunch from the saloon as they marched by. Tower's Fish Brand Store to the right advertised "Leggings, Overgaiters and Barefoot Sandals." Every window over the street seems to have been filled with onlookers.

Confederate cavalry general Nathan Bedford Forrest had been the most feared foe of the Union forces during the war, striking where least expected despite having no formal education or military training. Forrest's extraordinary capability as a battle tactician won him quick promotions, as well as foiling many unsuccessful Union attempts to capture or kill him. His philosophy of warfare was, "War means fightin' and fightin' means killin'." Forrest died in 1877.

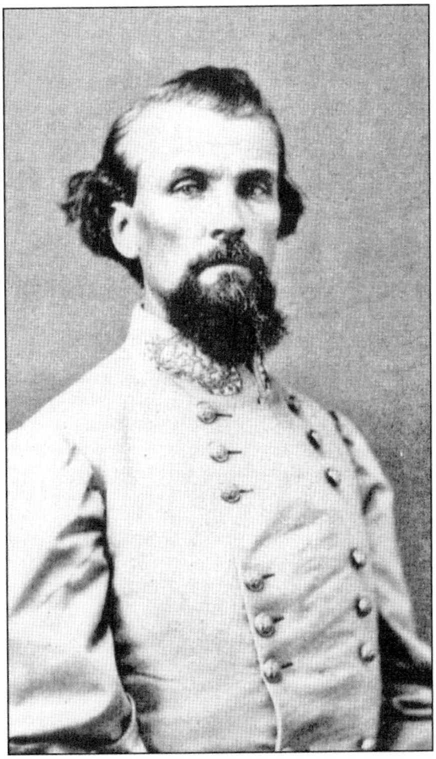

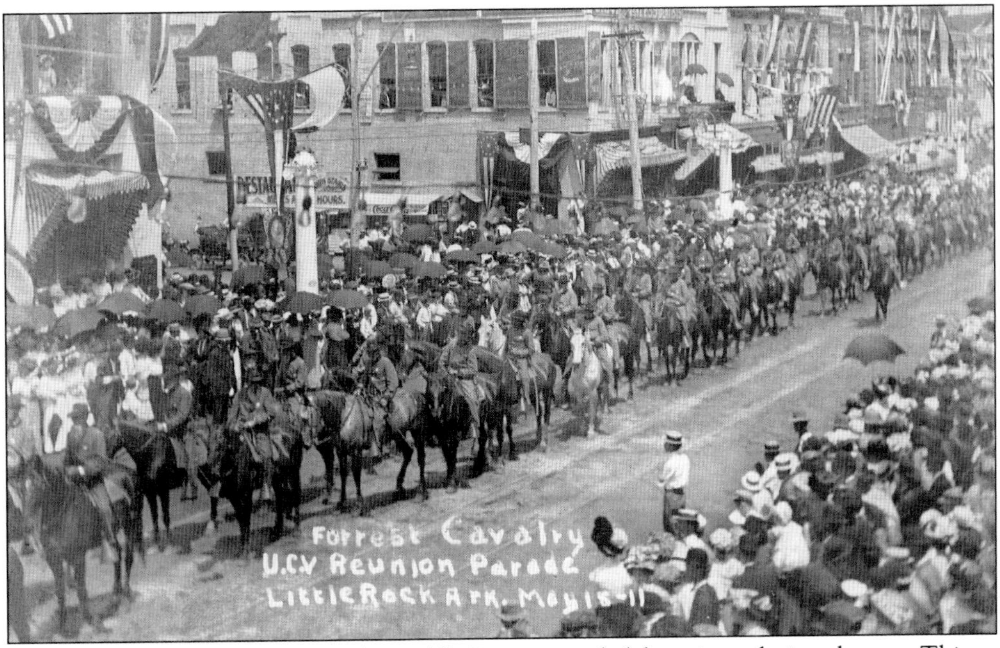

General Forrest, the "Wizard in the Saddle," was wounded four times during the war. Thirty-four years later, 200 of his mounted troops survived to ride together in the Little Rock parade, seen here passing the intersection of Main Street and Capitol Avenue. Their general's name was adopted by Forrest City, Arkansas, seat of St. Francis County, in recognition of the railroad in which Forrest had invested before the war.

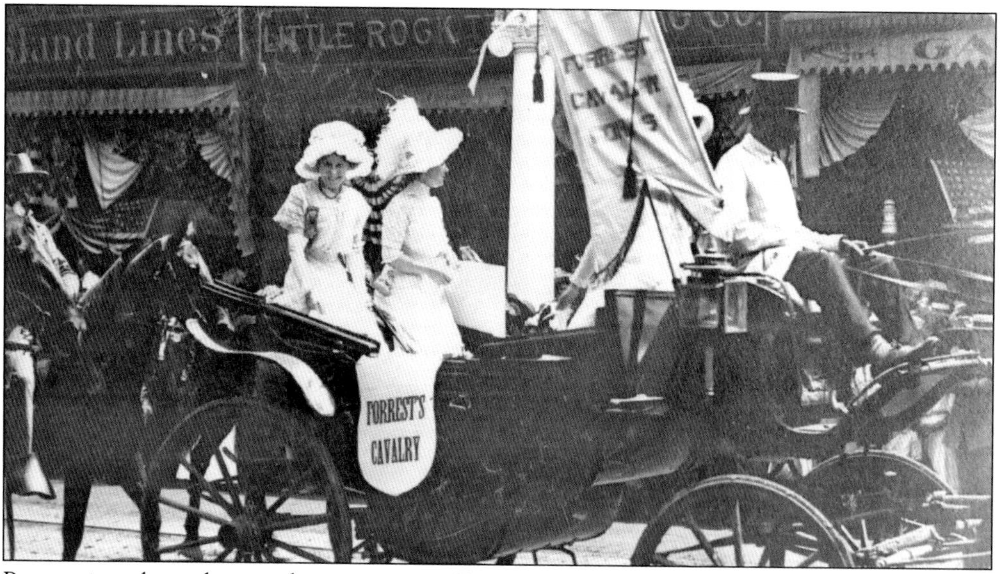

Progressing along the parade route among Forrest's mounted cavalry veterans were the unit's designated maidens, who rode in an elegant coach driven by a black man wearing a white coat and top hat.

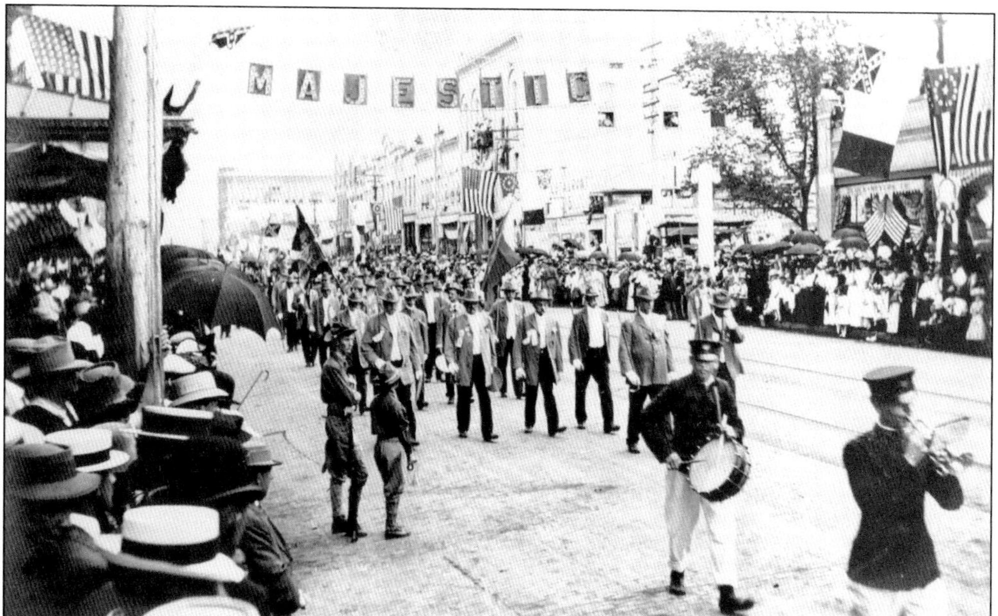

The band leading a group of veterans here is passing beneath a banner for the Majestic Theater. Standing just to the left on the edge of the street are two uniformed Boy Scouts, whose troop had been called into service to guide the elderly soldiers around town during the three-day reunion.

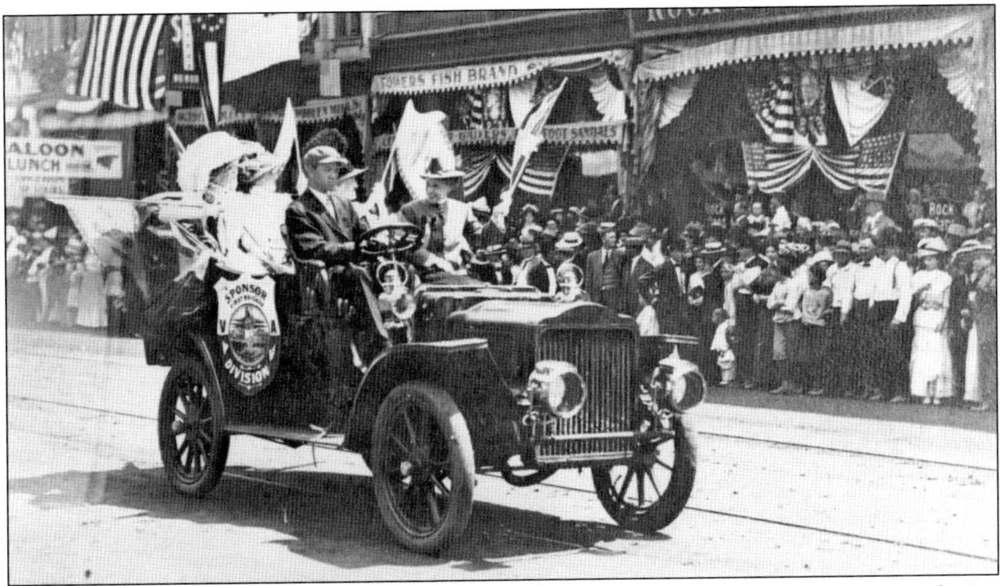

Mary Hall from Georgia, seated to the right of the driver, was a nurse and part-time scout during the war who was said to "have closed the glazing eyes of many a dying soldier" in Confederate field hospitals. "An unreconstructed rebel," she wore a belt with 11 gold buttons for the 11 Confederate states. At war's end, she had refused to take the oath of allegiance to the United States, perhaps because one of her brothers had died fighting the Union.

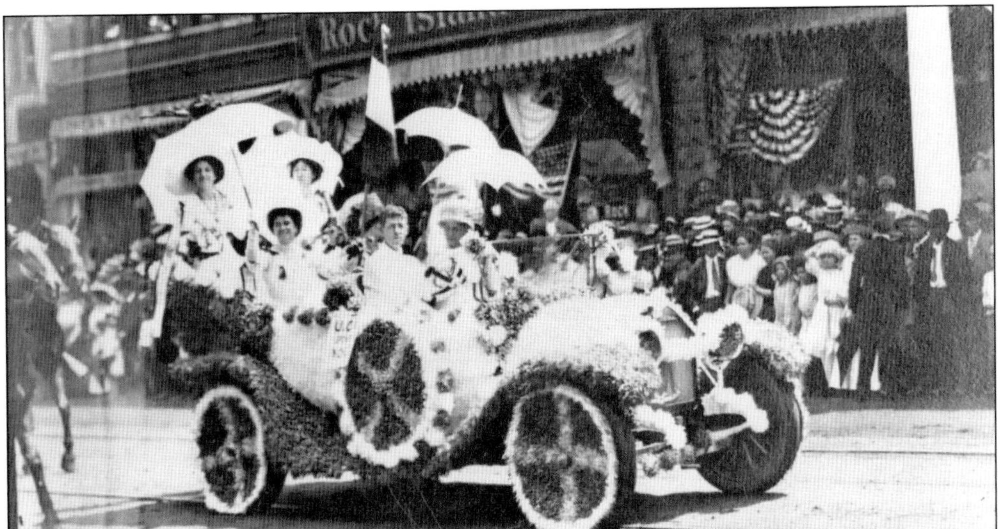

Among the 15,000 people in the parade was this group of smiling ladies in an automobile covered with flowers passing the Rock Island Rail Road offices on Main Street. The decorated vehicle contained Mrs. J. Griffith Edwards, organizer of the United Confederate Choirs of America.

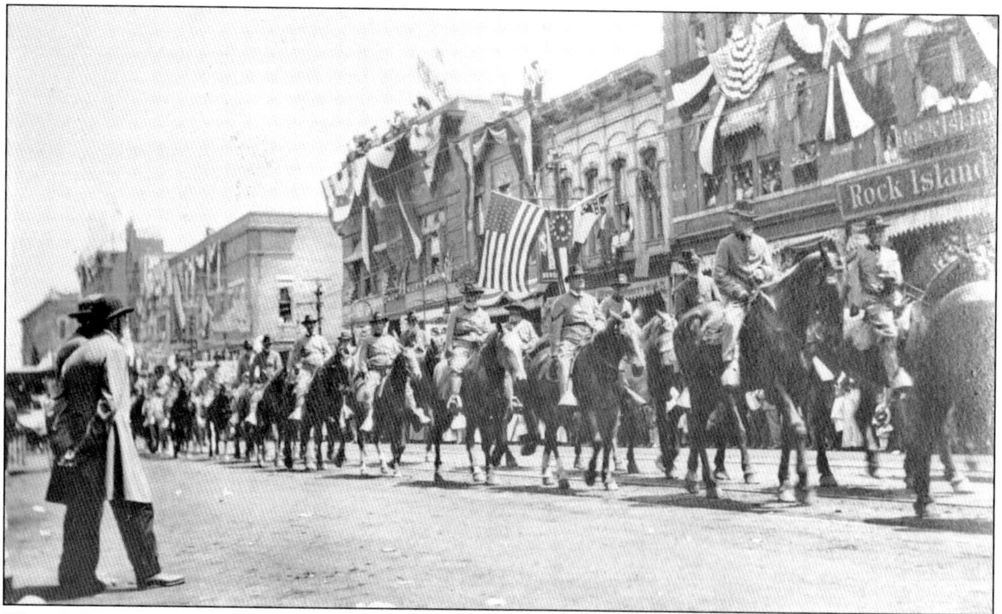

The *Arkansas Democrat* reported: "Sitting on the backs of their horses as proudly as they did when chasing the fleeing Unionists from a hard fought field, or marching with a sturdy step as they did when going to face the powerful batteries of Grant and Sheridan, the remnant of the veterans of the army of the Confederate States, that battled for four long and bloody years for a cause they held so dear, passed in review before 150,000 people along the Great White Way through the heart of Little Rock this forenoon, and heard the loving tributes of enthusiasm as each new detachment of the battle scarred and aged veterans swung into review. A tinge of sadness was added to the scene by the apparent realization of many of the old warriors that ere another Reunion is held many will have heard 'taps' and passed to the final roll call."

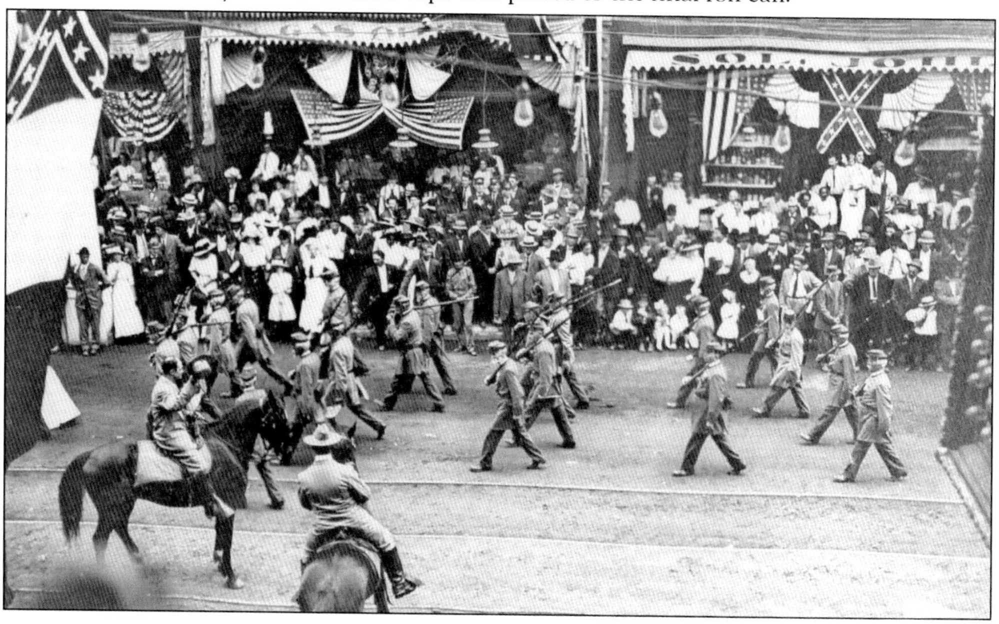

Try as they might, a few of the old soldiers were too infirm with age and the effects of their wounds of half a century before to march in the parade. These old soldiers were given places of honor along the parade route, as in this illustration from the *Arkansas Gazette* of a veteran holding his hat over his heart as the Stars and Bars passed in review. (Courtesy of the *Arkansas Gazette*.)

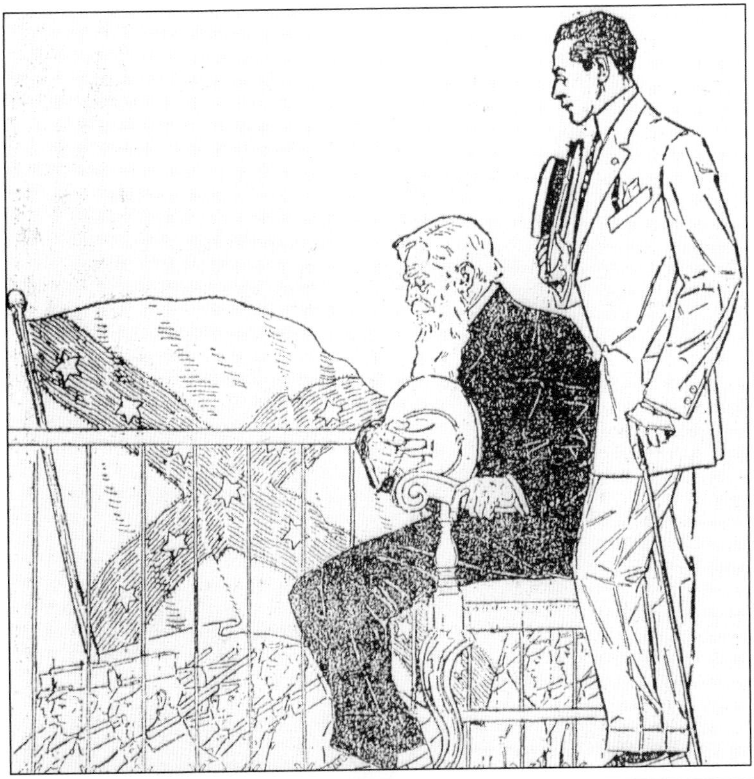

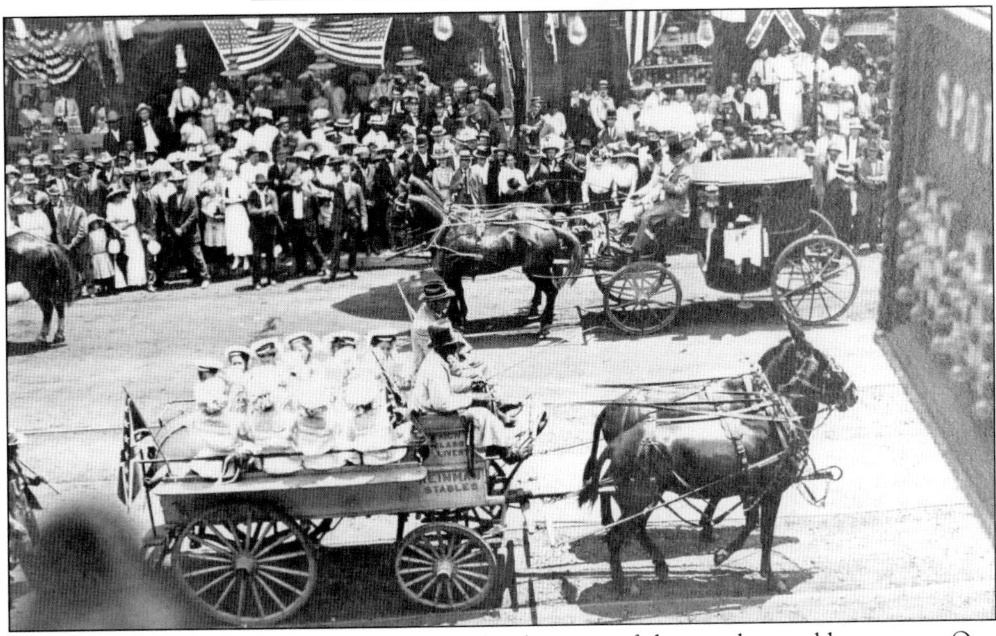

The ladies' wagon seen here stalled the parade when one of their mules would not move. One spectator shouted, "Build a fire under him." A powerful twist of the mule's ear by a burly policeman finally convinced the animal to get along. Elsewhere in the parade, a group of Texas veterans poked fun at the fact that the UCV seemed top-heavy with generals; they carried a banner reading, "We are the few remaining privates in the Confederate Army."

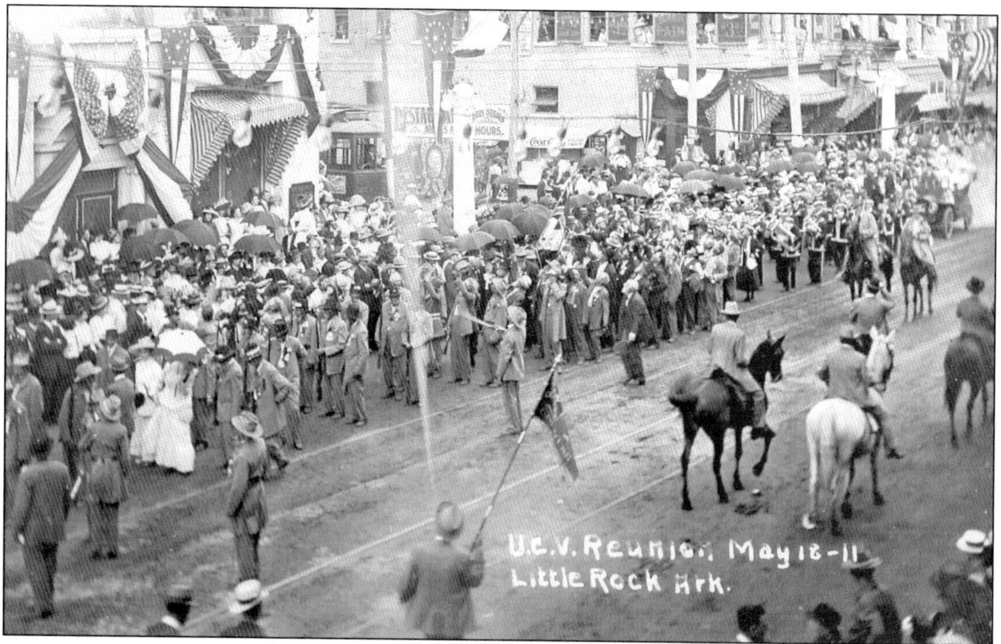

According to a reporter for the *Arkansas Gazette*, "Grizzled old warriors forgot their weight of years and scampered along the parade route as if they were boys of sixteen. Women, inspired by their love for the remnant of men in gray, walked with their honored sires from the time the parade formed for the march until it had completed the counter-march." The huge number of people in the parade necessitated the "counter-march," in which two columns marched in opposite directions on the same street. "Men in some instances, recognizing old comrades in another part of the parade, would fall out of line and hold impromptu reunions. It was a beautiful sight to see these displays of genuine affection and gratitude, and was especially impressive when the veterans themselves gave way to their emotions and literally hugged each other."

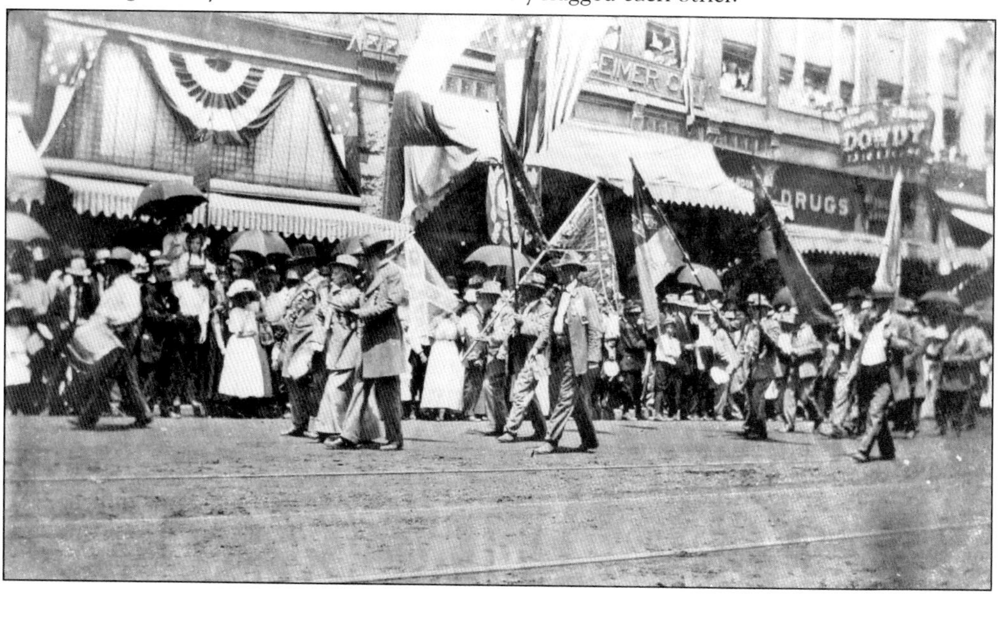

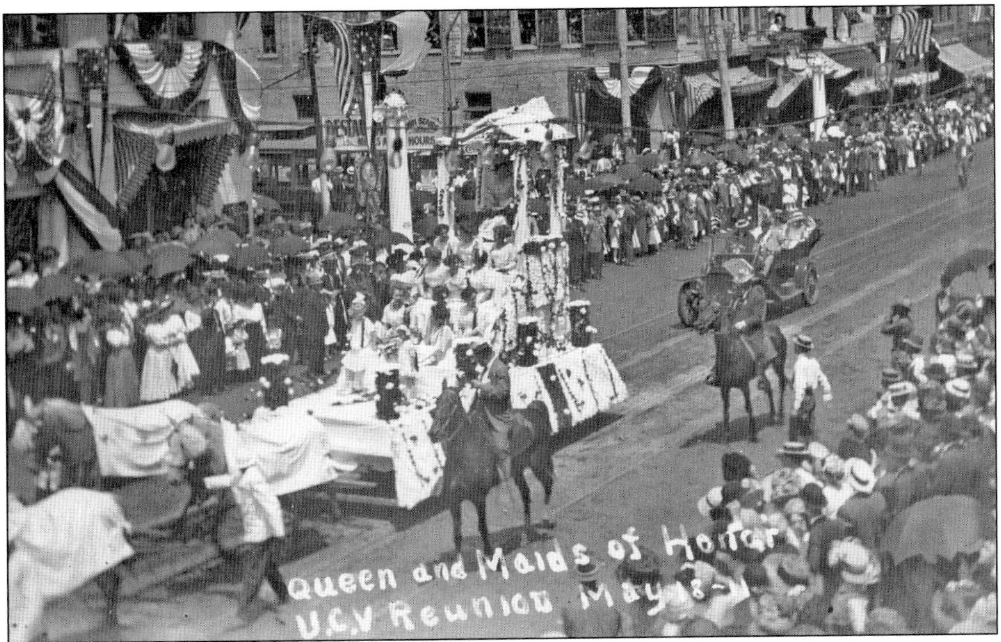

UCV Reunion Queen Kathleen Barkman and her maids of honor were borne along the route by four gray horses. The queen and her maids had helped play host at a variety of functions throughout the three-day reunion, including the closing evening's grand ball, at which they danced with many of the old soldiers.

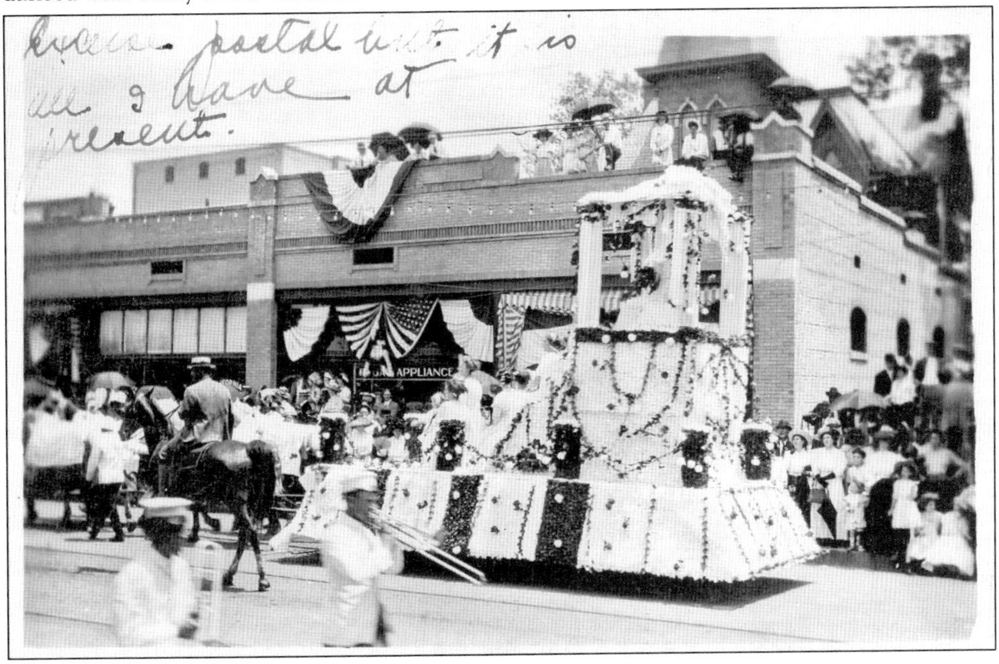

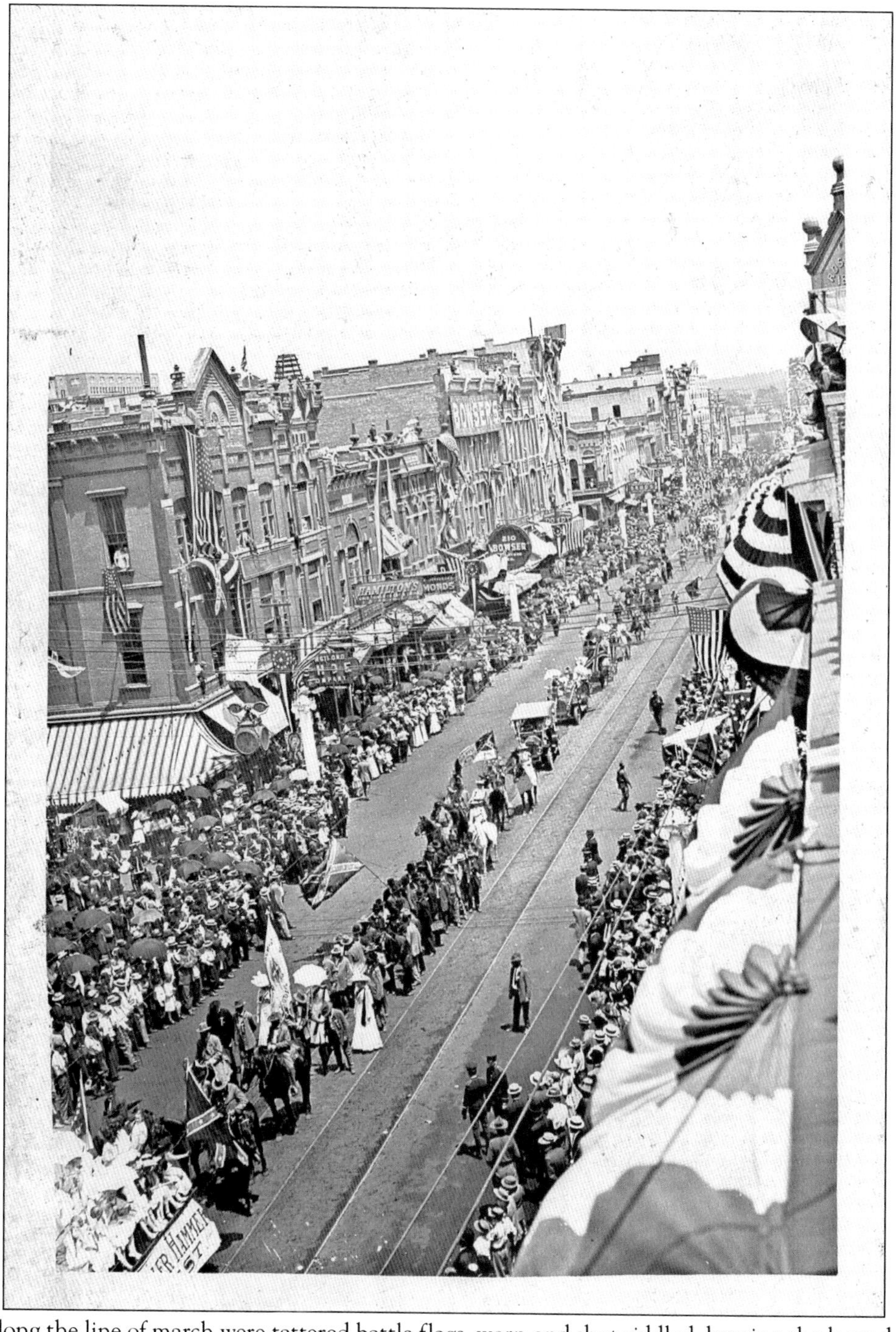

"Along the line of march were tattered battle flags, worn and shot-riddled, bearing the legend of their victories," according to the *Arkansas Gazette*. The parade stretched out here along Main Street included not just battle-damaged flags but also shot-riddled bodies in gray. A number of veterans were missing legs or had empty coat sleeves pinned to their breasts. Many noted an elderly black man pushing an equally elderly but more infirm gray-clad veteran in a high-backed wheelchair along the parade route.

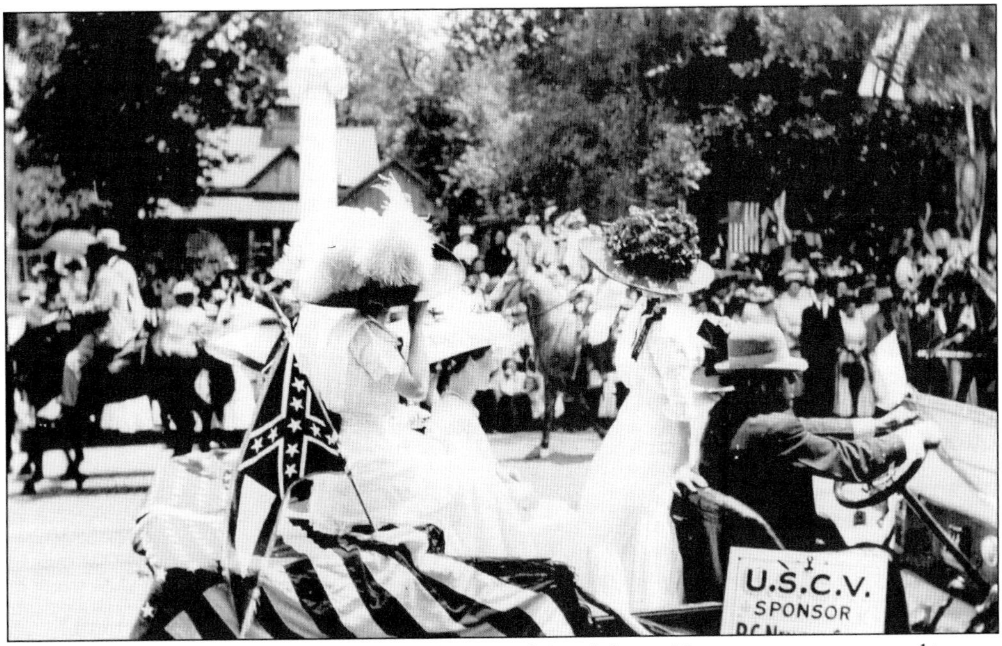

Little Rock's Robert C. Newton Camp of the United Confederate Veterans was represented in part by this automobile bearing three elegantly dressed women waving at the throngs of onlookers.

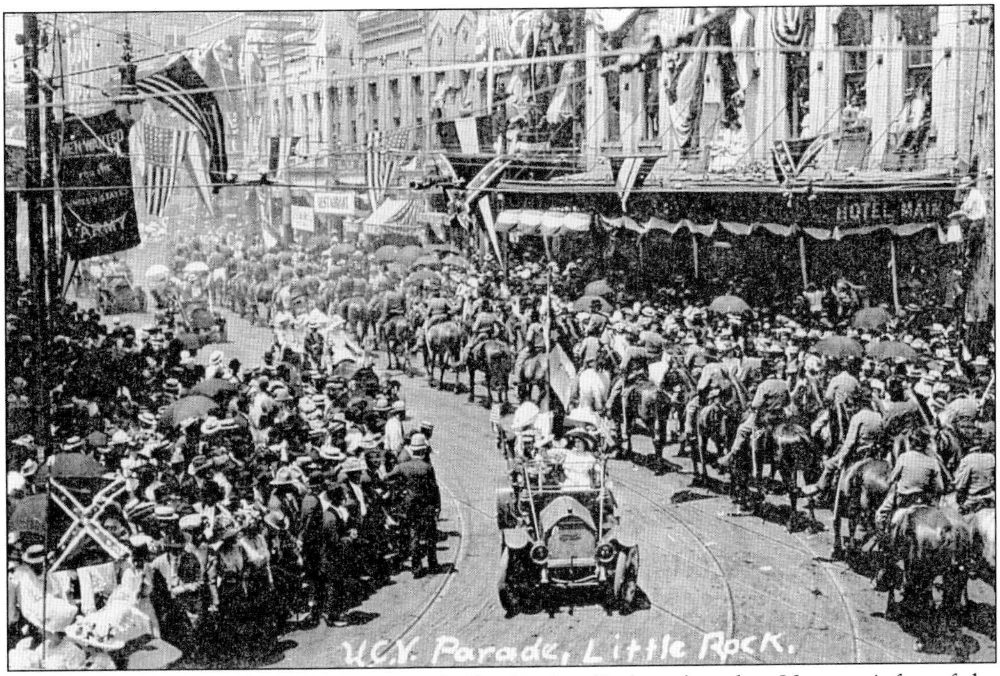

The parade reached Camp Shaver in Little Rock's City Park and made a U-turn. A few of the old veterans dropped out at the halfway mark, not able to make the return leg of the march that would terminate at city hall. Most, however, valiantly reformed their ranks and started back through the city with determination. The grandest parade ever held in Arkansas, before or since, was coming to a conclusion.

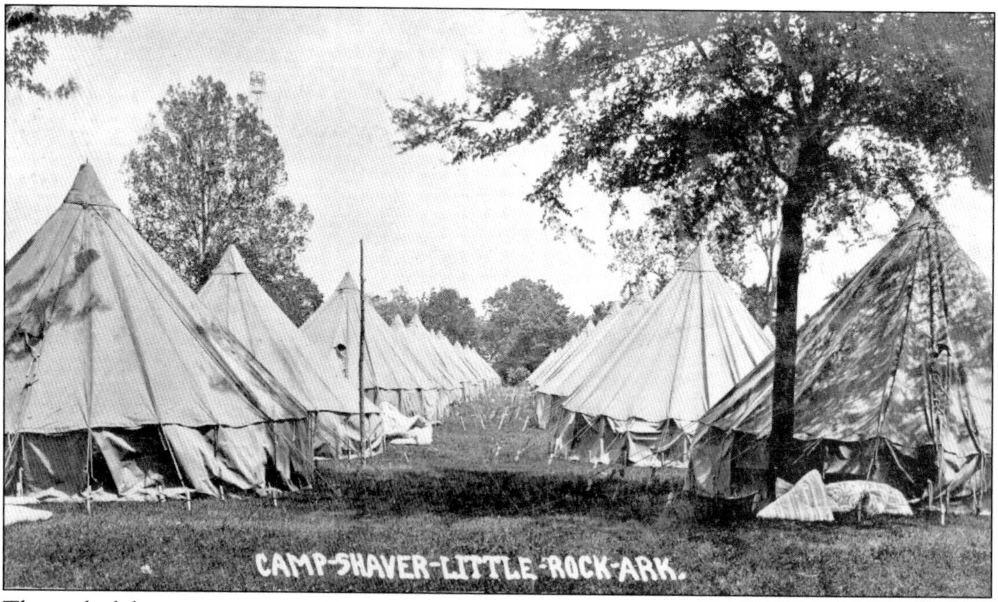

The end of the reunion was sad but brought one lighter note. The cleanup of Camp Shaver the next day prompted this comment by one source: "The collection of articles left by the veterans, in the language of General Shaver, 'Would make a monkey laugh.' Muskets, rifles, suit cases, grips, belts, trousers, vests, false teeth, pocket knives, spectacles and numerous articles were found in the tents after the veterans vacated."

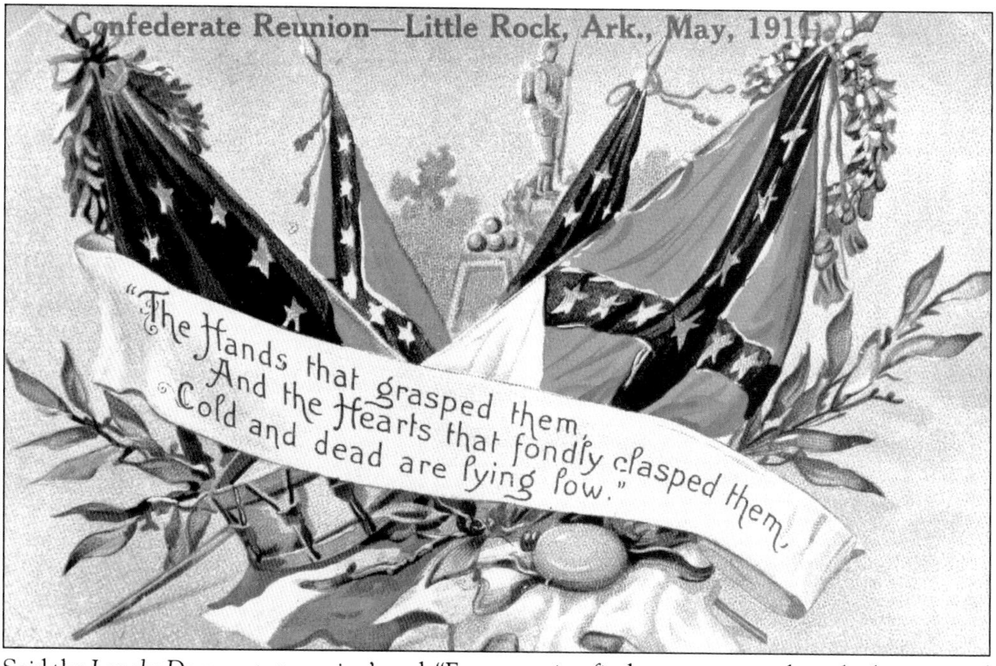

Said the *Lonoke Democrat* at reunion's end: "Every reunion finds a greater number who have spread their tents on Fame's eternal camping ground. They have long since turned over the crest of the hill of life and are fast approaching its foot. May their journey down it be amid the ministrations of friends, the peaceful shade of trees, the singing of birds, the perfume of flowers and may they at last sleep at the foot of the hill in that peace that passeth understanding."

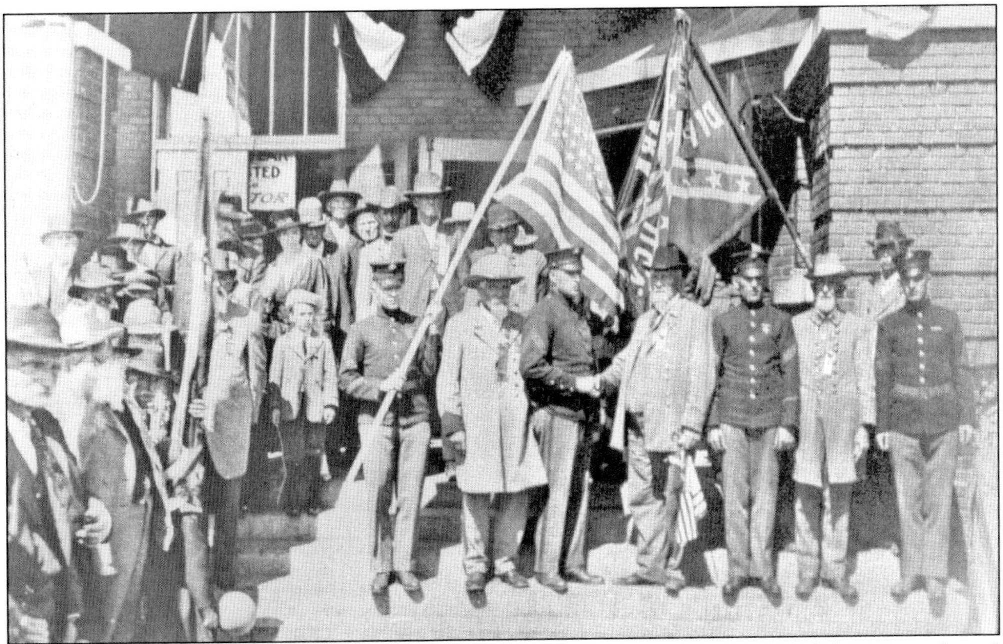

The theme of unity in the United States, amidst the celebrated glories of the remembered Confederacy, was a common note struck in speeches and sermons during the reunion events. This was demonstrated for a photographer near the conclusion of the UCV meeting. An old Confederate had posed, shaking hands with a U.S. Army officer from Fort Roots, as they stood beneath both the Stars and Stripes and the Stars and Bars.

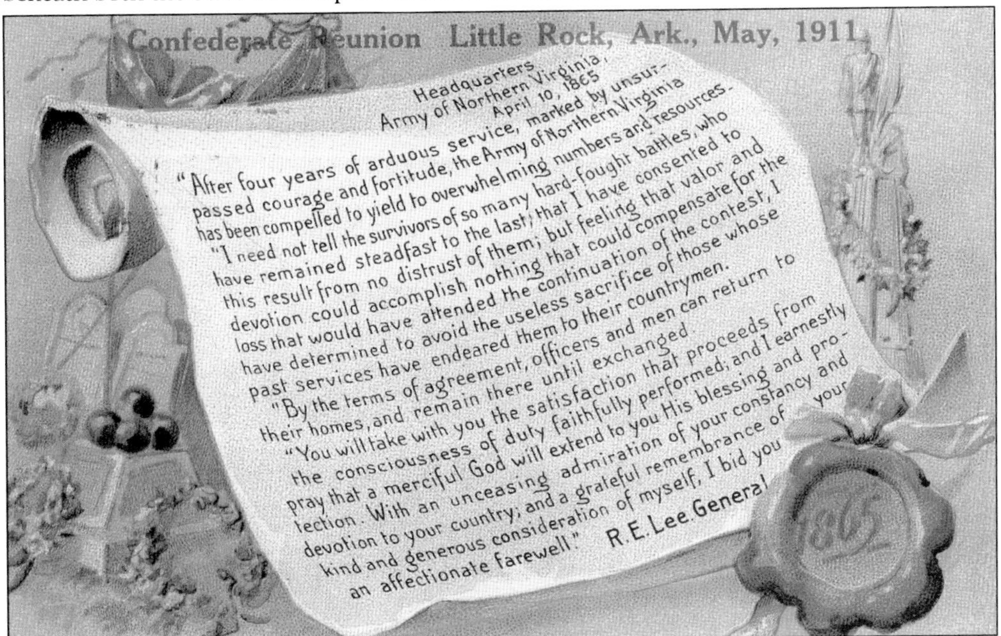

Many of the veterans carried home this postcard bearing Robert E. Lee's parting words to his troops after the surrender at Appomattox: "You will take with you the satisfaction that proceeds from the consciousness of duty faithfully performed, and I earnestly pray that a merciful God will extend to you His blessings and protection."

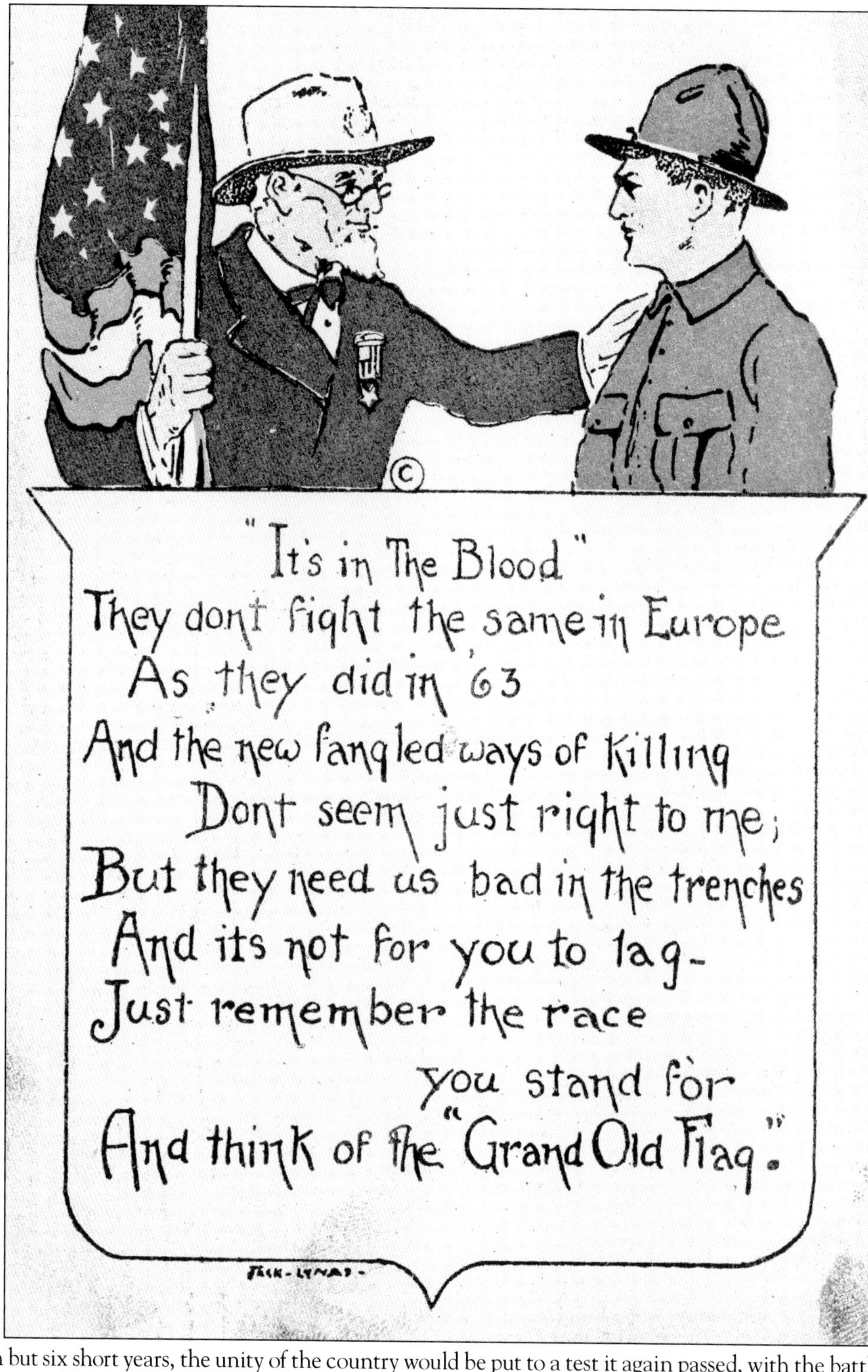

In but six short years, the unity of the country would be put to a test it again passed, with the battles against the Germans in France during World War I—the "War to End All Wars." The children and grandchildren of former Rebs and Yanks would fight side by side under a common flag.

Six

The Thin Gray Line Fades Away, but the Legacy Lives

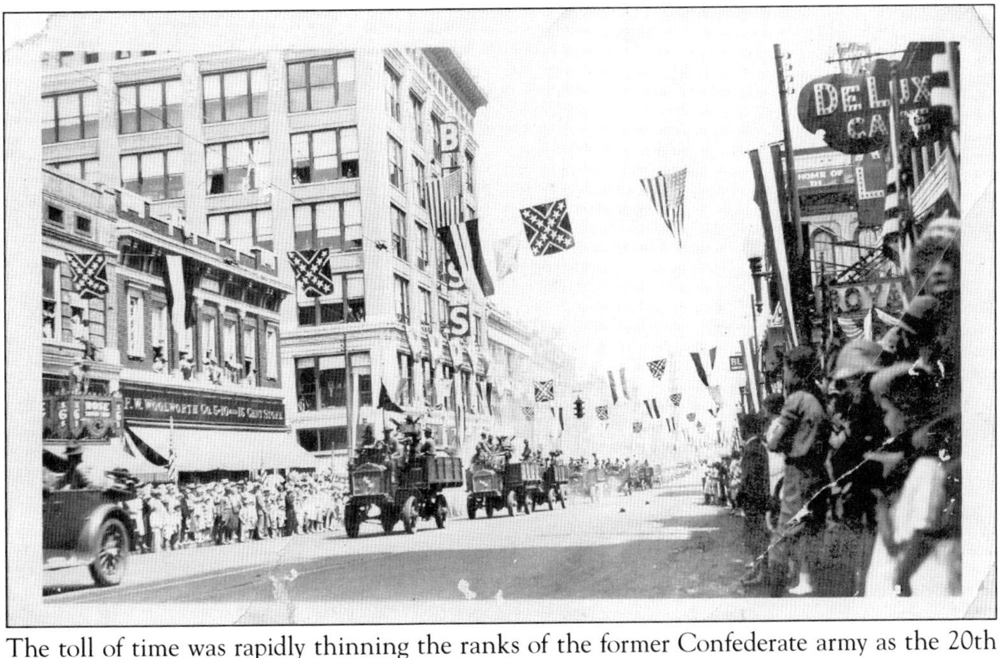

The toll of time was rapidly thinning the ranks of the former Confederate army as the 20th century moved along after World War I. As the thin gray line faded away, there would arise their sons, grandsons, and granddaughters, along with scholars, reenactors, and others who seek to keep those who fought alive in memory and heritage. Little Rock got its second chance to host the UCV reunion in 1928, when the youngest veteran in attendance was 78 and the oldest 99. The total attendance was only around 1,100 officially registered, though reports had as many as 3,000 present. The event included a five-mile parade that began in North Little Rock's Park Hill and ended on Main Street downtown, as seen here beneath the Stars and Bars.

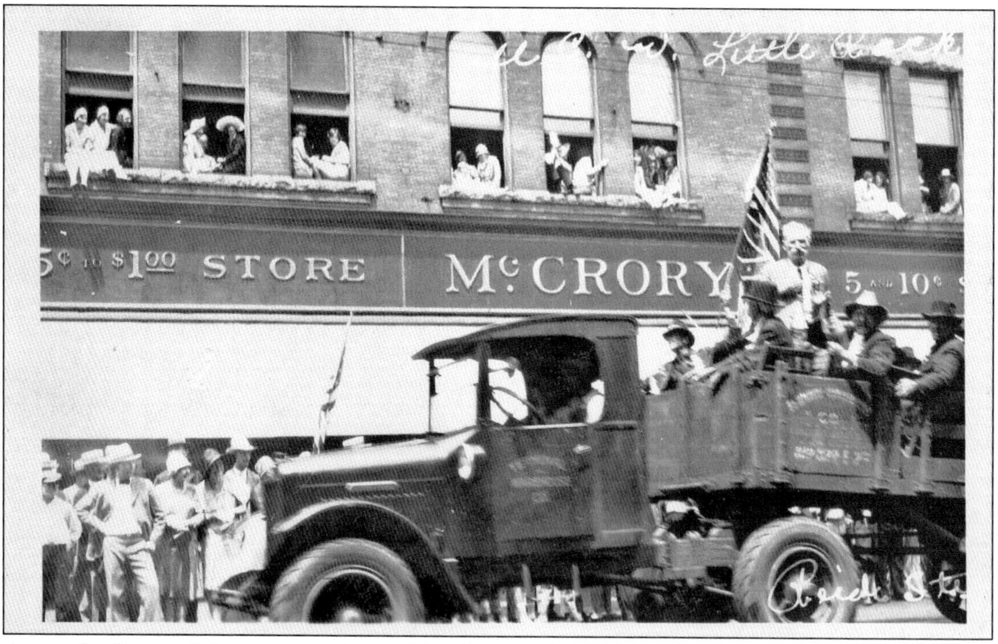

A parade climaxed the reunion, but unlike the parade of 1911, when most veterans marched or rode horses, in the 1928 parade, most of the now much-older vets rode in open-topped cars and aboard trucks. The reunion had a sad note when Gen. Zach Wardlaw of Utica, Mississippi, fell on the marble steps of the Marion Hotel and died of his injuries two hours later.

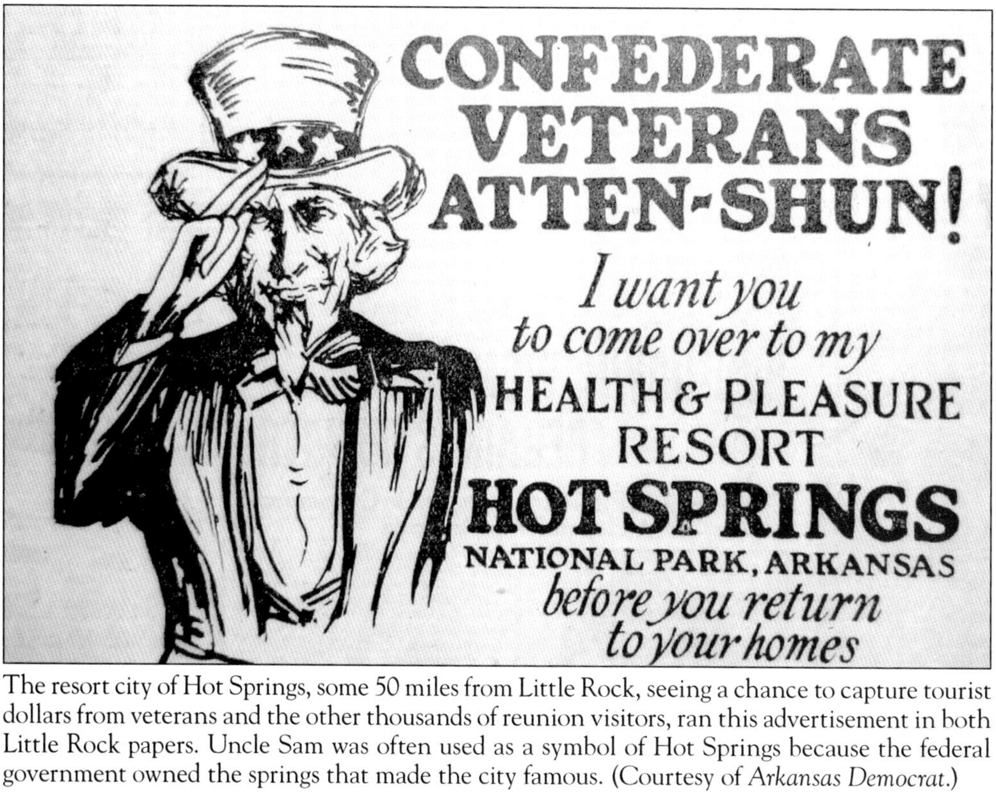

The resort city of Hot Springs, some 50 miles from Little Rock, seeing a chance to capture tourist dollars from veterans and the other thousands of reunion visitors, ran this advertisement in both Little Rock papers. Uncle Sam was often used as a symbol of Hot Springs because the federal government owned the springs that made the city famous. (Courtesy of *Arkansas Democrat*.)

Gen. Albert Goodwyn of Alabama, UCV commander in chief at the Little Rock meeting, had participated in the 1861 attack on Fort Sumter. He said, "My comrades, we are the rear guard of our unsurpassed army, all now facing the twilight. If there be any discord in our ranks, I plead with you by the memory of our common sacrifice, to discard all disharmony, so that as we cross over the river, we may be greeted by our advanced comrades as worthy brothers."

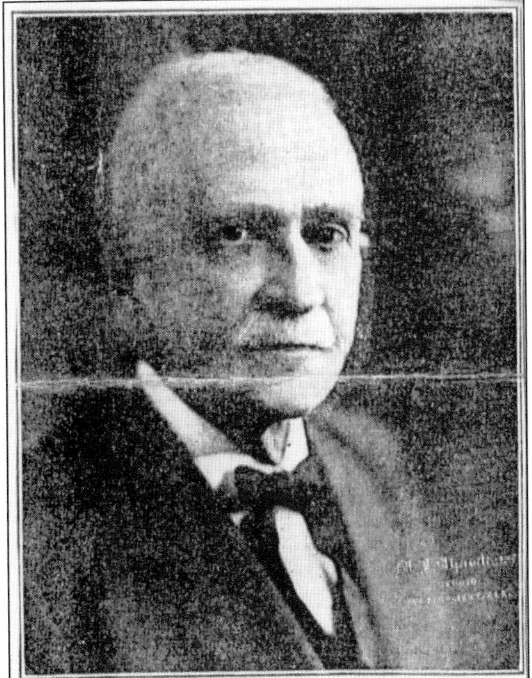

GEN. ALBERT T. GOODWYN, OF ALABAMA
Elected Commander in Chief United Confederate Veterans, Little Rock Reunion, May 8-11, 1928.

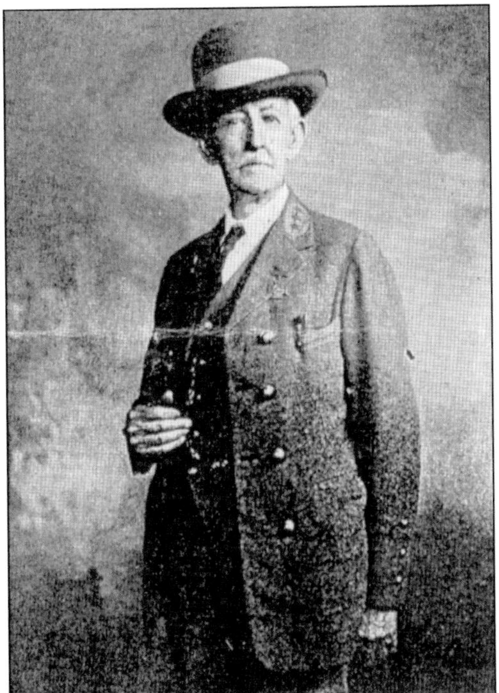

GEN. J. W. HOLLIS, COMMANDER ARKANSAS DIVISION, U. C. V.

Gen. J. W. Hollis led the Arkansas delegates at the 1928 meeting as the commander of the state's UCV division. He would have likely heard renditions of a new verse to an old song, penned at that meeting: "We are a band of brothers, native to the soil, fighting for the property we gained by honest toil. And when our rights were threatened, the cry rose near and far, Hurrah! For the Bonnie Blue Flag that bears a single star!"

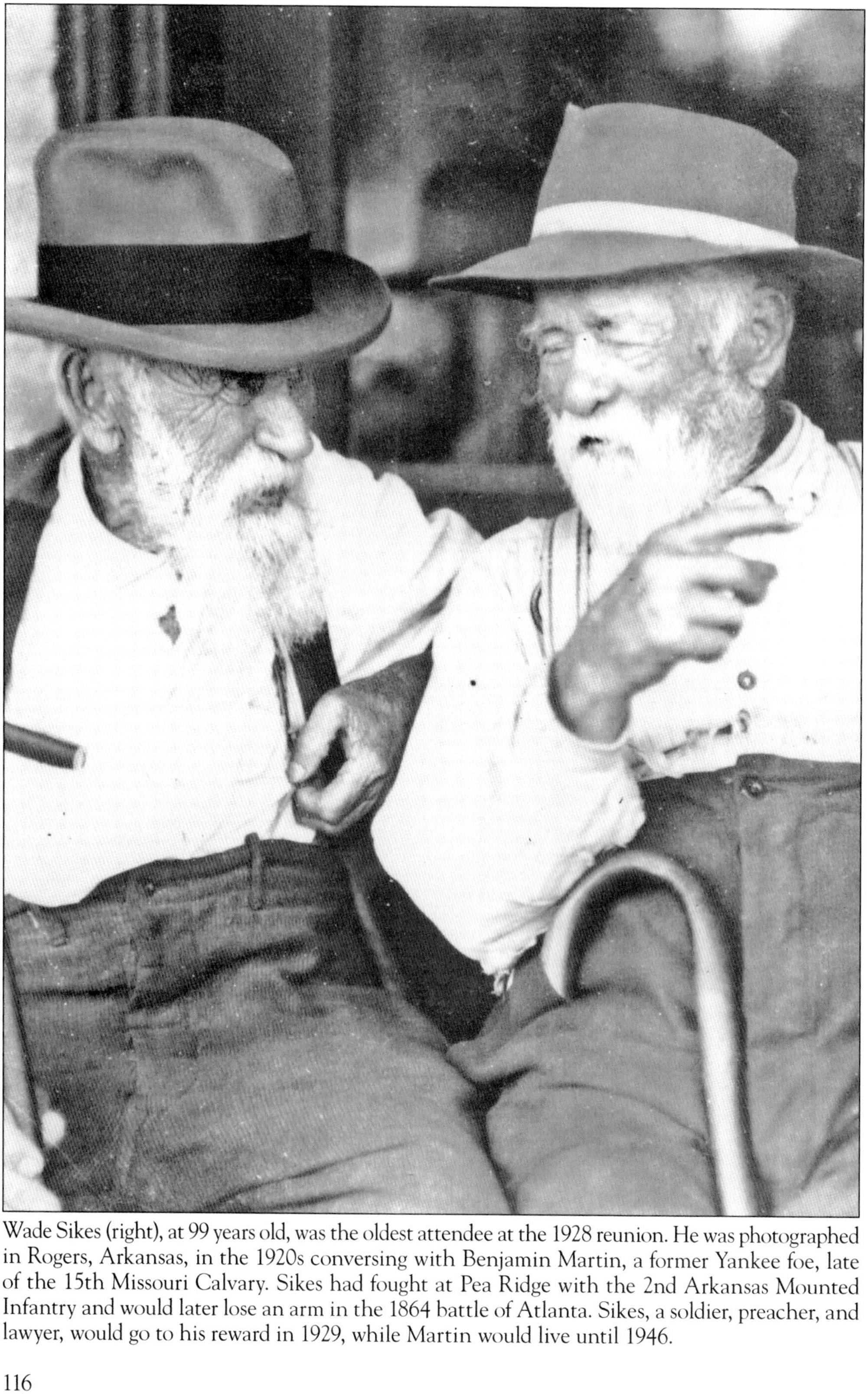

Wade Sikes (right), at 99 years old, was the oldest attendee at the 1928 reunion. He was photographed in Rogers, Arkansas, in the 1920s conversing with Benjamin Martin, a former Yankee foe, late of the 15th Missouri Calvary. Sikes had fought at Pea Ridge with the 2nd Arkansas Mounted Infantry and would later lose an arm in the 1864 battle of Atlanta. Sikes, a soldier, preacher, and lawyer, would go to his reward in 1929, while Martin would live until 1946.

In 1944, the UDC honored veteran William Jarrett on his 95th birthday. He was captured in 1863 at the age of 14 by Union troops occupying Randolph County; they threatened to shoot him for refusing to answer questions. His mother, recognizing the Union men as Germans from Pennsylvania, pleaded in German for her son's life. Jarrett marched off to war in 1864 wearing a gray uniform his mother had made by combining wool from black and white sheep to obtain a gray hue.

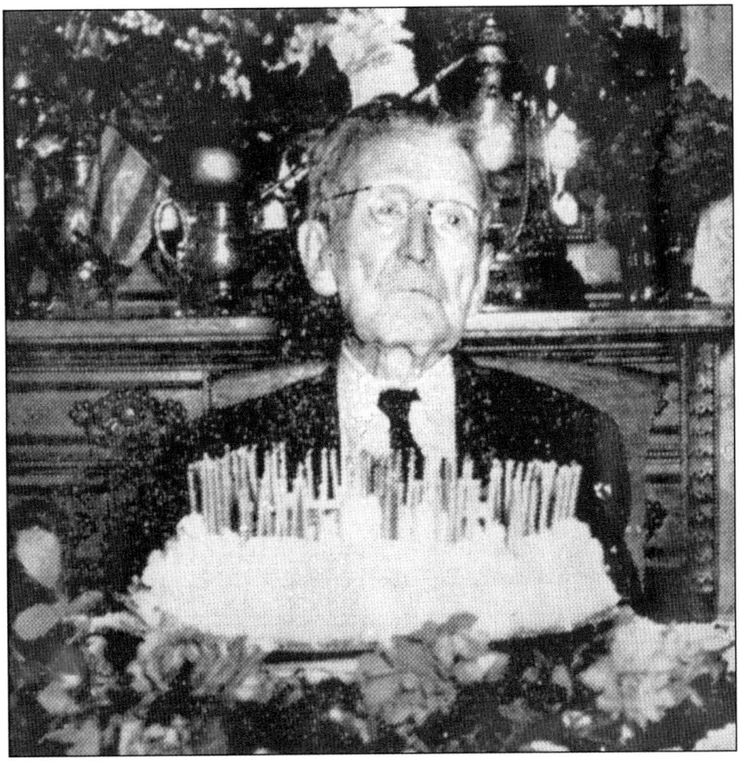

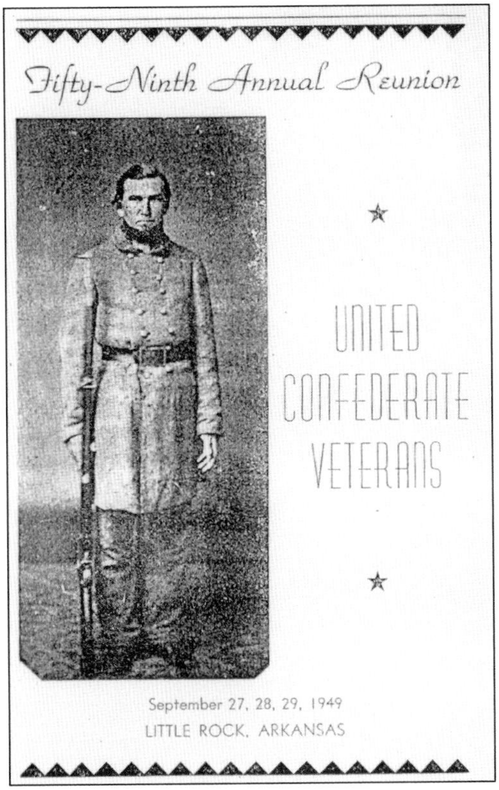

In 1949, Little Rock got its third and final chance to host the dwindling ranks of Confederate veterans. While 12,000 had attended the first Little Rock reunion 38 years earlier, 8 were expected for the third hosting, and only 4 were able to attend (their average age was 100.5 years). The SCV, again hosted by the Robert C. Newton Camp, reported that of the 600,000 original Confederates, only 28 were thought still living at that time.

CONFEDERATE REUNION DATES—SEPT. 27, 28, 29, 1949

OFFICIAL

Courtesy Card

INVITING you and your family to attend all functions of the 59th Confederate Reunion, including U. S. Marine Band Concerts and the Confederate Ball at Joe T. Robinson Auditorium on Wednesday Night, September 28th.

Confederate Reunion Committee

HEADQUARTERS — MARION HOTEL

As in 1911 and 1928, the venerable Marion Hotel was again the headquarters for the 59th annual UCV reunion. Arkansas governor Sid McMath, a Marine veteran of World War II, proclaimed "Confederate Week," saying, "These amazing representatives of another century will assemble for their 3rd and last meeting within Arkansas." He proclaimed that the Confederate flag be displayed in public places.

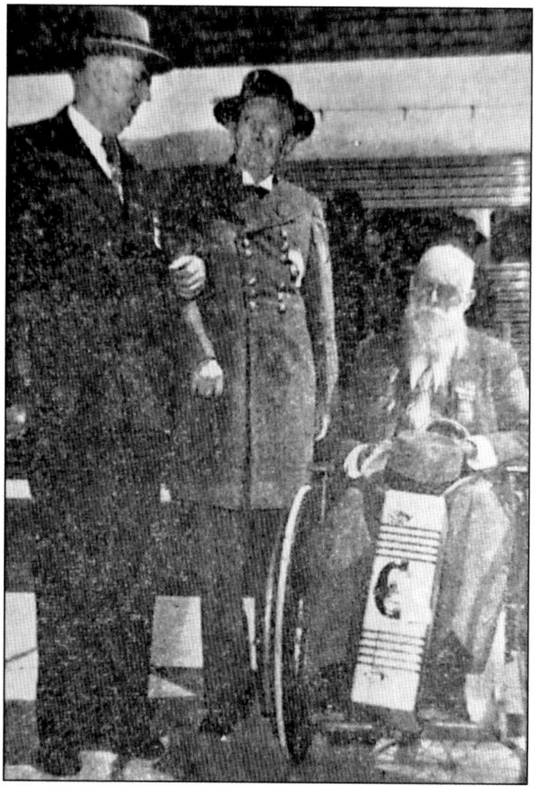

John Robert Thomas Reeves, of the Sons of the Confederate Veterans, greeted two arriving veterans at the train station in 1949. Uniformed Gen. James Moore of Alabama is in the center; in the wheelchair, with his suitcase held between his knees, is 100-year-old W. W. Alexander. It was noted, "Neither was able to get about without assistance but both had the fire of a school boy." (Courtesy of *Arkansas Democrat*.)

Gen. James W. Moore, the 98-year-old commander in chief of the UCV, told a reporter he was only 13 years old when he ran away from school and joined the Confederate cavalry. General Moore added that he was "still a young man" and that he still drove his automobile, except he couldn't see at night anymore. He claimed to be a graduate of Virginia Military Institute and to be the only person still living who had attended Robert E. Lee's 1870 funeral.

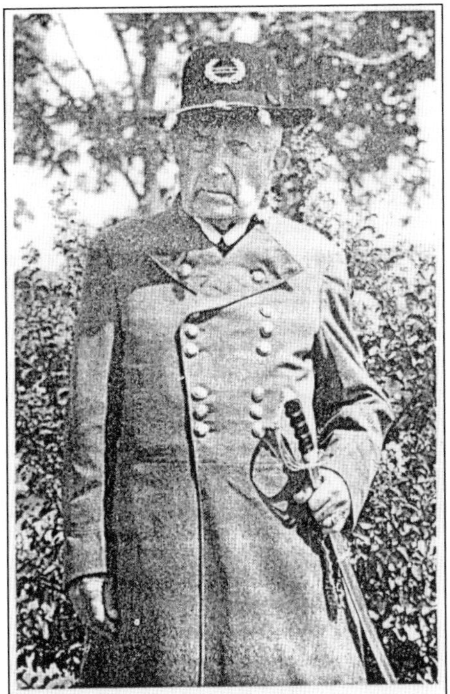

GENERAL JAMES W. MOORE
Commander-in-Chief, 1948-1949

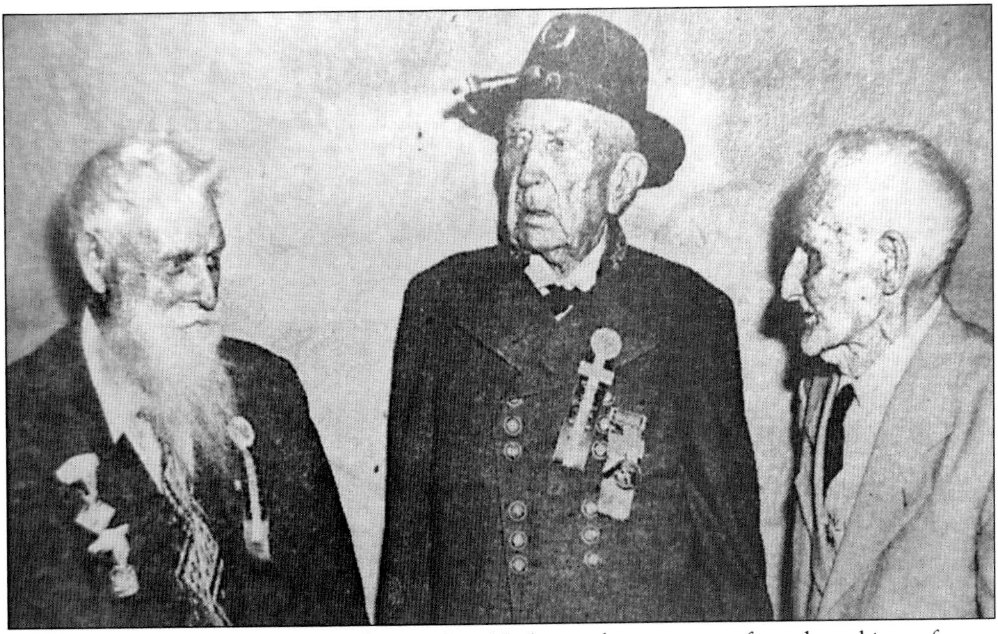

With only four veterans in attendance, the elderly gentlemen were often the subject of press photographers. W. W. Alexander, the 100-year-old veteran from North Carolina seen at the left in this photograph, laughed and said, "Bang! That didn't hurt me," when the camera's flashbulb went off. Commander in chief General Moore, in his well-decorated uniform, is standing in the center, with James Thrasher on the right. (Courtesy of *Arkansas Democrat*.)

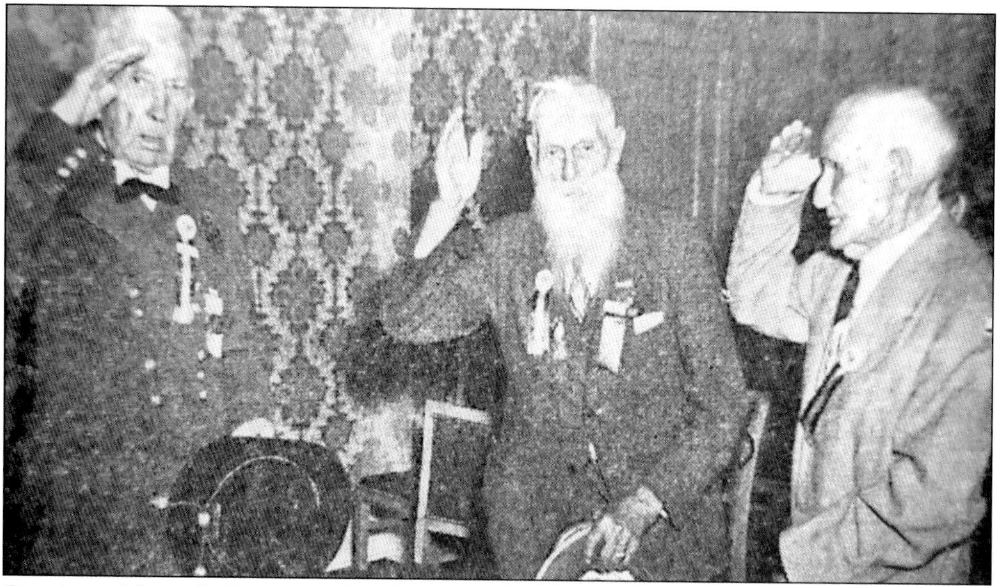

Gen. James Moore (left) receives the salute of fellow veteran James Thrasher (right) in recognition that Moore had been elected to the permanent post of UCV commander. With the ranks of the once-mighty army down to fewer than 30 in all the nation, the grim reality was that the future would hold no competition for the past. (Courtesy of *Arkansas Democrat*.)

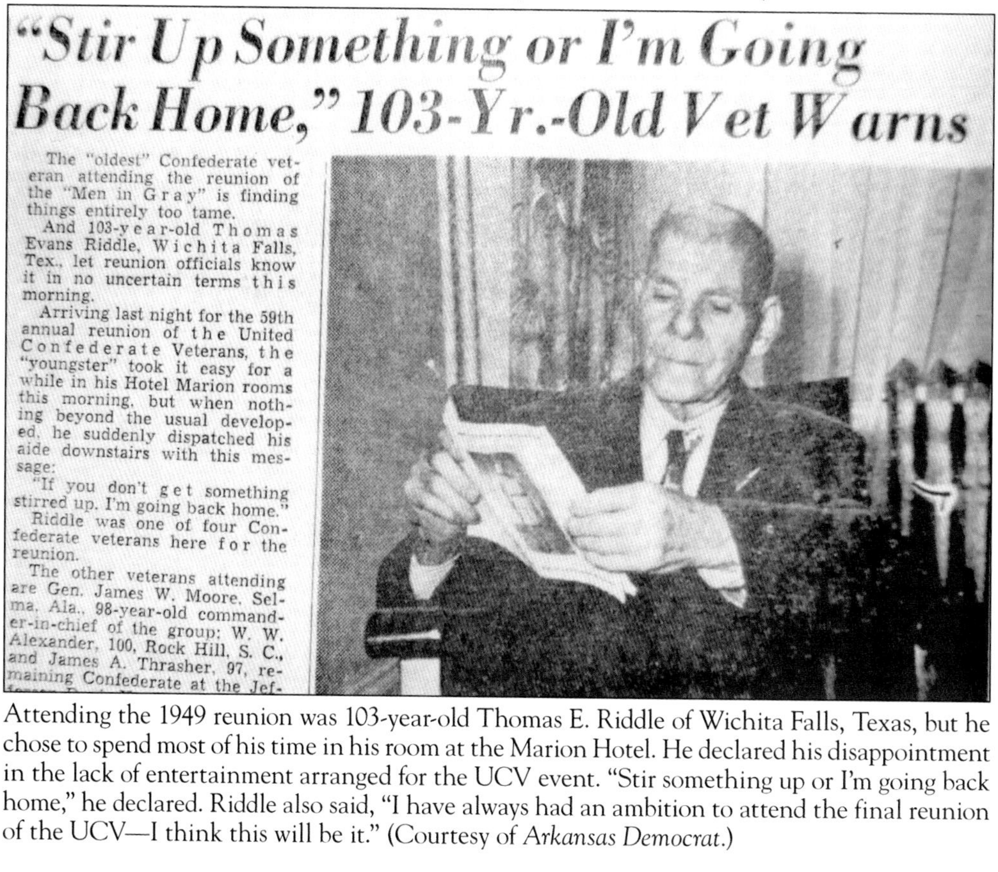

"Stir Up Something or I'm Going Back Home," 103-Yr.-Old Vet Warns

The "oldest" Confederate veteran attending the reunion of the "Men in Gray" is finding things entirely too tame.

And 103-year-old Thomas Evans Riddle, Wichita Falls, Tex., let reunion officials know it in no uncertain terms this morning.

Arriving last night for the 59th annual reunion of the United Confederate Veterans, the "youngster" took it easy for a while in his Hotel Marion rooms this morning, but when nothing beyond the usual developed, he suddenly dispatched his aide downstairs with this message:

"If you don't get something stirred up, I'm going back home."

Riddle was one of four Confederate veterans here for the reunion.

The other veterans attending are Gen. James W. Moore, Selma, Ala., 98-year-old commander-in-chief of the group; W. W. Alexander, 100, Rock Hill, S. C., and James A. Thrasher, 97, remaining Confederate at the Jef-

Attending the 1949 reunion was 103-year-old Thomas E. Riddle of Wichita Falls, Texas, but he chose to spend most of his time in his room at the Marion Hotel. He declared his disappointment in the lack of entertainment arranged for the UCV event. "Stir something up or I'm going back home," he declared. Riddle also said, "I have always had an ambition to attend the final reunion of the UCV—I think this will be it." (Courtesy of *Arkansas Democrat*.)

Despite veteran Riddle's complaint, there was some entertainment for the reunion on opening night at Robinson Auditorium and on two other occasions when the U.S. Marine Band performed concerts. Marine major William Santelmann, in charge of the band, greeted W. W. Alexander here after one performance. At a Marion Hotel breakfast sponsored by the UDC, Alexander demonstrated the famous rebel yell. (Courtesy of *Arkansas Democrat.*)

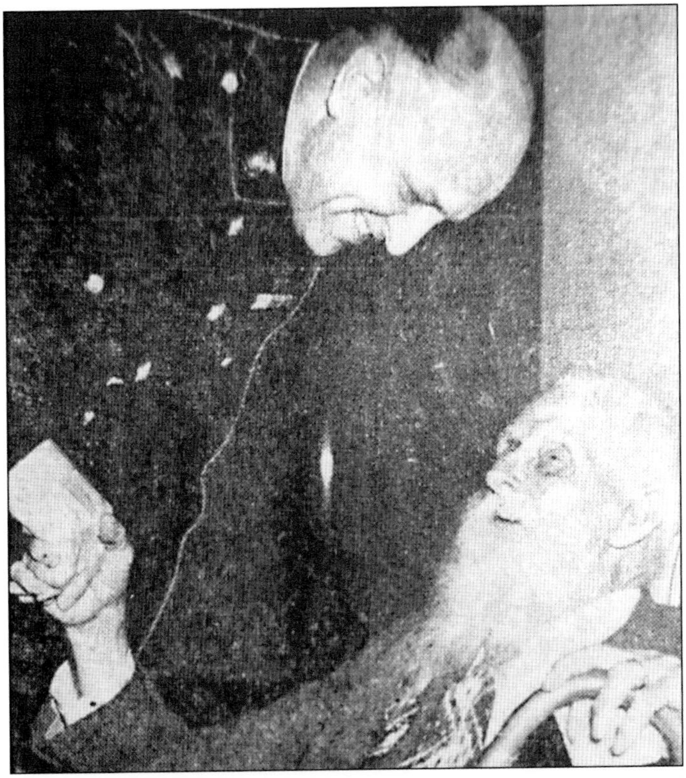

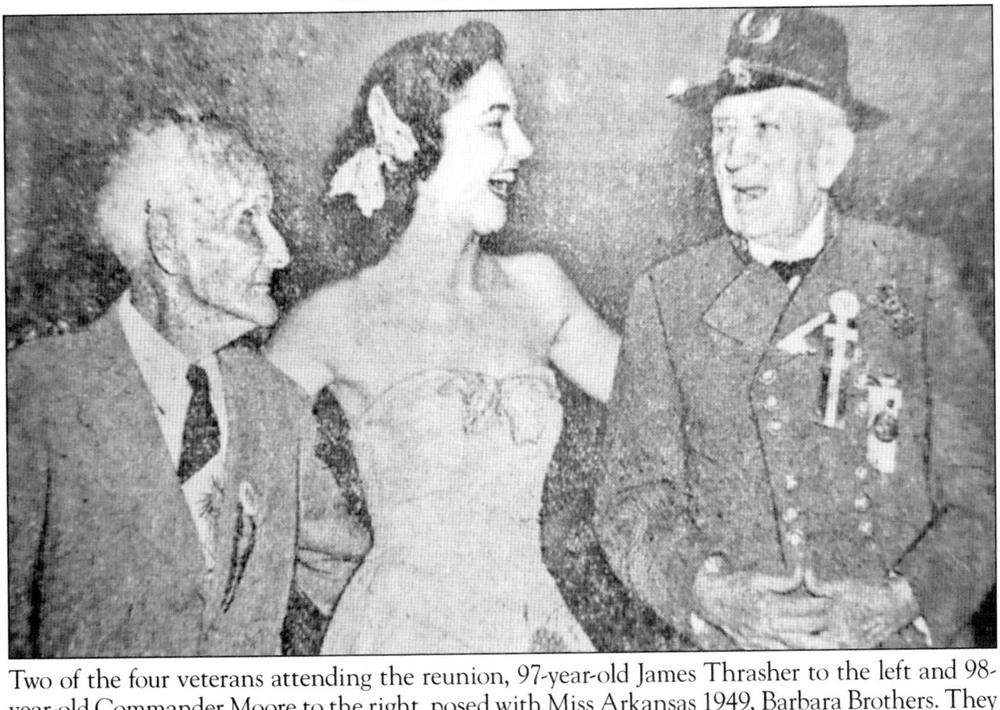

Two of the four veterans attending the reunion, 97-year-old James Thrasher to the left and 98-year-old Commander Moore to the right, posed with Miss Arkansas 1949, Barbara Brothers. They shared an open-topped Cadillac in the Main Street parade, which followed the same route that 12,000 old soldiers had paraded down 38 years before. (Courtesy of *Arkansas Democrat.*)

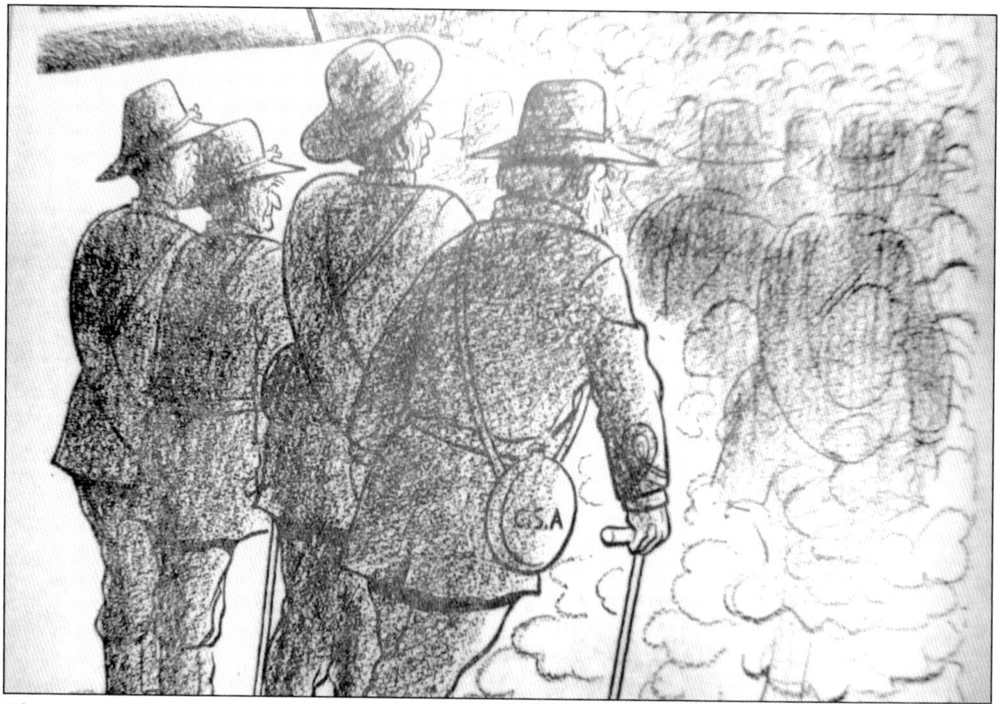

There would be two more reunions, in Biloxi in 1950 and in Virginia in 1951; never again would Arkansas host the event. Perhaps the most poignant closing note was this editorial cartoon from the *Arkansas Democrat* entitled "Rear Guard." The four veterans who made it to Little Rock were among the last, preparing to follow the 600,000 of their comrades who had already marched into eternity. (Courtesy of *Arkansas Democrat.*)

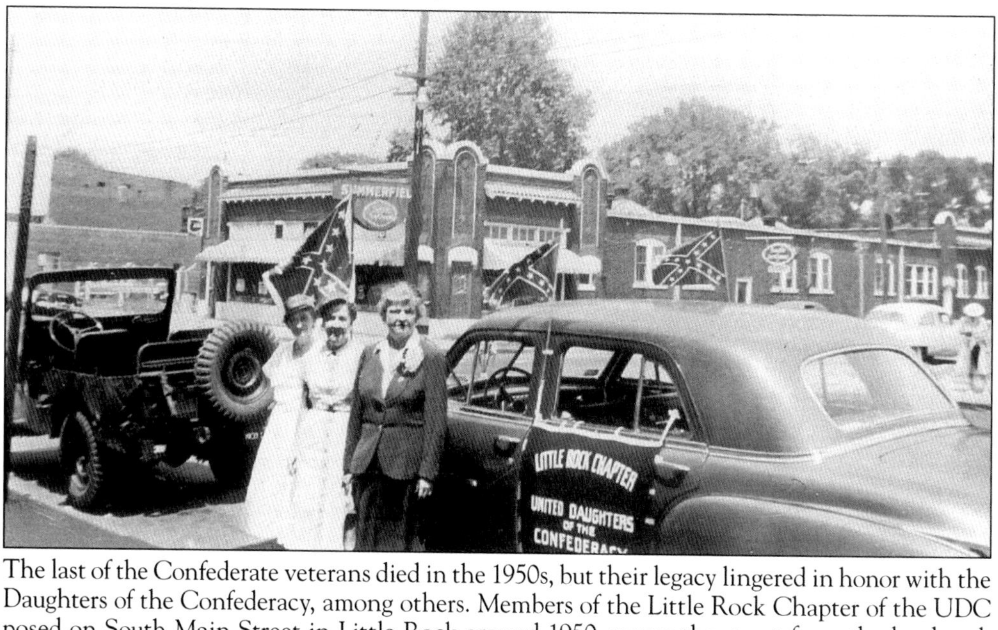

The last of the Confederate veterans died in the 1950s, but their legacy lingered in honor with the Daughters of the Confederacy, among others. Members of the Little Rock Chapter of the UDC posed on South Main Street in Little Rock around 1950, across the street from the landmark Summerfield's Ice Cream. Two of the women are wearing rebel caps, and the group's car is adorned with a banner and the Stars and Bars.

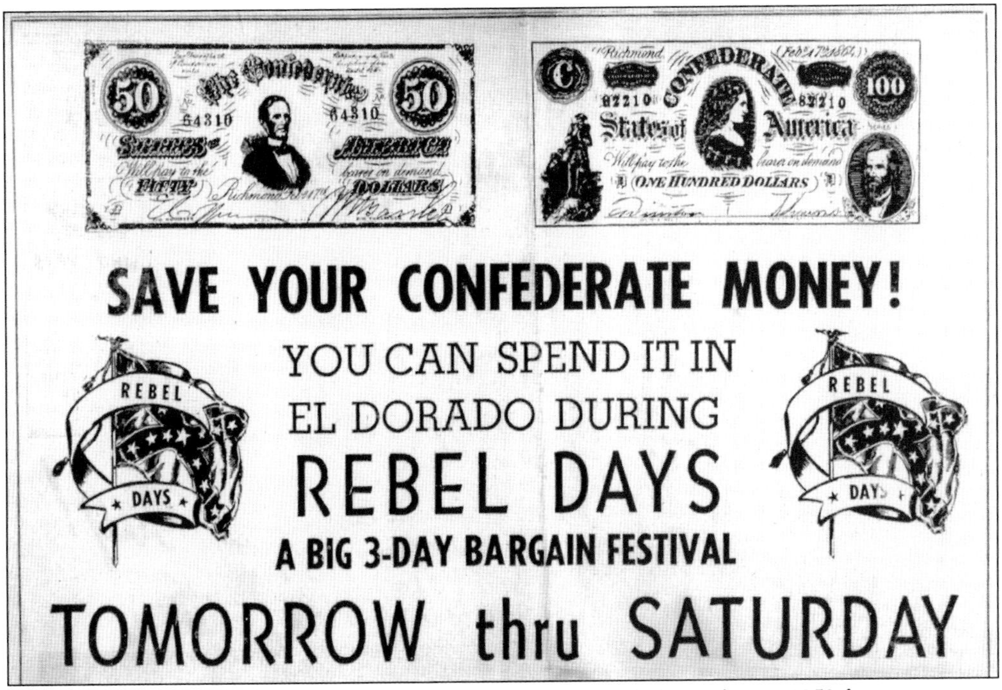

The merchants of the South Arkansas city of El Dorado banded together in 1952 for a newspaper promotion for "Rebel Days." Readers of the paper were instructed to cut out the authentic-sized Confederate currency and redeem it in participating stores for discounts on a wide variety of merchandise.

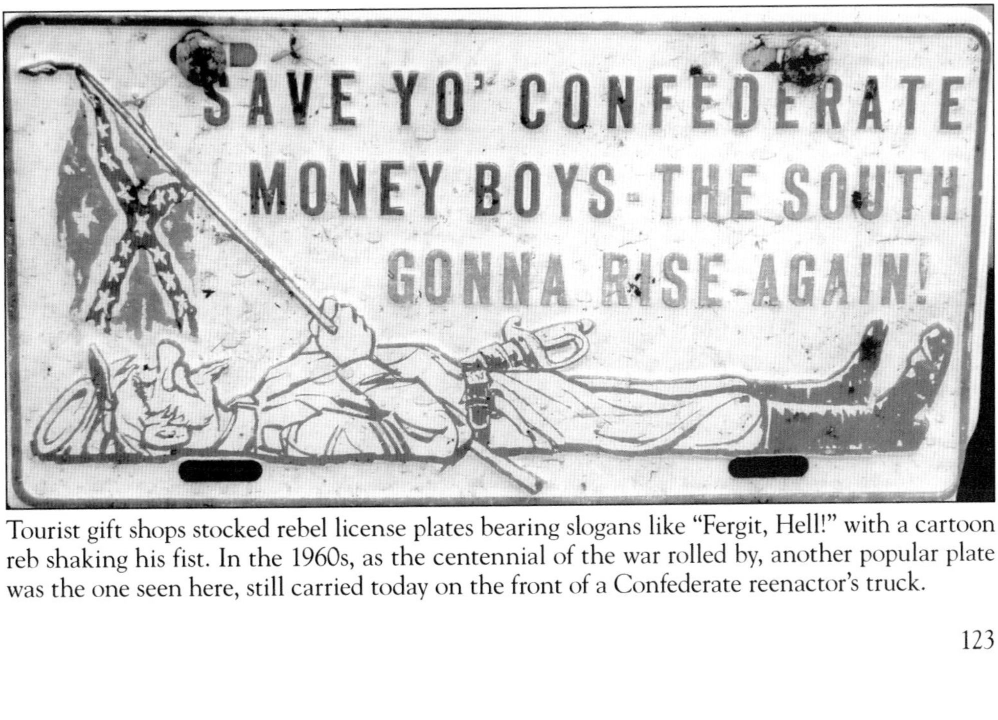

Tourist gift shops stocked rebel license plates bearing slogans like "Fergit, Hell!" with a cartoon reb shaking his fist. In the 1960s, as the centennial of the war rolled by, another popular plate was the one seen here, still carried today on the front of a Confederate reenactor's truck.

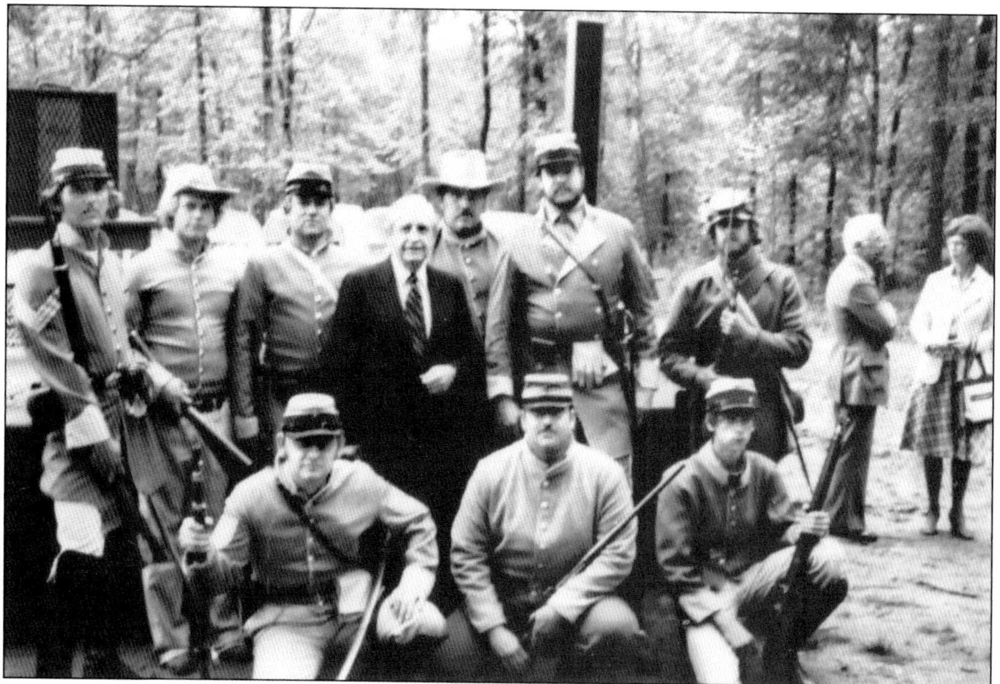

Some 500 delegates of the Sons of Confederate Veterans chose Little Rock for their 70th annual convention in 1965. They are visited here in a local park by Gov. Orval Faubus. (Courtesy of Butler Center for Arkansas Studies.)

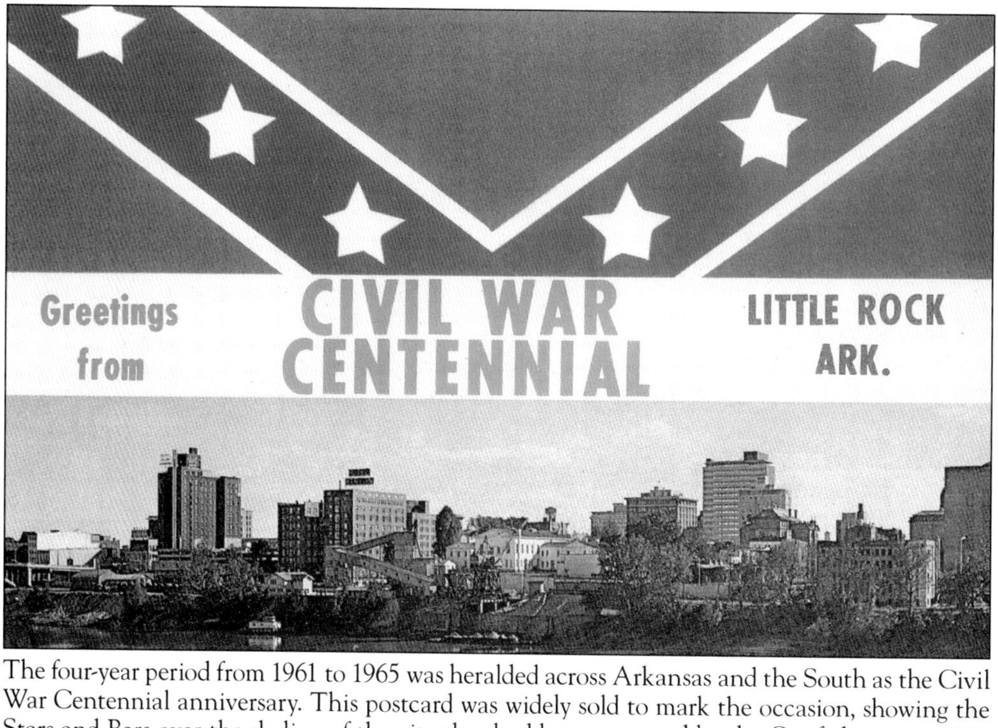

The four-year period from 1961 to 1965 was heralded across Arkansas and the South as the Civil War Centennial anniversary. This postcard was widely sold to mark the occasion, showing the Stars and Bars over the skyline of the city that had been captured by the Confederates in 1861 and retaken by Union forces in 1863.

By the 1980s, the Confederate flag and images of "Johnny Reb" had begun to be considered politically incorrect, though not in the North Arkansas town of Hardy. The picture above is the cover of the 1999 *Rebel* yearbook of the Highland School District. The student body elected "to end the last full school year of the century with renewed enthusiasm in all aspects of school life," having formed "Dixie Pride. . . . Breaking through to become the Rebels of the twenty-first century."

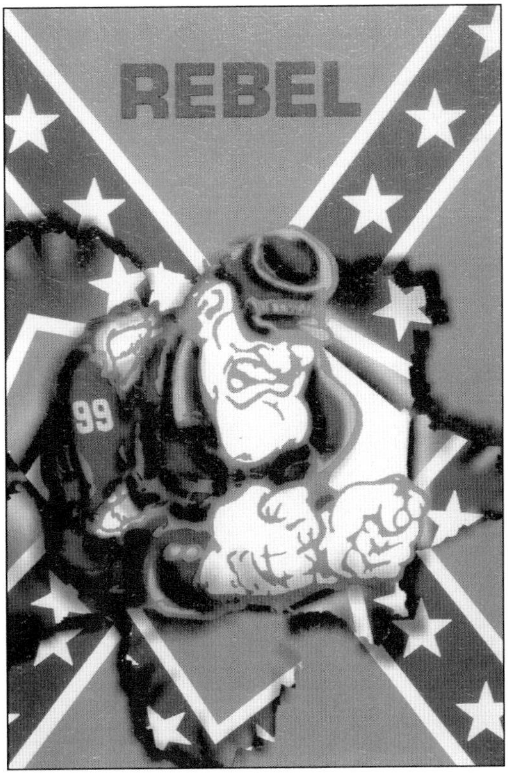

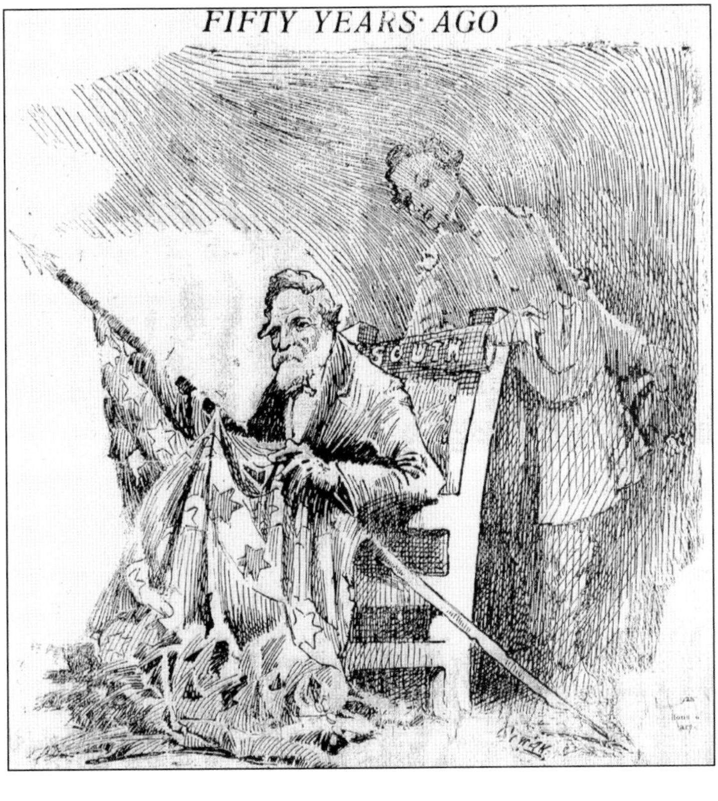

The spirit of the young soldier who marched off to war in 1861 looks over his shoulder at the aged, frail veteran he has become 50 years later. In this book, we have looked back more than a century to men who fought for what they believed but who later put aside their differences in peace and unity. It is hoped that the troubled world of today can do the same.

Closing Thoughts on Memory and Legacy

The men of the Arkansas Division Sons of Confederate Veterans are honored to have contributed to this presentation. It is a memorial to the ancestors who wore the gray during the War Between the States.

Even today, the Arkansas Division of the SCV carries on the traditions of their fathers, grandfathers, great-grandfathers, and great-great-grandfathers. We place military markers at Confederate soldiers' graves, march in patriotic parades, make speeches about our ancestors, and hold annual reunions as the Confederate veterans did until the last roll call mustered the final Confederate soldier home to be with his comrades of old.

As for our noble Confederate ancestors, their swords are sheathed now, their battle flags are folded three-corner, and the smell of powder is gone from the fields of thunder. The memory of these men who were seasoned veterans of so many hard-fought battles for "States Rights" will be etched in the hearts and minds of their descendants, the Sons of Confederate Veterans of Arkansas.

As we remember generals Fagan, Adams, Shelby, Thompson, Nelson, Govan, Marmaduke, Price, Forrest, Stuart, Jackson, and our beloved Patrick R. Cleburne, our thoughts go to what Gen. Robert E. Lee of the Army of Northern Virginia told us: "Duty is the most sublime word in our language. Do your duty in all things. You cannot do more. You should never wish to do less." The members of the Arkansas Division SCV will continue to do their duty to all Confederate soldiers that marched off to war and gave their all to the Cause!

We all have our crosses to bear in life, mine happens to be a Southern Cross
and I will bear it proudly forever!

—W. D. Honnoll; January 19, 1999

I want to personally thank Ray Hanley for undertaking such a noble project so that future generations will read and understand the true history of the men who wore the gray and fought for the South so long ago!

Respectfully as always,
W. Danny Honnoll
Arkansas Division Commander SCV
President, Arkansas Civil War Heritage Trails Foundation
Jonesboro, Arkansas

INDEX

Discover Thousands of Local History Books Featuring Millions of Vintage Images

Arcadia Publishing, the leading local history publisher in the United States, is committed to making history accessible and meaningful through publishing books that celebrate and preserve the heritage of America's people and places.

Find more books like this at
www.arcadiapublishing.com

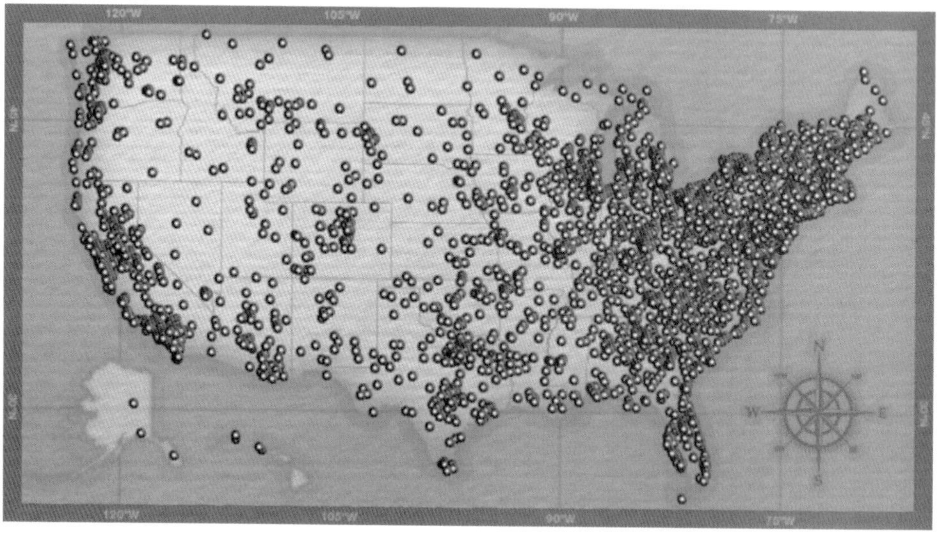

Search for your hometown history, your old stomping grounds, and even your favorite sports team.

Consistent with our mission to preserve history on a local level, this book was printed in South Carolina on American-made paper and manufactured entirely in the United States. Products carrying the accredited Forest Stewardship Council (FSC) label are printed on 100 percent FSC-certified paper.

MADE IN THE USA